FRONTIER SWASHBUCKLER

Missouri Biography Series
William E. Foley, Editor

WITHDRAWN

FRONTIER SWASHBUCKLER

The Life and Legend of John Smith T

Dick Steward

University of Missouri Press
Columbia and London

Copyright © 2000 by
The Curators of the University of Missouri
University of Missouri Press, Columbia, Missouri 65201
Printed and bound in the United States of America
All rights reserved
5 4 3 2 1   04 03 02 01 00

Library of Congress Cataloging-in-Publication Data

Steward, Dick, 1942–
    Frontier swashbuckler : the life and legend of John Smith T / Dick
Steward.
        p.   cm.—(Missouri biography series)
    Includes bibliographical references (p.   ) and index.
    ISBN 0-8262-1248-4 (alk. paper)
    1. Smith T, John, 1770–1836.   2. Pioneers—Missouri Biography.
3. Businessmen—Missouri Biography.   4. Frontier and pioneer
life—Missouri.   5. Missouri Biography.   6. Tennessee Biography.
I. Title.   II. Series.
F466.S854   1999
977.8'603'092–dc21
    [B]   99-43617
                                                                         CIP

⊗™ This paper meets the requirements of the
American National Standard for Permanence of Paper
for Printed Library Materials, Z39.48, 1984.

Designer: Stephanie Foley
Typesetter: BookComp, Inc.
Printer and binder: Edwards Brothers, Inc.
Typefaces: Galliard and Runic

Contents

Preface

C olonel John Smith T was a man unique in name and deed. The appellation "T," which referred to his Tennessee origins, gave his name a certain distinction, but it would have had little piquancy without his illustrious career to back it up. In the first three and a half decades of the nineteenth century, Smith T was one of the more notorious figures in Missouri. No single character spawned more myths and legends than the infamous colonel. However, by the onset of the twenty-first century his fame and reputation had faded from historical memory. This study attempts to illuminate his remarkable life and revise some of the stereotypical views of pioneer society.

Smith T was certainly one of early Missouri's most prominent men. He held positions of leadership in military, civic, political, and judicial affairs. His vast landholdings on both sides of the Mississippi, his roads, farms, mills, and mines, his salt-making facilities and shot towers, as well as a host of other economic activities, defy the egalitarian stereotypes of frontier democracy. But, as his mythic career suggests, he was more than simply a man of enterprise. His repertoire of violent activities included filibustering, dueling, and even murder. His dealings were so frenzied that he scarcely ever bothered to record them. Consequently, this biography was written without the aid of any of Smith T's personal and business records. Whether these records ever existed is still a matter of conjecture. Some of the colonel's descendants doubt that he ever took the time to assemble them. Others believe they were probably destroyed in a fire that in later years engulfed his granddaughter's mansion.

Despite these source limitations, the work on this book, with the assistance of some dedicated friends, continued. Providing valuable input and criticism throughout the course of this project was Martha Russell

Hervey. For more years than either of us would like to remember, Martha's patience, humor, encouragement, and advice have kept me focused on the task at hand. Good friends like that are hard to come by. Janice Muenks's keen eye was also helpful. Indispensable to the task at hand was Leah Treadwell, who typed and proofed the manuscript. Without Leah's unwavering help with so many technical problems, it is unlikely that this project would ever have come to fruition. Finally, thanks to Dr. James Goodrich and the State Historical Society of Missouri for the Brownlee Award and the financial assistance to defray some of the research expenses. All of their contributions are certain to have reduced the errors in this book, which, when discovered, must be placed squarely on the shoulders of the author.

FRONTIER SWASHBUCKLER

Introduction

Nowhere in the antebellum territories of the United States was the impact of the Tennessee Diaspora felt more strongly than in the Show-Me State. As one of the first trans-Mississippi members of the Union, Missouri was indebted to the Volunteer State for providing her with such favorite sons as Thomas Hart Benton and David Barton. One early Tennessee transplant, however, has over the course of the twentieth century lapsed into virtual obscurity. He was Colonel John Smith T—a lost legend of the Missouri frontier. At long last this is his story.

But first, a word of caution. Biography as historical genre pervades American frontier studies. For many in the academic profession, the conquest of the wilderness certainly provides a milieu for personal heroics. Historians, for their part, have capitalized on their subjects and have chronicled the deeds of their heroes and villains with style and verve. Perhaps some have been too enamored by the power of the individual and less cognizant of the forces that constrain as well as produce human achievement. Thus, some authors place their subjects in a position to overshadow an age and weave an indelicate balance between forces and men. Colonel John Smith T quite obviously did not dominate the nearly half century in which he struggled to make his imprint upon the western territory. In fact, by the modern age his name and deeds were all but forgotten. This work, although it attempts to resurrect the man as well as the myths, legends, and lore about him, will not try to make him larger than life.

In addition, it should be noted that biographical studies, unless the subject has failed or succeeded in accomplishing some dramatic deed, lend themselves more toward a theme than a thesis. Such is the case with Smith T. He accomplished no single grand objective. In point of

1

fact, one might argue that his greatest quest always seemed to be just beyond his grasp. The motif of this work, therefore, is somewhat less grandiose than a Carlyle biography. Succinctly put, for nearly fifty years the infamous colonel epitomized the restless and daring nature of the second generation of American expansionists.

The purpose of this biography is fourfold. First, it is to illustrate Smith T's checkered career and to document his successes and failures, especially as they affected Missouri life and culture. Second, it places him within the context of early American expansionism. The third reason for this work is to explain the hyperbole that surrounded his life, to clarify its functional role in pioneer Missouri, and to understand more fully why the above-mentioned myths, legends, and lore failed to capture the imagination of modern readers. The final reason is to interpret the pathways of progress not from a yeoman, egalitarian perspective, but from the viewpoint of frontier leaders such as Smith T who dominated the political economy of early Missouri. Collectively, it is hoped that the picture of frontier life that emerges from this biography will provide some additional insights into the political, economic, and social evolution of a pioneer society.

The Smith T saga does not conform very well to time-honored theories of frontier development. While Progressive historians emphasized yeomanry, individualism, democracy, and egalitarianism, the colonel's life exemplified opportunism and ruthless entrepreneurialism. Land grabbing, claims jumping, reckless speculation, and violence characterized many of his enterprises. In short, Smith T and other venture capitalists swiftly and radically changed Missouri's economy. The exploitation of natural resources and the integration of rural economies into larger national and international markets were just two examples of that transformation.

Violence accompanied these economic changes, and once again Smith T was in the vanguard of this turmoil. From his early days in Georgia and Tennessee to his formative years in Missouri, he was engaged in an ongoing struggle to retain his vast holdings. Challenges from Indians, squatters, rival government factions, and business competitors kept him embroiled in constant turmoil.

Smith T's career likewise challenges the theory of linear western progression. The frontier was not a successive pattern of settlements transforming the wilderness into civilization. Nor was each sojourn into these unchartered lands unique or exceptional. Movement of goods and persons did not flow in a single direction of "settlement westward." Unlike the stereotypical emigrant, Smith T did not sever his ties back East. This was no journey into an untamed environment from which he seldom if ever returned. His roots were firmly grounded in the states east of the Mississippi. For him, the wilds of Missouri were neither a final destination nor a point of embarkation. Rather, his varied and sundry business activities required constant vigilance and travel. The trans-Mississippi frontier served more as a benchmark than a final destination. Linkage, not severance, characterized his modus operandi. The isolation of the wilderness was more symbolic than real for Smith T.

In the process of nation-making, the role of Missouri pioneers and patricians such as Smith T was less one of taming the wilderness than of taking advantage of it. As a militia colonel and political leader, Smith T certainly had military and judicial responsibilities, but the self-appointed task of entrepreneurs such as the colonel was to consolidate American dominion over a territory with very divided loyalties. These mixed allegiances were to Great Britain, France, Spain, and various Indian tribes. The process of Americanization on the Missouri frontier was not so much one of conquest as it was of assimilation and acculturation. The Louisiana Territory was characterized not only by the size of the acquisition (which nearly doubled the size of the United States) but also by the suddenness with which it was acquired. Many of the inhabitants, European and Native American alike, had little time to adjust to shifting allegiances and new geopolitical strategies. If American leadership was to be exerted in these new areas, it would likely fall upon those enterprising individuals who by courage and ambition could establish an American identity on the fringes of Jefferson's empire of liberty.

Smith T's story, however, is more than merely political and business history. His was a life filled with danger, adventure, and violence. His fame stretched far and wide, and gave rise to some of the more colorful stories of the West.

The colonel possessed many of the character traits prized by early Missourians. He parlayed these qualities into a constellation of myths and legends that suited his various purposes. Yet, as this biography will suggest, the historical past and the mythical past were vastly different. To detail Smith T's life, the biographer must constantly separate the mythic from the real and juxtapose lost fact with forgotten lore. To many of Missouri's early mythmakers, John Smith T was a figure larger than life. Yet myths and legends, as this work will suggest, are not static concepts. In the end, the tales of this remarkable pioneer underwent such a considerable transformation that by the modern age they had lost most of their cogency.

John Smith T, in short, presaged Young America. Whether as a miner, speculator, judge, farmer, gunfighter, road builder, or military adventurer, his life epitomized the energizing spirit of the American West. In the process, however, his dreams of success usually intersected with a more sobering reality. Fame and a modicum of wealth punctuated a never-ending quest for power and personal fulfillment that was just beyond his grasp. His life, so varied and often reckless and violent, poses the difficult but rewarding task of disentangling the myths and legends from the historical record.

1. Tennessee Roots

Overlooking the Mississippi River not far from Herculaneum, Missouri, lie the white cliffs of Selma. During the early nineteenth century, these river precipices provided the setting for the shot tower in which one of the western country's most enterprising and daring pioneers, Colonel John Smith T, manufactured his bullets. The name "Selma" was derived from the poem "Fingal" by a Gaelic poet, Ossian, who composed it around the year A.D. 200. In the poem, Ossian described a placid and beautiful place, which he called Selma. In the eighteenth century, James Macpherson translated the poem into French and, according to one authority on early Missouri, it "became a must reading for those who read and spoke French fluently."[1] It was here on these cliffs that Smith T wished his final remains to rest at peace. But it was not to be. Over the years the grave became lost and nearly forgotten, just like the myths and legends that came to surround his life.

That Smith T's life story as well as the whereabouts of his final resting place are subject to controversy should not be all that surprising. Folklore had it that he buried $750,000 (probably in gold) in a twenty-gallon brass kettle near his home at Mine Shibboleth. The actual task of digging this pit was accomplished at midnight by a blindfolded slave who never knew where he dug. As the years went by, it did not take long for enterprising fortune hunters to comb not only Smith T's former residence some thirty miles away but his burial site as well. The confusion was in part compounded by his obituary in St. Louis's *Missouri Republican,* which placed him at the time of his death "at his new place on the river, below Ste. Genevieve." Actually, he died near Hale's Point in Tennessee; only later were his remains returned

1. Frank Magre to the editor of the *St. Louis Post-Dispatch,* March, 15, 1965, Frank Magre Collection, Herculaneum, Mo.

to his beloved cliffs of Selma. Relatives of the family maintained that Smith T and his granddaughter's husband, Ferdinand Kennett, were buried behind Kennett's mansion, called Selma Castle, and that both graves were looted and despoiled over the years.[2]

Facts were therefore an early casualty in the history of this knight errant of the Missouri Territory. But the controversy surrounding Smith T's death and burial was only the tip of the iceberg of misconception that began almost two hundred years ago. Perhaps the confusion is   for in death as well as in life, no other Missouri pioneer has   ded in as much mystery. But the myths and the legends of   re not buried with him in his eight-dollar wooden coffin.[3]   ment took place nearly a hundred years after his death. As   le is known for sure about him today, other than that few   s were as genuinely feared and admired in their lifetimes as   w have so inexplicably faded from our collective memories.   of Smith T was a legend that did not live. To tell his story   rate the man from the myth is one of the main themes of

      ith T was born sometime around 1770.[4] His proud father was Francis Smith. Lucy Wilkinson Smith was his mother. She was of the same Wilkinson family as the infamous General James Wilkinson, who later became implicated in the Aaron Burr conspiracy. This connection would later become apparent when Wilkinson and the Smiths teamed up once again in Upper Louisiana. Young Smith T was the fifth generation of fine Virginia stock, many of whom lived near Tappahannock. More than likely, his birthplace was a small plantation in Essex County, Virginia.

His grandfather, Colonel Francis Smith, had served in the Virginia House of Burgesses from 1752–1758. More than any other family

2. Mrs. Juels Quesnel to Frank Magre, n.d., in Magre Collection. Mrs. Quesnel was Kennett's granddaughter. Interview, Frank Magre, April 2, 1992, Herculaneum, Mo.; *St. Louis Globe-Democrat Magazine,* April 3, 1927.

3. Legal note, James White (administrator of John Smith T's estate) to John Brickey, Clerk, August 9, 1838, Probate Court Records, file no. 905, Washington County Courthouse, Potosi, Mo. Hereafter cited as Probate file no. 905.

4. Harry R. Burke, a relative and unpublished biographer of Smith T, believed him to be born around 1760 and to have fought at King's Mountain during the Revolution. See Harry R. Burke Papers, "Notes on John Smith T," Missouri Historical Society, St. Louis, 2. Hereafter cited as MHS. The 1770 birth date is ascribed among others by Snyder E. Roberts, *Roots of Roane County, Tennessee 1792,* 14.

Portrait of young John Smith T.
The boyish, refined features
became part of the legends
surrounding his life. Courtesy
of Missouri Historical Society.

patriarch, Francis Smith laid the foundations for the relative prosperity of future generations of Smiths. He had served in the colonial militia and had risen further up the ranks than his father, Captain Nicholas Smith. Francis held a number of civil as well as military posts in Essex County. While serving in these capacities, he amassed considerable holdings in land, livestock, and slaves. With the exception of a few faithful slaves whom he emancipated at his death, most of his inheritance was left to his second wife, Ann Adams Smith.[5] His first wife, Lucy Meriwether, had died, but not before giving him a son, whom he called Meriwether. With Ann he sired two other sons, Francis and William. To each of his two younger sons he bequeathed some property, as well as part of his most prized possession, his library.

John Smith T's father, also named Francis, spent a considerable amount of his life in Essex County. It was here that he met and married Lucy Wilkinson. The Smith estate, however, was not large enough or rich enough to sustain Smith T's father and uncles, as well as their progeny. In addition, the old tidewater aristocracy was in a struggle

5. Vallé Higginbotham, *John Smith T: Missouri Pioneer,* 2.

with a subtle and insidious enemy: the region's poor soil. The infertile soil forced many of them to seek new ground. Much of the Virginia soil neared exhaustion. Years of intensive cultivation, especially in tobacco, had severely limited the productive capacities of the land. To survive, one farmed the land harder, straining it to the breaking point. When that failed, one moved on to new land. Francis moved to Bedford County, Virginia, in early 1771. Shortly before the family's journey, Lucy gave birth to John.[6]

Francis's move to Bedford County was a typical response of the gentry class in the Upper South. As younger sons of the elite, they were continually pushed westward in search of land and profit. A restless spirit of movement and adventure would likewise characterize the life of John Smith T. Bedford County, however, proved to be only a temporary way station for Francis and his family. The real frontier, with its allure of lands abundant enough to create a new nobility, was Georgia. On the eve of the Revolutionary War, this southernmost colony held claims to lands stretching as far west as the Mississippi River. Its original royal charter, like that of Virginia, the Carolinas, Connecticut, and Massachusetts, extended to the Pacific Ocean.

During these twilight years of the British Empire in North America, colonial regulators imposed numerous restrictions on American immigration in the trans-Appalachian region. The Smiths, however, were not deterred. They, along with other native Virginians, showed little respect for British authority in moving into Wilkes County, Georgia, near the town of Washington, in late 1771. This was a full year and a half before the area was to be opened by his majesty's government for immigration. John Smith T, therefore, had a good teacher in his father when it came to claims jumping and disrespect for foreign authority. Before John's father could carry out his dreams of a western fiefdom, however, the Revolutionary War forced an unhappy postponement. Francis went off to war. Although he did not gain wartime notoriety like his brother, Meriwether, he served the Patriot cause faithfully and well.

John matured during a bloody age of revolution, war, and Indian massacres. As the eldest of three sons, the responsibilities of comforting

---

6. The best genealogical treatment is to be found in C. W. Coleman, "Genealogy of the Smith Family of Essex County, Virginia," 170–83. This was a reprint of the same article in the *William and Mary College Quarterly* 6, no. 1 (July 1897): 43–48.

his mother and holding the family together in the absence of his father would have fallen upon his young shoulders. Georgia's original imperial design as a buffer against Indian forays from Spanish Florida proved to be a constant source of anxiety during the conflict. Georgians had carried on a lucrative fur trade with the Indians to the south, and the war offered the Tories and the hostile tribes an opportunity to quell this fur market. One of the most significant of these provincial battles occurred at Kettle Creek. These raids were particularly savage, as was much of the guerrilla war in the South, and it would stand to reason that young John developed his first hatred toward Indians in these formative years.

In all probability, Smith T's youthful exposure to a world of violence led to his fierce independence and a penchant for dramatic action when it came time to defend himself, his possessions, and the family honor. In later life he was exceedingly fond of the kind of hunting shirts worn by veterans of the Revolutionary War as "a badge of honor."[7] Harry R. Burke, a distant relative of Smith T and a family historian, suggested that his ancestor's recollection of these early years was more than dim memories and that he personally identified with the Revolutionary cause. Throughout his entire life Smith T always maintained his staunch patriotism to the United States and never saw any of his expeditions and filibustering activities as disloyal or harmful to his country. Most leaders in the young Republic espoused westward expansion. They only disagreed as to the methods and timetable for such moves. Smith T saw nothing wrong in framing the question as a practical one rather than a theoretical exercise.

By the end of the Revolutionary War, young John had become imbued with his father's sense of western adventure. Georgia no longer held a valid title to those far-flung lands reaching to the Mississippi. These territories were now open to a host of land speculators who shared the Smiths' ambitions for profit. The new speculators had to contend with Creeks, Cherokees, Chickasaws, and Choctaws. These tribes had traditionally lived on and hunted these lands and were quite naturally reluctant to give them up. Notwithstanding these obstacles, the Smiths pushed onward.

One technique Revolutionary War veterans used to acquire new property was to petition the government for bounty lands in payment

---

7. Burke Papers, 2.

for wartime services rendered. In 1784, Francis sought such payments for duty for the time spent under the command of General Elijah Clark. He may also have sought land bounties at this time for John's services as well.[8] Francis Smith's speculation activities provided the young swashbuckler with his first exposure to the twisted and convoluted world of land claim controversies. In 1785, John accompanied his father and another prominent Wilkes County speculator, Zachariah Cox, to Muscle Shoals, in present-day Alabama. The prospect of a lucrative business in land sales and fur trading inspired the journey. But it was also a very risky venture. Georgia was reluctant to cede her western lands and would not formally do so until 1802. In the interim, the region saw corruption, greed, and fraud on a scale unparalleled in the history of land speculation. Among the more infamous of these transactions were the Yazoo land sales. Through bribery and deceit, a group of speculators had obtained from the Georgia legislature a tainted claim to that state's western lands.[9] The price for more than thirty million acres was a paltry one and one-half cents an acre.

Cox, a Georgia native and head of the Tennessee Land Company, had already founded a settlement at the bend of the Tennessee River in 1785. The young Smith T and his father had participated in the enterprise and thus were in a position to capitalize later in the Yazoo deal. Within a few years, Cox and his associates would receive from the State of Georgia, through the efforts of Senator James Gunn, a sizable part of the three and one-half million acres of land located near Muscle Shoals (sometimes referred to as the "Great Bend" of the Tennessee). The price paid for this land "transaction" was a mere $46,785. The project received support from the Holston settlers, especially John Sevier, who was a member of the corporation. In fact, at the outset of the venture, even William Blount backed the scheme.[10] Cox and his associates may have even received some financial backing from Robert

8. Most of the war rolls were destroyed or lost during and after the war and John Smith T does not show up on lists put together by the Daughters of the American Revolution. See Burke Papers, 3.

9. John F. Darby, *Personal Recollections of Many Prominent People Whom I Have Known*, 3.

10. Ibid., 3. Also see Governor William Blount to Secretary William Smith, April 17, 1791, in Clarence E. Carter, ed., *The Territorial Papers of the United States*, vol. 4, 55. Hereafter cited as *Territorial Papers*. Also see footnote relating to Zachariah Cox in ibid., 55.

Morris, James Wilson, Patrick Henry, Wade Hampton, and Robert Goodloe Harper.

Shortly afterwards, when Blount became governor of the Southwest Territory, he was officially "compelled" to oppose the company's plans because they violated treaty obligations with the Cherokee Indians as set forth by the U.S. government. The Spanish governor-general in New Orleans, Baron de Carondelet, likewise objected to the plans for fear that eventually the company might intrude into Spanish lands as well.

Despite the objections of the United States and Spain, not to mention the Cherokees, Cox persisted. His plans included not only land speculation through the Yazoo land grants but also the development of a commercial route between the Tennessee River and Mobile. This route would be a "short canal" connecting the Tennessee River somewhere above Muscle Shoals with the Tombigbee River. The projected canal would facilitate the shipping of produce by water to Mobile and eliminate the much slower and costlier route of going down the Mississippi River to New Orleans. The next step in Cox's plan was to build a blockhouse on an island at Muscle Shoals to defend a trading post as well as a myriad of other economic activities he envisioned. The Indians, however, had other ideas. In addition to Cherokee resistance, the party also faced the wrath of the Shawnee. Both tribes resented these intrusions into their best hunting grounds. Sometime in early 1791, they attacked and drove off Cox's party. All of the makeshift buildings, including the fort, were burned to the ground. Although it cannot be substantiated, it appears quite likely that Francis Smith and possibly his son were among Cox's besieged group.[11]

Shortly after the Indian attack, the American government, largely because of the enmity of General James Wilkinson, became increasingly hostile toward further intrusions into the area. Wilkinson may have seen Cox as an economic rival, or he may have been motivated by his divided loyalties to Spain, under whose payroll he was secretly enrolled.[12]

The late 1780s and early 1790s were years of apprenticeship for Francis Smith's eldest son. No doubt John kept a wistful eye on his father's farming and speculative activities as he acquired the trappings of

11. Thomas P. Abernethy, *The South in the New Nation 1789–1819,* vol. 4 (Baton Rouge: Louisiana State University Press, 1961), 154. George Penn Smith, Jr., "John Smith T. Fact and Tradition," 2. Burke Papers, 3.
12. Burke Papers, 3.

a formal education. Part of the time may have been spent at William and Mary College in Williamsburg, Virginia, where, according to legend, he not only acquired a degree but also mastered a classical education.[13] It is not possible to assess his intellectual progress as matriculation records, grades, and transcripts for the school were all lost or burned by British troops during the second war with England. Inquiries to the college have produced no tangible proof of his presence. We can only surmise that his college days were a brief respite from what otherwise was a lifelong quest for risk-taking, profit, and adventure. Smith T, after all, was not a man of letters. His reputation would be established as a "natural" aristocrat—a man born to lead by example, not by the accident of parentage. A classical education was important in the development of his mythic career, but he would gain his right to enhanced status and power by his frontier abilities.

John Smith T next emerged in the early 1790s as a budding entrepreneur of the West. On Christmas Day in 1789 he had made what was probably his first west-central Tennessee land purchase. The following year saw John and his brothers, Thomas and Reuben, involved in a number of lawsuits over land in Davidson County. On several occasions, he appeared in a Nashville court to prove his land deeds. Quite often, these problems arose because of squatters who settled without authorization on Smith T's land.[14]

He was also engaged in a number of land purchases in the eastern sections of Tennessee. He acquired from John Rice a 640-acre farm on the Caney Fork of the Cumberland River and another choice 5,000-acre tract nearby. He also was deeded 3,000 acres between the Clinch and Tennessee Rivers. Throughout the late 1790s, he amassed thousands of acres of land in eastern Tennessee.[15]

Furthermore, he continued to enlarge his holdings in the Tennessee Company. In time, he came to control the company, and by doing so was able to claim "the color of a title" to much of the northern half of the State of Alabama. Using this company as a medium, he

13. Frank Magre, "Chronology in the Life of John Smith of Missouri," 1; Roberts, *Roots of Roane County,* 14.

14. Carol Wells, ed., *Davidson County, Tennessee County Court Minutes 1783–1792,* 162, 171; Richard C. Fulcher, *1770–1790 Census of the Cumberland Settlements,* 19; Deeds, Tennessee Land Records, 1788–1793, Tennessee State Library and Archives, Nashville, 219–21. Hereafter cited as TSLA. Roberts, *Roots of Roane County,* 15.

15. Emma M. Wells, *The History of Roane County, Tennessee,* 20, 22.

was able to acquire a sizable investment in the infamous Yazoo Land Company. William F. Switzler, an antebellum Whig newspaper editor and historian of early Missouri, claimed that the U.S. government offered Smith T one hundred thousand dollars to settle his Alabama claim.[16] Smith T refused the offer, Switzler said, since his title to the land was already in litigation in the courts. In reality, Smith T's attorney, William Kelly, proposed the hundred-thousand-dollar settlement, but the government rejected the offer. In any event, the gamble did not pay off: the Supreme Court of the United States eventually decided against him and he lost the land.

But the young, enterprising pioneer was not content merely to speculate in chimeric land schemes. While continuing to claim the area around Muscle Shoals, Smith T widened the scope of his activities to include a system of river transportation on the western waterways. For a brief period, he owned a ferry that operated on the Clinch River. His ideas, many of which were from the wellspring of Zachariah Cox, were nonetheless bold and imaginative in both scope and intent. They were perhaps the first things that piqued the attention of Wilkinson. Both of Smith T's brothers were West Point graduates who served under his command. Undoubtedly, the wily general kept a watchful eye on Smith T's activities, mainly so that they would not conflict with his own enterprises. By 1796, Smith T was once again engaged with Cox in an enterprise of unusual boldness. The plan envisioned a series of settlements, including one on the Ohio River near the mouth of the Tennessee River and another at Muscle Shoals. The men intended to establish an inland waterway link to the Gulf of Mexico. Cox, with "the approbation" of James Garrard and John Sevier, the governors of Kentucky and Tennessee, respectively, commissioned Smith T to locate a hospitable site somewhere on the Ohio between the mouths of the Tennessee and Cumberland Rivers. The place chosen in February 1797 by Smith T was actually at the mouth of the Cumberland River in Kentucky. He or Cox named it, appropriately, Smithland. The town was designed as a substitute general depot for Muscle Shoals. A month after Smith T laid out the town, Cox, who believed that he had received

16. Burke Papers, 4; Gabe McCandles, "John Smith T: His Relationship to Smith-land, Kentucky," 5. "Col. John Smith T," Vertical File, MHS, 1; Magre, "Chronology," 1.

permission from Captain Zebulon Pike to settle the area, arrived with thirty-five men.[17]

Since the entire region swarmed with hostile Indians, Cox instructed Smith T to bring settlers and supplies by river. To ensure the safety of both, Smith T constructed a large boat replete with armaments and cannon. The boat was also intended to impress the Indians with the firepower of the reinforcements. Unfortunately, Captain Pike, acting most likely under orders from his superiors, refused, "for what cause he [Smith T] could not tell," to allow the boat to sail. Even after Smith T agreed to remove the armaments, the government still refused to allow it to move down the Tennessee River. In exasperation, Cox remarked, "Thus our infant settlement was left without provisions or supplies for defense." More than four hundred hostile Indians surrounded the small colony. Smith T nevertheless proceeded, traveling by land and without official sanction, to fortify the settlement. Although the first year or so was exceedingly harsh and dangerous, the small community continued to grow. Soon it had reached nearly 225 settlers. It has survived to this day and remains the county seat of Livingston County, Kentucky.[18]

Throughout the late 1790s, Zachariah Cox, Smith T's mentor, incurred even more wrath from Wilkinson. Wilkinson no doubt feared that the settlements might compete with his own trading monopolies. The general communicated to Secretary of State Timothy Pickering in 1798 that Cox still held aggressive designs on Indian lands and therefore violated the laws of the union. The warning reached the appropriate authorities, and the following year, while on a trading mission to New Orleans, Cox was arrested en route. The arrest, no doubt at the behest of Wilkinson, was made by Winthrop Sargent, governor at Natchez. Wilkinson also warned the Spanish governor, Manuel Gayoso, that Cox posed a danger to the Spanish dominions. At the time of his arrest, Cox had a sizable number of men under his command. These potential filibusterers, who perchance had designs on Spanish territory, were disbanded.[19]

17. McCandles, "John Smith T," 1–2. J. S. Buckingham, *The Eastern and Western States of America*, 58, 75. Abernethy, *The South in the New Nation*, 155–56.

18. McCandles, "John Smith T," 2–4.

19. Secretary of State Timothy Pickering to Governor Winthrop Sargent, December 10, 1798, in *Territorial Papers*, vol. 5, 53. Burke Papers, 4–5.

Hounded by both the U.S. and Spanish governments and repeatedly arrested by the authorities, Cox's power was broken. By the time Smithland was firmly established, Smith T had emerged as the dominant figure in the Tennessee Company. Despite the federal government's objections and the opposition of the Chickasaw and Cherokee tribes, the small town survived.[20] In spite of its many problems, Smithland became a center of activity, both legal and illegal. One of its more notorious transients was Samuel Mason and his family of river pirates.

Of all the characters who crossed paths with Smith T, none were more mystifying than Samuel Mason. Born in 1750, he was a descendant of the distinguished Mason family of Virginia. During the Revolutionary War he became an officer in the Continental Army and a decorated war hero. What possessed him to become one of the most notorious pirates during the age of the flatboats remains a mystery. For a while, the Mason clan plied their trade near Cave-In-Rock, a refuge for Ohio River criminals some eighty-five miles below Evansville, Indiana, and fifty miles above Paducah, Kentucky. After being forced to flee this hideout, the Masons sought out Smithland as a safe haven from which to operate.[21]

Other river pirates, such as the infamous brothers "Big" and "Little" Harpe, had robbed and killed settlers and then headed for Smithland. The Harpes' father had been a North Carolina Tory; after the war they had moved westward in search of easy prey. Their crimes were particularly cruel and heinous. One contemporary likened them to "death and terror." For obvious reasons, therefore, Smithland's inhabitants forced these unwelcome parties westward toward Spanish territory. They eventually settled near the little Mississippi River town of New Madrid. From here, Mason, his sons, and the Harpes became the "scourge of the Natchez Trace." For a while, Mason acted with impunity in the Spanish territory. Eventually, however, he was killed and his severed head, encased in Mississippi mud, became a grotesque reminder of the wages of sin.[22]

20. Abernethy, *The South in the New Nation*, 157–58.
21. Frank R. Prassel, *The Great American Outlaw: A Legacy of Fact and Fiction*, 65.
22. James Hall, *Sketches of History, Life, and Manners, in the West*, vol. 2, 87. For other descriptions of the Harpes see James Hall, *Letters from the West: Containing Sketches of Scenery, Manners, and Customs; and Anecdotes Connected with the First Settlements of the Western Sections of the United States*, 265–82; Prassel, *Great American Outlaw*, 66.

Meanwhile, Smithland was experiencing other vexations. Originally, it had been designed to serve as a conduit for trade downriver toward the settlement at Nashville or upriver to towns around Frankfort and Lexington. The plan even included a charter for a canal to eliminate portage between distribution points.[23] The system ultimately envisioned nothing less than a virtual commercial monopoly of the entire region. The plan, grandiose and a bit too impractical, collapsed like so many early western business ventures.

Another of Smithland's problems was an attack on the town by an army unit allegedly under orders from General Wilkinson. Wilkinson claimed it was in response to the aid and comfort given to the Masons and other undesirables by Smithland's inhabitants. The attempted arrest of the river pirates, he contended, would push them into Spanish territory and make them more vulnerable to apprehension. The assault on Smithland, however, was more than likely made after its uninvited guests had already been forced to move. Most probably, the attack was to safeguard the general's plans for his own commercial monopoly in the region. In any event, the hostilities on the Cumberland made Smith T realize how formidable a foe Wilkinson could be.

In the late 1790s Smith T left Smithland and moved back to eastern Tennessee. While working in the backwaters of the trans-Appalachian frontier, Smith T could buy and claim land, then wait for future settlers to come. By preceding many of the more settled farm families, he positioned himself well. He could anticipate increases in the value of the best lands and control along the way many of the mill sites, springs, and salt deposits, all of which had a great potential for profit. And, as he acquired the land, he gained valuable experience, which he would later put to good use in the wilds of Missouri. It was in Tennessee that he, along with Meriwether Smith, helped found the town of Kingston, which is today the county seat of Roane County. The first land sale recorded in the county was by Smith T to a certain John Rhea. While at Kingston, he purchased a large number of slaves. He also invested in the Cumberland Turnpike. Furthermore, he continued to stake his claim to one-half of the northern section of Alabama.[24]

Burke Papers, 5–6; Otto A. Rothert, *The Outlaws of Cave-In-Rock,* 37–38, 60–61, 94, 291–93.

23. Burke Papers, 4.

24. Ibid., 6; Herbert L. Harper, "The Ante-bellum Courthouses of Tennessee," 16–17; Magre, "Chronology," 1; *DeSoto Press,* November 18, 1963.

It was also here in "the mountain grandeur" of Kingston that John Smith T fortuitously met Nancy Walker, a young woman of "education and refinement." The two perhaps first met when Smith T, who had been given several slaves by his father, sold them to the Reverend Sanders Walker. The Walkers had migrated to Tennessee from Ogelthorpe County, Georgia. The Reverend and his wife, the former Sarah Lamarr, had six children, including Nancy, who was born in 1774. By the time of his death in 1805, Reverend Walker had amassed a considerable estate consisting of land, slaves, and a still that he bequeathed to his "beloved wife." In addition, he had willed some of his property to each of his children. By marrying Nancy, John put himself in the position of inheriting a considerable amount of property.[25]

John's choice of a mate was one of the most sensible decisions of his life. Nancy was a young woman of gentle personality and strong character. She was a devout Christian and fond of her Bible. Considering that her future husband tended to treat religion lightly, the marriage was somewhat out of character. What she saw in the young swashbuckler was a fierce determination to succeed, a fine family pedigree, and unusually fine-chiseled features that gave him a boyish demeanor. It was not an altogether deceptive physiognomy. Despite his combativeness, Smith T remained a devoted and caring husband. And, for all his wandering escapades, he always returned to Nancy, his bedrock of comfort and stability. In this respect, he departed from the many frontiersmen who slept with Indian or slave women. Unlike some members of his class who strayed from the chivalric code, he remained loyal and devoted to his wife. His passions and excesses were material, not sensual. His faults were part of his success. He was the prototype for the American character of acquisition, diversity, and expansion.

Throughout her married life, Nancy extended hospitality to the many friends and acquaintances of her husband. She was, according to Smith T's biographer, Vallé Higginbotham, "serenely engaged in the domestic duties and skills of the time," active in the training of servants and slaves, and devoted to the education of their only child, Ann, and later to their grandchildren.[26]

The exact date of Nancy's arrival in the Missouri Territory has not been completely resolved. Nor, for that matter, has the date of her

25. Higginbotham, *John Smith T,* 20–21.
26. Ibid., 21–22.

husband's arrival. She may have made some trips with her husband to this wilderness outpost but, in all probability, she did not take up permanent residence there until sometime around the end of the War of 1812. Her only daughter, Ann Smith T, for example, met and married her first husband, Captain David S. Deadrick, while he was stationed at "Southwest Point," a military post across the river from Kingston. The reason for Nancy remaining in Tennessee was obvious. The Kingston home would have been positioned somewhere in between the growing number of land tracts held by her husband. These holdings, by 1800, would have encompassed land in Spanish Louisiana, Georgia, Alabama, and Roane, Knox, Bedford, and Marion Counties, Tennessee.

Smith's southeast Tennessee political connections were enhanced in 1797 when his sister, Ann Adams Smith, married Peter Early. From 1802 to 1807 Early served as a U.S. Congressman from Georgia, and from 1813 to 1815 he was the governor of the state.[27] His Georgia connections were likewise strengthened by his association, again by relatives and their marriages, with Governor Wilson Lumpkin. Other political allies included the Brown brothers, Robert T., Thomas, and John. The latter two served as his agents in Roane County, while Robert T. accompanied him in 1798 to the Missouri Territory. John's brother, Thomas Adam Smith, married Cynthia B. White, who was the daughter of General James White, the founder of Knoxville. Once, when a relative of General William White believed that Smith T had not been treated like a gentleman by Sam Houston and his friends, he challenged Houston and fought a near fatal duel with him.

By 1790, the American frontier was moving rapidly west, and John Smith T was not far behind. American settlements had breached the crest of the Appalachians and were moving down the rivers and valleys on the other side. The western border consisted of a broad zone stretching south of Albany and down to Knoxville. It was a hinterland nearly eight hundred miles long and one hundred miles wide. Called the trans-Allegheny frontier, it lasted until the Mississippi Valley frontier was created by the Louisiana Purchase. In this wilderness region, the average population density ranged between two and six settlers per square mile.[28]

27. Kenneth H. Thomas, Jr., "Georgia Family Lines," 34–35.
28. Frederic L. Paxson, *History of the American Frontier 1763–1893*, 45.

It should be noted that John Smith T was no Daniel Boone. He did not explore, trap, or hunt in the uncharted wilderness. Nor was he usually in the vanguard of conquest, i.e. of taming the forests and vanquishing the native tribes. His arrival on the frontier came in the third stage of settlement, namely the occupation stage when the dialectic of civilization and barbarism was often played out in desperate, violent fashion. This stage of makeshift political alliances, conflicting land claims titles, reckless speculation, and enterprising capitalism was the world in which he thrived. Community life was in its formative stage, and he hoped to shape it to his advantage.

Although most of the commercial activity in early Tennessee centered around the towns, Smith T embodied the frontier, pioneer life. His entrepreneurial talents depended on the emergence of capitalism and towns, but his fame rested largely on the myths and folklore of the country. The Smith T iconography was the rifle, dirk, and pistol, not the carriage, home, or personal library. The talents that afforded him fame were shooting skills, not mining or speculative dexterities.

Even before he achieved fame in the wilds of Missouri, the outline of his redoubtable career had taken shape. His was the task of matching the natural wealth of land and resources with the capital, manpower, and political connections requisite for economic success. It was a tenuous marriage of imperial capitalism and pristine naturalism. As the consummate opportunist, he employed tactics gained in previous business experiences to take advantage of specific local conditions. Whichever type of wealth he tried to exploit, whether riverways, turnpikes, slaves, salt springs, mills, land claims, lead, or overland trade, he derived the dynamics from the political economies of earlier, more established settlements. These future cities were the areas that thrived on the natural resources of the frontier.[29] The social values he espoused—a vibrant entrepreneurial spirit, rugged individualism, and a willingness to use whatever type of force necessary to achieve his objectives—were also sequential elements of earlier frontier experiences. He attempted to replicate the social and political structures of the past, and he operated best in a gray area somewhere between wilderness conquest and

29. For an intriguing view of the "resource frontier" thesis see Richard Slotkin, *The Fatal Environment: The Myth of the Frontier in the Age of Industrialization 1800–1890,* chap. 3.

failed to pay the taxes on the property, the court ordered that it be sold by Knox County Sheriff Robert Houston to the highest bidder. It was purchased by George Wescott, John Ramsey, and Solomon Marks, but they too failed to meet payment on the taxes. Once again, Sheriff Houston sold the property at the Knoxville Courthouse. This time the highest bidder was John Smith T. His bid, approved by Judge Archibald Roane, was registered on September 7, 1803.

The fifty thousand acres of land (which had been cleared of title by a treaty with the Indians in 1798) were indeed a valuable acquisition for the young entrepreneur. His enhanced stature in the community as one of the county's largest taxpayers made him an ideal juror. Court records show that he was summoned each year from December 1802 to December 1804 for jury duty. In addition, he, his brother Reuben, and Meriwether Smith all joined Captain Hugh France's Militia company for Roane County in 1802.[32]

The Kingston tract afforded Smith T the funds to finance a myriad of other operations. In the late 1790s and early 1800s, records indicate that he sold considerable amounts of the land for a good profit. Records also indicate, however, that he oftentimes appeared in court for relief against squatters and other unauthorized persons who settled upon his lands. Since many of these individuals refused to leave peacefully, it sometimes became necessary for him to resort to force of arms against them. Yet a perusal of the criminal records of that day indicated no indictments for murder or any other violent crimes against him. In almost all cases, the court supported his side. Some cases, however, were settled out of court, with Smith T covering the expenses. Throughout these turbulent years he relied upon the assistance of Reuben and a small but loyal coterie of gunmen to ward off intruders. He would repeat this experience at violence and gunplay with even greater results a few years later in the Missouri Territory.

Smith T was also cultivating a new set of political connections in eastern Tennessee. In 1799 he obtained an appointment as a justice in Knox County, no doubt through the good offices of John Sevier. Three years later the Tennessee legislature established Roane County, and Smith T was appointed as a commissioner to supervise the erection of a courthouse, prison, and stocks at the county's main town, Kingston.

32. Mable H. Thornton, *Pioneers of Roane County, Tennessee 1801–1830*, 7, 13–14.

It was here that he further planned to persuade the same legislature to make Kingston the permanent state capital. The possibility that the town would become the capital held also the promise of a fortune to be made in rising land values on his vast holdings in the area. The Tennessee House of Representatives in fact convened briefly in Kingston in 1806–1807 and for one day, September 21, 1807, deigned the town as the state capital. Smith T, however, was by then in Missouri and personally unable to take charge of the lobbying efforts. Subsequently, the legislature moved the capital to Knoxville.[33]

It was at Kingston that Smith T enjoyed "the greatest notoriety among the pioneers." One contemporary historian, citing a nineteenth-century account, said of him, "An excellent shot, he fought several duels and killed many people at the slightest provocation."[34] No actual dates, places, or names of the deceased for these killings were presented, however, to substantiate the accusations. At first glance, it would appear that the myths and folklore about Smith T were transplanted from Tennessee to Missouri. But it should likewise be noted that the Goodspeed's histories, the same series of publications that did so much to popularize John Smith T in Missouri, also published the same type of historical genre in Tennessee. It therefore is difficult to trace how much of his reputation followed him to Missouri and how much was created in the new territory and transported back to Tennessee.

Rehistoricizing the early folklore of Smith T forces the researcher to focus on a variety of questions designed to demystify the subject: Where and how did the stories begin? Who wrote the accounts, and why? What was the historical accuracy of the myths and legends? How does one trace the cultural evolution of the myths and legends as they developed over a span of nearly two hundred years of development? And finally, what was the historic imprint and consequences of these stories? Folklore, as well as myth, relied heavily upon metaphor and narrative to identify in symbolic form the outline of frontier villains and heroes. In fact, the tall tales of Smith T's daring feats metaphorically reflected and conditioned a system of values that defined and sanctioned behavioral patterns of enterprising frontier capitalists for years to come.[35]

33. Burke Papers, 6; Harper, "The Ante-bellum Courthouses of Tennessee," 16–17.
34. Harper, "The Ante-bellum Courthouses of Tennessee," 17.
35. For the influence of frontier metaphors see Slotkin, *The Fatal Environment*, 19–24.

Another facet of Smith T's life that gave him added fascination was his unusual name. While in Tennessee, he added the celebrated "T" behind his name to distinguish himself from the hosts of John Smiths who frequented the rugged land. Not only was the name very common, it was the alias of countless scoundrels and outlaws. The "T" also obviated the endless joking, "So you're the man that Pochahontas saved." As a legal and distinctive signature it was also a practical device that settled questions of false identification.[36]

With a new appendage to his name and a growing reputation for intrepid action, Smith T made plans to expand his activities farther west. The late 1790s was in fact an opportune time for a different type of venture. First of all, Smith T would perhaps never again have the support of such a powerful and devious figure as Wilkinson. The general's hostile forays on Smithland, as well as his other intrigues to curtail Cox and his young partner, had been somewhat forgiven and forgotten. Necessity bred strange fellowships on the frontier. What made the healing process more palatable was the dream of a western palatinate in Upper Louisiana. To accomplish these designs, Smith T needed Wilkinson's support. Although neither man could have known that Spanish Missouri would soon be under the American flag or that the general would be named its first governor, the schemes of filibustering and lead mines had an irresistible lure.

Second, John Smith T, by temperament and upbringing, was well suited to filibustering. For men of the Southwest frontier, the inclination to dabble in foreign intrigue came more easily than for men of the Northwest. Here in the foothills of the southern Appalachians, English, Spanish, French, and Indian alliances and conspiracies were made and broken with Byzantine regularity. Conspiracy was the order of the day. With the seat of national power weak and remote, the likes of Wilkinson, George Rogers Clark, John Sevier, William Blount, Richard Henderson, and James Robertson professed their loyalty to the union but seldom allowed their patriotic duty (as they saw it) to conflict with their personal ambitions. This was the makeshift world of John Smith T—a western reliance on individualism and egotism. Thrown upon their own initiative and resources, early pioneer leaders saw little inconsistency in their pursuit of public and private rewards.

36. Burke Papers, 6. Higginbotham, *John Smith T,* 2.

A third reason for his trans-Mississippi move concerned the political and social climate of Tennessee. Its "vexatious period of youth and adolescence" had ended, and the region was maturing rapidly.[37] In 1796, it became the sixteenth state of the union. Granted, it was far from "civilized" in a modern sense, but Smith T nevertheless believed that his landholdings and other speculative ventures were secure enough to diversify his activities. It was a fateful decision, not only for him but for his adopted land, Missouri.

37. Paxson, *History of the American Frontier,* 91.

2. To the Western Frontier

J ohn Smith T arrived in Missouri during the twilight years of the Spanish Empire in North America. Unlike many of his fellow compatriots, he realized that the lands east of the Mississippi would not contain for long the American desire for expansion. Many Americans in both the political and scientific communities in the late eighteenth century believed that the terms of the 1783 settlement ending the Revolutionary War would meet the demographic needs of the new nation well into the next century. As for the trans-Mississippi West, most would have agreed with Henry M. Brackenridge's 1811 assessment that "the natives will probably remain in quiet and undisturbed possession, for at least a century." No doubt European and Native American powers were less sanguine. Nevertheless, they too hoped that the trans-Appalachian West would occupy American expansionist energies for years to come. Such was not the case. The American Diaspora continued unabated, and by 1800 many of these restless and "fearless" adventurers had crossed the Mississippi River and arrived in Spanish Missouri.[1]

John Smith T had always cast a covetous eye toward Spanish lands. In the last years of Spanish rule in Missouri, perhaps in 1797, he had ventured into the territory to seek his fortune. It was there that his first adventure into the convoluted world of Spanish intrigue began. Three overriding factors lured him to the wilds of Missouri. First, the land was the point of departure for expansion westward to the Rockies and beyond. It was also the logical starting point for commercial and demographic penetration into the Spanish Southwest, especially Texas. Second, the area held vast natural resources for future exploitation.

1. Henry M. Brackenridge, *Journal of a Voyage up the River Missouri*, 235. William V. N. Bay, *Reminiscences of the Bench and Bar of Missouri*, 115.

Some of the most important of these included farmland, furs, salt springs, lumber, and ore. The last of these, ore, led to the third and most important reason for Smith T's venture into Missouri. This was the abundance of lead, which was vital to all military expeditions that might be directed against the Indians or any foreign power that might challenge the United States' supremacy in the West. "Perhaps," wrote Captain Amos Stoddard, the officer who received possession of Upper Louisiana for the United States, "no part of the world furnished lead ore in greater quantities and purity."[2]

Smith T was not the only American pioneer attempting to cash in on Spanish lead. His greatest competitor, Yankee miner and entrepreneur Moses Austin, had arrived at roughly the same time in the territory. Unlike Austin, Smith T had little or no direct knowledge of lead mining. His inexperience did not deter him from jumping into the new business. Under the watchful eye of Spanish authorities, his debut was relatively auspicious. In fact, he may have been one of the last group of Americans to enter the territory legally. In 1795 the Baron de Carondelet had instructed his subordinates "to maintain great watchfulness" over these newly arriving guests.[3] Smith T was certainly a man who needed watching.

By 1797–1798, Spain had seen almost enough and had begun to slow down the flow of immigrants. In September 1797, the governor general of the Province of Louisiana, Don Manuel Gayoso de Lemos, issued a series of regulations designed to curtail the speculative nature of American settlers. Article 14 of the regulations stated that henceforth, new inhabitants would be forced to forfeit their land grants if within one year of their arrival they had not settled upon the land and within three years had not cultivated six of every one hundred acres. Article 15 further stipulated that no settler could sell or transfer his land until he had raised three crops.[4]

2. Gilbert C. Din, "The Immigration Policy of Governor Esteban Miró in Spanish Louisiana," 155–75. In his *History of Southeast Missouri* (vol. 1, 60), Robert S. Douglass called Smith T "one of the most dangerous men in the history of the state." U.S. Congress, *American State Papers, Documents, Legislative and Executive, of the Congress of the United States in Relation to the Public Lands*, 189–91.

3. Baron de Carondelet to Don Francisco Rendon, August 27, 1795, in Louis Houck, ed., *The Spanish Regime in Missouri*, vol. 2, 406.

4. General James Wilkinson to Secretary of State James Madison, November 6, 1805, in *Territorial Papers*, vol. 13, 254–55; Gilbert C. Din, "Spain's Immigration Policy in Louisiana and the American Penetration, 1792–1803," 270–72.

Before the American Revolution, Spain had welcomed American guests as an imperial buffer to English expansion from across the Mississippi. But she belatedly realized that the cure may well have been worse than the disease. Spanish authorities recognized that the Americans were multiplying like the proverbial loaves and fishes, and that social unrest could easily lead to a call for political independence. American settlers were already changing the face and complexion of the territory, and they were becoming increasingly restive and independent. One example of this was that fewer and fewer settlers were going through the formalities of accepting Catholicism as the price of admission.

Because of the Spanish misgivings toward her less-than-polite guests, Smith T's early years in the Ste. Genevieve district were marked by few incidences of violence. Like the majority of his compatriots, he "projected no filibustering enterprise; no schemes of a revolution." He confined his activities mainly to purchasing small land grants in areas that contained lead deposits. He did not resort to strong-arm tactics or otherwise take the law into his own hands. As a case in point, he loaned money to a certain David Strickland, who had obtained a Spanish land grant on Breton Creek. When the debt was not paid in early 1803, Smith T sued in the Ste. Genevieve courts and won the case. His gentlemanly demeanor was no doubt due to the watchful eye of the Spanish and the harsh punishment meted out to would-be revolutionaries. Still, he chafed under Spanish rule. No doubt he shared the sentiments of a fellow filibusterer, William D. Robinson, who believed that Spanish policy had long been "a steady, systematic course of injustice and outrage towards the unfortunate Americans."[5]

Smith T had set no timetable for revolutionary activities in Missouri. No doubt he, along with most westerners, shared Thomas Jefferson's

5. For a description of early Ste. Genevieve, see Thomas Ashe, *Travels in America Performed in 1806* (London: William Sawyer and Co., 1808), 288–90. For genealogy, see A. B. Kennett to William Boyce, October 14, 1914, Miscellaneous File, Collection no. 3096, Joint Collection, University of Missouri, Western Historical Manuscript Collection, Columbia, Mo., and State Historical Society of Missouri Manuscripts. Hereafter cited as WHMC. Also see Laurence M. Hyde, *Historical Review of the Judicial System of Missouri* (Kansas City: Vernon Law Book Co., 1952), 3. John Clark, *"Father Clark" or the Pioneer Preacher: Sketches and Incidents of Rev. John Clark*, 227. Higginbotham, *John Smith T,* 4. *American State Papers,* vol. 2, 373; Timothy Flint, *Recollections of the Last Ten Years,* 203–14. William Davis Robinson, *Memoirs of the Mexican Revolution,* 1; Herbert S. Parmet and Marie B. Hecht, *Aaron Burr: Portrait of an Ambitious Man,* 234.

belief that Spanish control over these lands, and especially the Mississippi River, "perpetually exposed" the United States to commercial danger. A danger that loomed even larger, however, was the fear, also expressed by Jefferson, that Spain would be "too feeble to hold" these lands "till our population can be sufficiently advanced to gain it piece by piece." Smith T of course hoped to speed the day of delivery. Not surprisingly, there was considerable consternation in both Missouri and Washington when rumors began to circulate about the possible transfer of the Louisiana Territory to Napoleon. Historians are very familiar with Jefferson's remark that on that date the United States must marry itself to the British fleet. The cession of Louisiana and the Floridas, he wrote to Robert Livingston on April 18, 1802, "works most sorely on the United States." It would, he further argued, "restrain her forever within her low-water mark." But the president also believed that American demographics would ultimately defeat the French general. The victory would come, he wrote, when "we shall have planted such a population on the Mississippi as will be able to do their own business." These hardy Americans, he further elaborated, would obviate "the necessity of marching men from the shores of the Atlantic."[6] Jefferson's remarks clearly indicated that he supported expansionist activities, provided of course that they were channeled into activities consistent with American policy. What he would shortly object to would be unauthorized filibustering escapades led by self-serving adventurers or political adversaries. The name of Aaron Burr, vice president of the United States and confidant of Wilkinson, immediately comes to mind.

The filibustering schemes of men such as Burr, Smith T, and Wilkinson were hatched in the last years of Spanish rule. These dreams of empire, however, were still in their infancy when Smith T confronted the more pressing and immediate problem of Moses Austin and his virtual monopoly of the lead mining district. Austin had accomplished his immediate objective when the Spanish gave him nearly a square league of the territory. Due to his powerful position, Austin did not

6. For a short description of these events see Noble E. Cunningham, Jr., *In Pursuit of Reason: The Life of Thomas Jefferson*, 260–68. Also see Third Annual Message to Congress, October 17, 1803, and Thomas Jefferson to Robert Livingston, April 18, 1802, in Philip S. Foner, ed., *Basic Writings of Thomas Jefferson*, 349–54, 656–57. Thomas Jefferson to A. Stuart, January 25, 1786, in Julian Boyd, ed., *The Papers of Thomas Jefferson*, vol. 9, November 1, 1785, to June 22, 1786, 218. Bernard DeVoto, *The Course of Empire*, 392.

initially perceive Smith T as a dangerous foe. Nor did he anticipate the turmoil that would soon be unleashed. His lack of suspicion was somewhat natural since these years of Spanish rule were only preparatory ones for the man from Tennessee. While laying the groundwork for his filibustering schemes by acquiring some lead mines, Smith T spent most of his time commuting back and forth to Kingston, Tennessee, and to Wilkes County, Georgia.

Austin recognized the extent of Smith T's economic challenge when the latter claimed 10,000 arpents that had originally been granted to Captain James St. Vrain. Contained within this tract of land were the Bellefontaine mines, Mine à Liberty, and Mine Shibboleth. The latter was located approximately eight miles from the town of Potosi. It was here that Smith T set up his major mining operation and his place of residence. For Austin, Smith T's presence at Shibboleth was uncomfortably close. In addition to these tracts, Smith T claimed that he had been granted 1,000 arpents of mineral land near Mine à Breton. This mine was the heart and soul of Austin's enterprises and the place of his residence, Durham Hall. Smith T, however, had only begun to make his presence felt. He also claimed 300 arpents at Doggett's mines, 250 arpents on McKee's branch, which took in the McKee mines, 300 arpents at Renault's mines, 300 arpents at Mine à Robina, and numerous other small claims dotting the countryside. He also purchased a concession near Old Mines. Salt springs were considered almost as valuable as mining property, and many of the springs were also claimed by him. Likewise, he attempted to take possession of many mill sights and lush stands of timber. One historian of the Lead Belt recalled, "If ever a swashbuckler, opportunist and peculiar combination of kind friend and bitter enemy ever lived, it was John Smith T."[7]

To what extent his acquisitions in Missouri were ends in and of themselves or means to a larger plan cannot be fully ascertained. Nor is it likely that the exact connection between Wilkinson, the other possible intruders into Spanish territory, and Smith T will ever be fully understood. Perhaps even they had not formulated exact details. In the

---

7. Deed, James St. Vrain to John Smith T, August 16, 1806, Recorder of Deeds, Book A, Indirect, August 16, 1806, Ste. Genevieve Courthouse, Ste. Genevieve, Mo., 106. A fuller description of this sale will be provided in a later chapter. James A. Gardner, *Lead King: Moses Austin*, 117. Henry C. Thompson, *Our Lead Belt Heritage*, 46. A listing of the major mines in Washington County can be found in Henry R. Schoolcraft, *A View of the Lead Mines of Missouri*, 65–66.

Statue of Moses Austin,
Smith T's chief rival for control
of the lead mining district.
Courtesy of State Historical
Society of Missouri, Columbia.

late 1790s, the plan of action may have included an initial attack on
Upper Louisiana using supplies of lead, men, and foodstuffs procured
by Smith T's sojourns into Missouri.

The Missouri Territory was awash with schemers, voyageurs, and
filibusterers who dreamed of distant empires. Another notable figure
besides Austin who had arrived quite early in Missouri was William
H. Ashley. Although best remembered for rationalizing the fur industry, Ashley also discovered potassium nitrate in a number of eastern
Missouri limestone caves. Activities at the caves included the purifi-
cation of saltpeter, which was then taken to Mine Shibboleth. At the
mine, Ashley added charcoal and sulfur to make gunpowder.[8] Lead
and gunpowder were of course two essential ingredients in any type of
military adventure.

8. David B. Gracy II, *Moses Austin: His Life*, 100–108; Richard M. Clokey, *William A. Ashley: Enterprise and Politics in the Trans-Mississippi West*, chaps. 1–2.

Whatever the nature of these schemes, the course of the empire shifted with Jefferson's 1803 purchase of the Louisiana Territory. Missouri no longer required benevolent liberation from an Iberian yoke. Safely under the American flag, she was no longer a prize to be won by filibusterers such as John Smith T. This did not mean, however, that Smith T relinquished his dream of empire. In fact, the acquisition of Missouri provided him and his cohorts with a safe haven from which they could launch even deeper forays into New Spain. Spanish lands had become all the more attractive because of the common misconception at the time that the plains and prairies due west of Missouri were infertile. The evidence usually presented to support this thesis was the treeless terrain, which suggested that it could not sustain viable agricultural activities. Hence would-be expansionists scanned the southwestern horizons for future settlements as they began the full-scale exploitation of Missouri's soil, timber, minerals, and fur without foreign impediments. The Missouri lead country now took on a different look. Smith T, for his part, had most likely viewed the Missouri venture from its beginnings both as a means and an end. Considerable fortunes could be realized from its land and lead. But it also proffered the possibility of a southwestern fiefdom of unfathomable riches. Geopolitically, Missouri was ideally suited as the springboard for filibustering expeditions aimed at targets as distant as California or Mexico City itself.

After the Louisiana Purchase, the Missouri Territory was administered by Governor William Henry Harrison from Vincennes, Indiana. Vincennes, however, was a long distance away. Dissatisfied with this organization, the new citizens petitioned for a more suitable arrangement. In early 1805, Washington bowed to their demands and established a trans-Mississippi government called the Territory of Louisiana, with the capital situated at St. Louis. Missouri was now a first-class territory. Courts and military commands were set up in the five major towns: St. Louis, St. Charles, Ste. Genevieve, Cape Girardeau, and New Madrid. Amos Stoddard, who served in an acting capacity as administrative head, was replaced later in 1805 by a territorial governor, General James Wilkinson.

Jefferson's appointments of Wilkinson and Dr. Joseph Browne, the brother-in-law of Aaron Burr, as territorial secretary were an unexpected boon to the plans and fortunes of John Smith T. First, they provided an opportunity for a full-scale challenge to Austin's supremacy in the lead district. Perhaps in anticipation of the coming power struggle, Austin wrote to Wilkinson in July 1805 that Smith T was attempting to have him removed from office and marked for "disappointed ambition." Second, it allowed Smith T to extend his political influence to St. Louis by aligning him with the Creole faction through the good offices of Wilkinson.[9] The general, always an admirer of the rich and powerful, had thrown in with the French, anti-republican forces in St. Louis. Since many of the French stalwarts opposed Austin, Smith T was able to form some valuable political allies through his connections with Wilkinson. Third, and most important, Wilkinson's appearance on the Missouri frontier accelerated the timetable for the filibustering schemes that both men had earlier planned. With the governor as an ally, Smith T set out to take advantage of the confused situation surrounding the Spanish land grant titles and to get control of the lead necessary for their military undertakings.

Compounding this volatile situation was an ambience of greed and reckless ambition created by the influx of American immigrants into Missouri. In addition, Spanish authorities had not taken adequate steps to secure valid land titles in Upper Louisiana. For example, land that had been granted to individuals had not been subjected to tax levies. The lack of good tax records no doubt made proof of ownership and title more difficult to ascertain after the territory was transferred to the United States. But that was not all. Spain granted two kinds of land concessions, one called "floating," the other referred to as "special." Special concessions specified the exact location of a grant and the amount of land, measured in arpents, which the grant entailed. Floating concessions had no specific boundary and had not been subject to survey. The only detail specified was the quantity of land granted. Usually the land lay vacant but held some promise of mineral wealth or agricultural productivity. The petitioner was not required to settle immediately on the property. Further complicating the matter was the common practice of detaching floating concessions into parts and parcels so as to cover new diggings. Under the circumstances prevailing

9. Moses Austin to James Wilkinson, July 22, 1805, vol. 1, pt. 1, 1765–1812, Moses Austin Papers, Barker Library, University of Texas, Austin. For Wilkinson's connections with Creoles such as the Chouteaus, see William E. Foley and C. David Rice, *The First Chouteaus: River Barons of Early St. Louis,* 126; Weston Arthur Goodspeed, *The Province and the States,* vol. 4, 17–18.

in the late eighteenth century—the vast amount of land, administrative and logistical inefficiencies, the scarcity of population, and absence of land surveyors (no regular land office ever existed and Spain did not send a surveyor until 1795)—floating concessions, which were far more common than special concessions, seemed a practical course of action. Of more dubious reasoning, however, was the policy enacted in 1798 that no land titles issued by the Spanish lieutenant governor in the territory could become valid until sanctioned by the royal intendant in New Orleans. This proscription made complete titles so rare that only eighteen existed in all of Upper Louisiana. In addition, the last two lieutenant governors, Zenon Trudeau and Carlos DeLassus, exacerbated the problem by granting unusually large and conflicting tracts to their friends and favorites. Most landowners, therefore, bought and sold incomplete titles and never tried to go through the time or expense of procuring a complete one.[10]

Much of the violence in Missouri after 1803, especially in the mineral region, revolved principally around these land disputes. There were complete and incomplete titles, titles in varying degrees of completion, Indian titles, squatters with no titles, and floating and special concessions, as well as fraudulent and conflicting claims. The mining country lent itself to speculation, since conventional wisdom held that all private claims would be adjudicated before new public land would be offered for sale. It therefore behooved every interested party to acquire all types of private claims ranging from the bona fide to those of dubious validity.[11] But what began as purely legal and economic disagreements soon grew into points of honor. Confrontations increasingly became personal as each individual and faction, convinced of the rightness of their own claims and aware of the potential wealth to be amassed, perceived other contenders as perfidious and deceptive. It was a world tailor-made for a man such as Smith T to exploit.

10. David D. March, *The History of Missouri*, vol. 1, 210–11, 212–15. Henry M. Brackenridge, *Recollections of Persons and Places in the West*, 214. For Judge J. B. C. Lucas's perspective on Spanish land grants, see J. B. C. Lucas to Abner Leacock, November 10, 1817, in John B. C. Lucas, ed., *Letters of Hon. J. B. C. Lucas from 1815 to 1836*, 22–25. Also see Lucas to William Crawford, November 9, 1820, ibid., 33; Lucas to Philip B. Barbour, January 20, 1820, ibid., 90–92. Hereafter cited as Lucas, *Letters*.

11. March, *The History of Missouri*, 215. William E. Foley, *The Genesis of Missouri: From Wilderness Outpost to Statehood*, 143.

Another potentially explosive situation was the Indian problem. Amos Stoddard wrote to President Jefferson and cautioned him about the Osage Indians, who "yearly plunder the inhabitants." The following year, Wilkinson also reported to Secretary of War Henry Dearborn on the seriousness of the Indian situation and Spain's complicity in the matter. The "savages," he wrote, continued to jeopardize the frontier and defy his forces. Spain, he added, would erect strong barriers of hostels to oppose the United States in time of war and "harass our frontier in time of peace." The Indians, who outnumbered the white settlers "ten to one," would continue to menace the settlers because their "habits of life, put it out of our power to destress or destroy them."[12]

Aware of both the Indian problem and Missouri's vast wealth, as well as the violent extremes to which some men would go to achieve their personal fortunes, U.S. officials at various levels of government took steps to exert control over the territory. Stoddard became the first official to try to establish order. Even he, however, became thoroughly captivated by the land's potential. His report to Jefferson on June 16, 1804, alluded to the quantity and purity of the lead ore. The abundance of this mineral, enough to supply the United States and Europe, he went on to add, could make a miner forty or sometimes a hundred dollars a month. It could also make the United States rich and powerful. By the time of Stoddard's report, the contest for mineral supremacy in the district had already begun, and Stoddard fully supported Moses Austin. Austin, he said, was "better calculated" to give reliable information on the mines than any other person. Although he provided Jefferson with surprisingly full details on Mine à Breton (Stoddard called it Burton) and other mines in the area, he did not once mention John Smith T or his holdings.[13]

Jefferson, duly impressed by Stoddard's report, informed Congress of the findings on November 8, 1804.[14] Meanwhile, Stoddard decreed that all public records must be turned over to him to be authenticated. On March 26, 1804, Congress declared that only Spanish grants issued before the October 1, 1800, Treaty of San Ildefonso were valid. Judges

12. *American State Papers*, Public Lands, vol. 1, 189–91. General James Wilkinson to Secretary of War Henry Dearborn, December 30, 1805, in *Territorial Papers*, vol. 13, 357–58.
13. *American State Papers*, Public Lands, vol. 1, 189–93.
14. Ibid., 188.

and lawyers sprang into litigation the following year with the establishment of a new territorial government and a new March 2 land law that established a land commission with inordinately tight guidelines to review the claims.

At roughly this same time, Wilkinson arrived in St. Louis as territorial governor. Historians still debate why the president selected such an untrustworthy individual for such a delicate position. No doubt Jefferson's reasons were both political and military. The president owed Wilkinson and his supporters a payback, and he also believed the presence of a high-ranking military officer would have a stabilizing effect on the frontier. Obviously, Jefferson erred, for Wilkinson instead quickly entered the fray. He ordered the district commandant, Major Seth Hunt, to stop all illegal mining on government lands.[15] Perhaps Wilkinson believed that Hunt would enforce the orders selectively and allow the general's allies such as Smith T to continue mining disputed property. In any event, the instructions backfired. First, the miners rose up in protest against a policy that countermanded their traditional rights. Second, no government official could have expeditiously determined the legitimacy of the conflicting claims.

The plot thickened even more when Hunt sought to enforce Wilkinson's instructions against John Smith T. The commandant, an ally of Moses Austin, unquestionably had proved himself persona non grata to the governor and his faction. On June 30, 1805, Hunt inexplicably ordered Smith T off a tract of land that the colonel had purchased from the commandant himself only a year before! The land in question was a five-hundred-acre floating concession Hunt had purchased for seventy-seven dollars as part of an estate sale of Pierce Blott. The tract had been purchased prior to the March 26, 1804, law for ascertaining and adjusting titles and claims. The March law had divided the Louisiana Territory into two districts, provided for the establishment of a government in Missouri, and imposed a moratorium on unauthorized settlers on public lands. The difficulty at the time, however, was that Missouri was not legally or administratively capable of ascertaining or adjusting the claims issue.

Hunt's order gave Smith T only forty-eight hours to comply. It also forbade him to dig minerals, erect houses, cut timber, or engage in any

15. William E. Foley, *A History of Missouri, Vol. I, 1673 to 1820*, 101–2.

other economic activity on the disputed property. The same day, Hunt wrote Wilkinson and reported that Smith T held several floating and antedated concessions that were in defiance of U.S. law.[16]

No doubt Hunt hoped that his eviction orders would lead to the diminution of Smith T's power as he struggled with Austin. Already, Hunt warned the governor, Smith T had started other "unlawful and unauthorized" settlements on the Grand River. If he did not obey the eviction order, wrote Hunt, then Smith T would be removed by force. Since Hunt had no militia organized for such purpose, he requested that federal troops from Kaskaskia be brought in to enforce his orders.

Smith T had no intention of complying with Hunt's dictums. On July 8, 1805, he wrote Wilkinson and assured him that there had been no breach of law. What had particularly angered Hunt and Austin, he asserted, was a small tract of land near Mine à Breton that he had claimed and on which he had found lead. This tract, along with the Hunt land, would make, the colonel believed, a "suitable plantation" as well as a good mine. Austin, he claimed, "wishes to add my little possession to his own" and along with Hunt had sought to deprive him of character and property. Smith T also insisted that he had tried to get his holding surveyed but that Hunt had blocked the effort. Finally, he produced deeds of transfer signed by Lieutenant Governor Charles Dehault Delassus for the land purchased from Hunt.[17]

The quarrel between Hunt and Smith T served as the pretext for Wilkinson to move against Hunt, whom he did not trust. It also gave Smith T an opportunity to drive a wedge between Austin and Wilkinson. Since Hunt was allied with Austin, any action that brought discredit to one would undoubtedly affect the other. Wilkinson, like Smith T, quickly took advantage of the situation. On July 5, Wilkinson wrote Smith T that Hunt's eviction order had given him "sensible concern." Although the *Territorial Papers* contain no evidence indicating that Wilkinson showed his friend all of the formal communications he had received on the case, it seems clear they realized that Hunt and Austin posed a serious challenge to their short-range, as well as long-range, ambitions.[18]

16. Seth Hunt to John Smith T, June 30, 1805, and Hunt to Governor James Wilkinson, June 30, 1805, in *Territorial Papers,* vol. 13, 208–9.
17. Smith T to Wilkinson, July 8, 1805, in ibid., 210–11.
18. Wilkinson to Smith T, July 5, 1805, in ibid., 210.

On July 16, Hunt angered Wilkinson when he objected to the governor's sharing the commandant's orders and documents with Smith T. Two days later, in a letter to Hunt, Wilkinson chastened him for helping to create the "vindictive personal factions" that were racking the territory while the governor was trying to promote reconciliation. He further criticized Hunt's purchase and sale of a concession that he now claimed was illegal. Finally, in defense of Smith T he wrote, "I advise you to accommodate your controversy with Mr. Smith, whose character and connections are respectable, and whose influence is in unison with the policy of our administration."[19]

During the next month or so, the governor prepared his case against his recalcitrant subordinate. Depositions, certificates, and testimonies by Dr. Andrew Steele, Rev. James Maxwell, John Price, Robert Wescott, Joseph Kimbell, J. V. Garnier, and Alpha Kingsley all verified Hunt's insubordination. Dr. Steele's warnings of Hunt's actions were all the more poignant since he, along with Smith T and others, was involved in the filibustering schemes that were being concocted.[20] On the basis of these accusations, as well as on the rumor that Hunt had also charged Captain Amos Stoddard of "mal-conduct," Wilkinson ordered Hunt to not leave the territory until an official inquiry into the charges had been made. By this time Hunt realized that his attacks against Smith T had sealed his fate with the governor. Perhaps he realized too that an earlier admonishment by Wilkinson to tread lightly on Smith T because he "may give value to the object in quest of which he seems adventuring" had subtle overtones which he did not at the time fully understand.

On August 31, Hunt wrote Wilkinson that he had "very little interest in the affairs of Louisiana" and desired to leave "with a determination not to return." Wilkinson was not in a forgiving mood. He ordered Hunt's arrest and wrote to Secretary of War Dearborn to argue Smith T's innocence. Wilkinson further stated that Hunt had "leagued himself with men of at least dubious character, in opposition to what he [Hunt] stiled the French faction." Furthermore, he wrote, the young

19. Hunt to Wilkinson, July 16, 1805, Wilkinson to Hunt, July 18, 1805, in ibid., 212–13.
20. See ibid., 214–18, especially Dr. Andrew Steele to Wilkinson, September 9, 1805, 214–15.

upstart had "stigmatized" his character and "adds menace to insult, and contempt to menace."[21]

What particularly incensed Wilkinson was the spirited defense Hunt put up against both him and Smith T. Smith T, Hunt claimed, was an "intruder" on public lands and his "very respectable standing" in Tennessee had no bearing on the case. He went on to add that no distinction or favors should be shown "between either high or low, rich or poor, influential or obscure." Smith T, Hunt charged, was the first violator of the law, and unless he was stopped, more unauthorized settlers would follow. An example should be made of Smith T, and "every disposition to infringe the laws should be nipped in the bud."[22]

Hunt and Austin found a new ally in late 1805 when J. B. C. Lucas, appointed by President Jefferson as the territorial judge, arrived in the western country. On November 19, 1805, Lucas reported to Secretary of the Treasury Albert Gallatin that Smith T had violated federal law and that Wilkinson knew it. Furthermore, the governor had done nothing about these infractions because Smith T had found lead ore on the illegal lands. The letter appeared to suggest that Lucas suspected some type of plot had been hatched between Wilkinson and Smith T and that lead played an important part in it. Some other motive besides Smith T's respectability, Lucas intimated, had led the governor to support him.[23]

On February 13, 1806, Lucas again wrote to Gallatin about Hunt's travails. As the judge saw it, Hunt was a "republican" who had tried to stop "the intrusion of John Smith" on lands belonging to the United States. For his efforts, he had been arrested by the governor and not released until early February. Before he could leave the Missouri Territory, however, Hunt was challenged to a duel by one of Wilkinson's officers. The differences were "amicably settled," but the following day, Lucas reported, the governor's son sent another challenge. Hunt responded by telling the young man that his quarrel was with his father and that he would duel only with him. Nevertheless, two officers the very same day

---

21. Wilkinson to Hunt, August 22, 1805, Hunt to Wilkinson, August 31, 1805, Wilkinson to Dearborn, September 8, 1805, in ibid., 214, 205–7.

22. Hunt to Wilkinson, September 5, 1805, in ibid., 223–25.

23. For Lucas's Republican ideas, see Hugh G. Cleland, "John B. C. Lucas, Physiocrat on the Frontier," pt. 1, 1–13, pt. 2, 87–100. Judge J. B. C. Lucas to Secretary of the Treasury Albert Gallatin, November 19, 1805, in *Territorial Papers,* vol. 13, 287–89.

bore another challenge from the governor's son. When Hunt refused to receive it, one of the officers cudgeled him. During the struggle, Benjamin Wilkinson, a nephew of the governor, also entered the fray. Less than an hour after this altercation, another officer arrived at Hunt's home and "beat him again." Not satisfied with this humiliation, the same officers posted Hunt as a coward, a poltroon, and a scoundrel. Hunt responded to the postings by challenging the abusive officers, but Wilkinson refused to allow the duels to take place.[24]

According to Lucas, the violence spilled over into St. Louis when the Wilkinsons and their cadre of officers, "armed with swords and pistoles," forced a prominent attorney, Edward Hempstead, to sign a certificate in favor of the governor. This systematic intimidation, Lucas added, was intended to silence critics of Wilkinson. Lucas further believed that he too was marked to "be mobbed or assassinated," but he had refused to flee as his "honnour and independence is more precious to me than my safety." Men such as Wilkinson and Smith T, he bellowed, would not or could not intimidate him or keep him from carrying out the law of the United States, especially when it came to unauthorized settlements of government lands.[25]

Hunt and Austin also tried to solicit the support of a prominent group of gentlemen referred to as the "anti-junto" faction. Besides Lucas, the group contained other large land speculators such as editor Joseph Charless, David Barton, William Russell, and Rufus Easton. Most of these elites had come to the territory after the Louisiana Purchase and thus "did not stand to profit from the vindication of Spanish land grants."[26] The anti-junto factions in St. Louis and Ste. Genevieve did little to curtail the speculative land greed of Smith T. Nor, for that matter, did anyone else. In all fairness to his enemies, it does appear that virtually every economic aspect of Smith T's life revolved around greed and exploitation. Land speculation involved the exploitation of the less fortunate of the pioneers, who either could not afford to buy large tracts of land or could not hold on to their property without the assistance of organized gangs of thugs and ruffians. But land hunger

24. For an example of Hunt's posting, see Public Letter of William Keteltas, n.d., in ibid., 253.
25. Lucas to Gallatin, February 13, 1806, in ibid., 445–47; J. B. C. Lucas to Charles Lucas, November 12, 1807, J. B. C. Lucas Collection, MHS.
26. Duane Meyer, *The Heritage of Missouri: A History,* 169.

was not confined to the large speculators. Oftentimes squatters and small farmers settled on the land without authorization and thwarted the rights of later migrants. Acquisitiveness, therefore, cut across all economic lines.

Land was not the only exploitable commodity in Smith T's scheme of things. Slaves were to be worked on the land and in the mines, while Indians were to be dislodged from their native lands. Partnerships were used and then discarded when deemed expedient. Many of his filibustering activities, which will be detailed later, were designed to exploit weaknesses in the defenses of his foes. His mining operations also had to be exploited quickly and ruthlessly lest the ore, finite in quantity, be claimed and extracted by others. The recklessness and violence that permeated the mineral area were permanent reminders that mining civilizations were inherently unstable. Their ephemeral nature made them ideally suited to greed, and attracted the type of violent men who could survive on the mining frontier. Nor does it take much historical imagination to see how a miner's assault on the environment could easily be transformed into an assault on persons and property.

Smith T operated with great dexterity in the field of floating concessions. He also wielded the force necessary to keep his claims. The St. Vrain claim was a case in point. St. Vrain was the brother of Lieutenant Governor Delassus. In 1796, he had received two sizable land grants, one totaling ten thousand arpents. Smith T had taken an incomplete title to these lands, the most notable of which were the lead mines at Shibboleth and Bellefontaine. These mines proved very profitable, and he would for the next thirty-five years be involved in litigation and violence to hold onto them.

Years later, in the case *John Smith T vs. The United States,* Smith T finally had his day in court. His petition, which had been decided unfavorably by the Missouri courts, was taken under advisement by the U.S. Supreme Court in 1830. Nearly six years later the court upheld the Missouri court ruling and declared Smith T's land claims invalid, mainly on the grounds that the tracts had been located by private, rather than public, survey. In its ruling, the court declared that "Spain never permitted individuals to locate their grants by mere private survey." Furthermore, the court declared that Congress had not contemplated favorably awarding any of the claims litigations unless the various procedures in the land transfer were in accordance with the laws and usages of Spain.[27]

Ironically, the court's ruling, which finally laid to rest the St. Vrain grant, occurred in the same year that Smith T died. Yet for the better part of a quarter century, his tactics bankrupted many small claimants who could neither challenge him in court nor physically fight him for the land. His tactic was to move onto disputed lands, claim them, obtain a writ against the tenants, tie up ownership in the courts, and continue working the mines. In some cases, by the time the dispute was settled, he had virtually exhausted the ore, and the point of ownership had become moot. Initially, the government seemed unwilling and later unable to deter him.[28]

Yet for all his chicanery and combativeness (historian David March called his tactics "illegal and shameful"), John Smith T rose in stature. Compared to his principal adversary, Moses Austin, Smith T became a virtual folk hero among many of his contemporary frontiersmen. Austin, by contrast, had alienated many of the small miners as well as the prominent French families in the district. "The French," Rufus Easton confessed to Austin, "are violently prejudiced against you" and they "will not be ruled by a rod of iron." Austin had obtained large Spanish lead titles in 1797–1798, just before Spain stopped the practice of granting claims out of fear that too many Americans were flocking to Missouri. Therefore, after 1800, many would-be miners were relegated to working for Austin or squatting on land to which they held only precarious claims.[29]

Another point of friction between Austin and his detractors pertained not only to the quantity of lead he controlled but also to its ultimate destination. Some critics exploited the fact that much of the lead during the later years of Spanish rule ended up in arsenals in New Orleans and Havana. Since Americans on the frontier oftentimes faced hostile Indians, allegedly armed and abetted by Spain, Austin's earlier entrepreneurial ventures were construed by some as unscrupulous and traitorous.[30]

27. Louis Pelzer, "The Spanish Land Grants," 13–14, 34; Roberts, *Roots of Roane County,* 16.

28. March, *The History of Missouri,* 252.

29. Ibid. Rufus Easton to Moses Austin, July 29, 1805, Rufus Easton Papers, MHS. Clokey, *William A. Ashley,* 12.

30. James H. Perkins, *Annals of the West: Embracing a Concise Account of Principal Events Which Have Occurred in the Western States and Territories,* 675–76.

Many denizens of the mining area were also alienated by Austin's revolutionary mining techniques. He had used many of these procedures previously in Virginia. Prior to his coming to Missouri, the French settlers farmed the land and in the off-season extracted the lead by skimming off three to four feet of soil. Usually their hard work enabled them to produce enough of the mineral to buy food and farm supplies. Austin initially used shaft mining as a substitute for surface excavation. Although he later abandoned the technique, he had by this time displaced many of the French part-time miners. In addition, he constructed a smelting furnace and a factory to make shot and sheet lead. He carried out further vertical integration of his operation by means of a company store, flour mills and sawmills, and a blacksmith shop. He built a road from Mine à Breton to Ste. Genevieve; thus he was positioned to use the Mississippi River as an outlet to markets in the United States and beyond. To symbolize his newfound wealth and status, Austin constructed, as his domicile, Durham Hall, a stone house on his Mine à Breton site. This tract consisted of one square league of approximately 4,250 acres. To many, Durham Hall was "the most impressive private residence" in all the territory, but to many others it was also a source of envy and anger.[31]

Political power accompanied Austin's rising economic fortune. After the American transfer, the nabob of Durham Hall became chief justice of the Ste. Genevieve Court of Common Pleas. At approximately the same time, he ordered all miners to evacuate his properties and to cease all unauthorized mining activities.[32] John Smith T, however, was not easily intimidated, especially when he had the secret backing of the territorial governor. As his running battle with Hunt suggested, it was Smith T who had initiated the trouble with Austin by purchasing and attempting to work a floating concession in the very heart of Austin's empire, Mine à Breton.

The feud between the two most powerful men in the mining area continued to grow until by 1805 it finally reached the point of no return. A veritable civil war commenced, with each lead mogul possessing a personal army loyal only to his own commands. "The war,"

31. Floyd C. Shoemaker, *Missouri and Missourians: Land of Contrasts and People of Achievements,* vol. 1, 140–43, 11.
32. Foley, *Genesis,* 90, 164–65; Foley, *History,* 101.

wrote Austin associate Thomas Oliver to lawyer William C. Carr, "rages higher and more high in our little district," with Smith T attempting to represent himself as just another squatter. Austin, reported Oliver, was "in a hell of a pet" and was "determined to make a spirited defense" against him. Throughout this period, a virtual reign of terror existed, with the Ste. Genevieve district "divided" between the Austin and Smith T factions. In one rash move on July 4, 1806, Smith T and his men unsuccessfully attacked Mine à Breton in hopes of commandeering Austin's cannon. The cannon, a three-pounder by Austin's recollection, had been his first line of defense in 1802 against an Indian attack, and he had no intention of giving it up without a spirited defense. On another occasion during the mineral wars, Thomas Scott, an Austin supporter, attacked Smith T with a knife and was arrested. He was defended by William C. Carr. Scott's stay in jail, however, was brief. He was quickly released by Judge Lucas, who, not surprisingly, found no cause to hold him.[33]

The ever-escalating level of violence forced a very uncomfortable meeting between the mineral region's two most powerful protagonists. Unfortunately, the face-to-face meeting between Smith T and Austin only led to more acrimony. Smith T accused Austin of murder, and Austin promptly filed suit for slander. In a letter written to Smith T one month after the colonel's assault on Durham Hall, Austin accused his bête noire and the Rev. James Maxwell, an Irish priest brought by the Spanish to minister to the faithful, of trying to ruin his family. Maxwell, fond of card playing and horse racing, was a natural ally of Smith T. The priest was himself a major land speculator who claimed immense tracts under Spanish grants. Maxwell had not been involved in the attack on Durham Hall, and Austin did not accuse him. His letter was directed straight at Smith T. "I have don [*sic*]," confessed Austin, "what every man of honor ought to have don," and that was to not recall the past.

33. Thomas Oliver to William C. Carr, July 29, 1805, William C. Carr Papers, MHS. Judge Lucas always maintained that "nabobs" such as Smith T were in fact the ones pushing "the industrious and poor" settlers and miners off their land. See Lucas to William Crawford, November 9, 1820, in Lucas, *Letters,* 33. Timothy Phelps to Moses Austin, August 6, 1807, and Frederick Bates to Moses Austin, September 12, 1807, Austin Papers; Carl J. Ekberg, *Colonial Ste. Genevieve,* 156. Moses Austin to Judge Lucas, July 6, 1806, Legal Notes of J. B. C. Lucas, July 8, 1806, Lucas Collection. Austin maintained to Judge Lucas that it was Smith T who, while drunk, attacked Scott with a knife. Also see William C. Carr Notes, 1806, ibid.; Court Order, July 15, 1806, and Lucas to Gallatin, August 5, 1806, in *Territorial Papers,* vol. 13, 556–57, 559.

But, he told Smith T, the favor had not been reciprocated. Now, he added, "the laws of our country will determine whether you are justified or not." If men do justice to each other, he concluded, then "no man can dishonor himself." The letter was a bold and courageous effort on Austin's part, but it did not have the desired effect. Perhaps the letter's intent was mitigated in part by a remark allegedly made by Austin to another influential miner, William Perry, in which he accused Smith T of murder. This prompted the colonel to in turn sue Austin for slander. He asked for an award of ten thousand dollars. "We will meet," Austin retorted, at the "Bar of Justice."[34]

Austin's inclination to meet in court rather than on the field of honor prompted a letter from his friend William C. Carr suggesting that "a man of character" might have to take direct action "to maintain unsullied his reputation." Fortunately for Austin, the temptation to challenge "this monster," as he referred to Smith T in a letter to Rufus Easton, abated. In this same letter, Austin spoke of Smith T as a man "universally detested" but of such "daring" as to be able to wreak more havoc than forty men. Smith T had already challenged Hunt to a duel, but so far, Austin added, he had "thought proper to keep his room." An almost inevitable sense of tragedy gripped Austin as he wrote of his enemy. Some may give him God-like qualities, he wrote, for "truly he is a god, but a god of darkness." As to the letter itself, Austin fearfully cautioned Easton to burn it "if you wish me well."[35]

Since the small miners and many of the French Creole families considered the mines common property, Austin's earlier preemption of the land put him at odds with a majority of the district's members. The circumstances played directly into Wilkinson's and Smith T's hands. They solidified their political position with the French in the mining district and then extended their alliance to include Creole families in St. Louis such as those headed by Bernard Pratte, Charles Gratiot, and Auguste Chouteau. They further widened their political circle by easing tensions with some of the rival elites in the territory such as Edward Hempstead.[36] And the governor fired Seth Hunt as

34. Moses Austin to Smith T, August 7, 1806, Austin Papers; Gracy, *Moses Austin,* 113; Legal Notes, July 1806, Lucas Collection.
35. William C. Carr to Moses Austin, August 12, 1806, Austin Papers. Moses Austin to Rufus Easton, August 14, 1805, Easton Papers.
36. Easton to Moses Austin, July 29, 1805, Easton Papers; Burke Papers, 7; March, *The History of Missouri,* 195.

commandant and ordered his arrest, thereby eliminating a valuable ally of Austin's.

In addition, Wilkinson publicly exposed Hunt's condemnation of Smith T—a tactic that Austin believed showed Smith T had "obtained great credit" with the government officials. Although Austin did not seem to be aware of the family connections between Wilkinson and Smith T, he realized that he too was being condemned without a trial. Still, he mistakenly persisted in the belief that in the end public opinion would side with him, since the behavior of Smith T, as he so distinctly observed, "would draw resentments from a stone." In the interim, however, Austin pondered how he was to respond to his family and friends who were "daily branding me with a want of resolution to meet the abuse daily offered to myself and friends."[37]

Austin's trust in Rufus Easton, however, was badly misplaced. Only two weeks before Austin's cryptic letter to him, Easton had voiced confidence in Governor Wilkinson's ability "to conciliate the old inhabitants of the country" and to "restore harmony." The governor, Easton wrote, "is a fine man and one who will do justice." Austin, on the other hand, cautioned Easton, was "too much heated" and was thereby playing into the hands of his enemies. As to Wilkinson's predisposition toward Smith T, Easton believed it to be from the colonel's "character and influence" in Tennessee.[38]

If Easton had any inkling that the Smith T–Wilkinson connection went any further than Smith T's Tennessee roots, he did not convey it to his so-called confidant, for Easton, like most upper-class Missourians, was not above some intrigue and deceit. Ambition outweighed loyalty, and Easton, who later became a U.S. territorial delegate from Missouri, did not want to burn his political bridges with Wilkinson or to commit himself totally to the Austin side in the mineral wars until a clear-cut victor could be ascertained. Moreover, Easton had an account against John Smith T in the amount of $980.40 for legal services rendered to him from 1809 through 1814. During the aforesaid period, Easton handled perhaps as many as fifty legal transactions for Smith T, including the lending of money. It is not unlikely that their relationship reached

37. Thomas Oliver to Carr, July 29, 1805, Carr Papers; Moses Austin to Easton, August 14, 1805, Easton Papers.
38. Easton to Moses Austin, July 29, 1805, Easton Papers.

back to the early days of the mineral wars, when Austin believed that Easton was his ally. Easton, however, broke with Wilkinson sometime after September 1805. The rupture was caused by Easton's refusal to join the conspiracy hatched by Burr and Wilkinson.

After Hunt's dismissal as commandant, Wilkinson next removed Austin as chief justice of the Ste. Genevieve Court of Common Pleas and appointed Smith T in his stead. The Court of Common Pleas was a trial court for most of the civil actions in the region. It also performed many district administrative functions. The Court of Quarter Sessions, which Smith T also headed for a while, was a trial court for most criminal cases, except capital offenses, which had to be tried by a general court. Even without this position on the Court of Quarter Sessions, Smith T's judicial positions put him in a very powerful position. Smith T was also appointed lieutenant colonel in the militia. In his judicial capacity as judge, said one account, he assumed virtually complete control of the region, ruling "with the scepter of a tyrant, no man daring to oppose him." Tales abounded of how Smith T and a small army loyal only to him would ride heavily armed into Ste. Genevieve, whence, seated at the bench with his trusted rifle draped across his lap, he would dispense "justice." Besides his legal duties, he was militarily responsible for regional safety and welfare. As lieutenant-colonel of the militia, he kept a watchful eye on the frontier and the possibility of Indian invasions. He demanded a strict accounting by his junior officers of the strengths and military status of their companies. In the interim, Smith T "continued to amass thousands of acres of land and the minerals interred in their veins."[39] Plans to use these resources in conquest of a greater southwestern empire were, so far, progressing smoothly.

Austin, however, proved to be a more formidable and resilient adversary than expected. Allied with him during these turbulent years

39. State of Missouri, *Treaty of Cession Laws of a Public and General Nature of the District of Louisiana, of the Territory of Louisiana, of Territory of Missouri and of the State of Missouri up to 1824,* vol. 1, 2–15, 57–64; William F. English, *The Pioneer Lawyer and Jurist in Missouri,* 48. Joseph Browne, Secretary of the Territory of Louisiana to Thomas Jefferson, July 14, 1806, in *Territorial Papers,* vol. 13, 545–48. *Kansas City Journal,* August 7, 1896. John Smith T to David Murphy, February 7, 1807, David Murphy Papers, MHS. Document, Frederick Bates, December 30, 1807, James Fordyce Collection, MHS. There are certificates of land claims to more than three thousand arpents by Smith T and hundreds of arpents claimed by his brother, Reuben.

The territorial divisions in early Missouri, c. 1812.

was John Rice Jones. Jones was a pro-slavery entrepreneur living in Kaskaskia, Illinois, during its territorial stage. He had been introduced to Austin during Austin's first visits to Missouri, and in fact he assisted Austin's efforts to settle in the lead district by serving as a go-between with the Spanish government. In 1810, two years after his son was killed in Illinois, Jones moved to Mine à Breton. In the following years he became a joint owner of some mines with Austin. This arrangement obviously put him at odds with Smith T and the small miners.[40]

Although previously stripped of his political authority by Wilkinson, Austin still possessed other powerful allies, especially in St. Louis. Realizing the futility of legal satisfaction in the Ste. Genevieve courts,

40. Floyd C. Shoemaker, "David Barton, John Rice Jones and Edward Bates: Three Missouri State and Statehood Founders," *MHR* 65, no. 4 (July 1971): 533–35.

Austin helped instigate a new way to preoccupy Smith T. This tactic called for Austin supporters such as James F. Scott and Elisha Baker to sue the colonel for assault and battery as well as false imprisonment. Some of these men, including Baker, were illiterate. Court records in Ste. Genevieve indicate only an "X" for Baker's signature. It is more than likely that Baker and the others served in Austin's volunteer force. Normally, these men were represented by Austin's attorney William C. Carr. The cases, however, were not to be tried in Ste. Genevieve but in the General Court in St. Louis under the jurisdiction of Judge Lucas, an Austin ally. Lucas no doubt delighted in ordering the sheriff of Ste. Genevieve to bring Smith T to St. Louis to stand trial. Although these legal actions did not result in any great harm, they no doubt distracted Smith T during the height of the mineral war.[41]

Austin also resisted, by means of his own private army, all attempts by Smith T and his henchmen to wrest his mineral empire from him. Stabbings, shootings, and killings, including attempts on Smith T's life, continued throughout the mining district war. On another occasion, Smith T was struck by a rifle ball and while thus immobilized was slashed with a knife. Before the assailant could finish his nefarious deed, the colonel's men pulled him off their boss and killed him instantly. The mineral war was indeed a near complete breakdown of law and order.[42]

These early territorial days were not only filled with episodes of reckless physical intrepidity but also were highlighted by many instances of bold and daring economic ventures. Like his arch rival Moses Austin, Smith T undertook some remarkable steps to vertically integrate his mineral enterprises. In 1806, he and Robert Browne joined in a partnership called W. H. Ashley and Company. Browne was the son of Joseph Browne, Wilkinson's territorial secretary. Ashley served as the principal partner.

Although Smith T provided most of the limited amounts of principal, the partnership depended in large degree upon infusions of credit. Browne played the least active role of the three, but provided political

41. Litigation, Miscellaneous Cases, May Term 1807, August Term 1809, Territory of Louisiana, 1804–1812, Record Group 1, Box 4, General Court Case Files, Missouri State Archives, Jefferson City, Mo. Hereafter cited as General Court, MSA. Three other men, Darius Shaw, James Whittlessee, and Darius F. Scott, also sued Smith T and apparently won some substantial judgments against him.
42. March, *The History of Missouri*, 229. William E. Foley, "The American Territorial System: Missouri's Experience," 416.

influence and some money. The operation's main objective was not extraction of lead, but the purchase and sale of it. In a day and age when hard currency was in short supply, the company's lead would be used in frontier communities as a medium of exchange.

Austin's control over the region's political economy had begun its dramatic decline, and Smith T was determined to use every means possible to hasten its further demise. Ashley's biographer, Richard Clokey, has called Smith T a "violent and devious man." The characterization no doubt was true. But in all fairness, more sinners than saints frequented the rough-and-tumble world of early Missouri. Clokey, however, correctly assessed Smith's motives in the partnership as both "another phase of his struggle with Austin" and "the future base of his commercial empire."[43] One of the factors counted upon by the partners to weaken Austin's grip was demographic. After the pacification of the Osage Indians in eastern Missouri, the pace of immigration quickened. New mines and other economic activities such as farming, timber cutting, and road building signified the end of Austin's monopoly. These new settlers and miners nevertheless needed supplies to maintain their economic independence.

The Ashley, Smith T, and Browne company devised a plan to offer itself as a "commercial agent" moving supplies to and from the mines and Ste. Genevieve. They would buy, on credit, the mining tools, foodstuffs, and agricultural supplies for the miners from the merchants of Ste. Genevieve. These products would thereupon be transported over forty miles of formidable roads to the mining area. Here at the mines, the partners would sell or exchange their wares for lead. The lead would then be transported back across the roads to prospective buyers on the Mississippi River.[44] Smith T also planned to build the roads. The business venture envisioned some of the vertical and infrastructural aspects of Austin's enterprises, except that Ste. Genevieve and not Mine à Breton would be the source of supplies. The other part of the plan was Smith T's hope that the operation would obviate the miners' dependency on Austin and thus further reduce his hold on the region.

Using his connections with Governor Wilkinson, Smith T connived to get Ashley an appointment as a justice of the peace in the lead region.

43. Clokey, *William A. Ashley*, 13.
44. Ibid.

Wilkinson also agreed, at Smith T's urging, to commission him a captain in the territorial militia. In the meantime, Browne was busily at work in the territorial capital winning friends and gaining influence to help the trio carry out its designs against Austin.[45]

The enterprise never achieved the success its founders envisioned. Part of the problem was the perennial lack of adequate capital, extremely high overhead expenses, and the unsettled economic and political climate that inhibited business growth. Smith T, however, did not give up on the idea of a road linking the mines to the Mississippi River. In fact, this scheme would become one of his most daring and successful business ventures. It would be called the Selma Road.

45. Ibid.

3. *The Road to Selma*

To keep abreast of Austin's ever-expanding enterprises, Smith T had decided that he too must construct a road from his mines to the Mississippi River. The choice for the ultimate destination of the road was Selma. His love for the surrounding white cliffs caused him to remark to his family that he would like to be buried there. The beauty of the place later prompted his granddaughter and her husband, Ferdinand Kennett, to construct their home and grave sites on the same spot. Their domicile was called Selma Hall. Kennett completed the home in the mid 1850s, nearly two decades after Smith T's death. Smith T obviously never saw the full magnificence of the home. In fact, the structure built by his descendants, because it rivaled any home built in antebellum Missouri, came to be called Kennett Castle after its first owner. But to no small degree it was Smith T's business ventures that made the construction of this mansion possible. In essence, it was his determination to rationalize the lead mining industry and to defeat Moses Austin that laid the foundation for Selma Hall.

Lead had played a prominent role in the mining region long before Austin and Smith T challenged each other for supremacy. Native Americans had traded the "heavy metal" as far north as Canada and as far south as Central America. Realizing the riches that the lead deposits offered, the Indians resisted the first French attempts to raid one of their primary sources of wealth. Nonetheless, by the 1720s the French had ensconced themselves in the mineral region. For nearly a hundred years the pioneers used lead as legal tender or exchange. All in all, in the first 250 years of lead mining, roughly seven billion dollars' worth of the heavy metal was extracted from east-central Missouri.[1]

---

1. Frank Magre, "Tracing the Old Selma Trail from Lead Mines to River Bank," unpublished paper, n.d., 2, Frank Magre Collection. Hereafter cited as Magre, "Tracing the Old Selma Trail."

At first the French moved raw lead, mostly large surface chunks, along scattered trails to an "entrepot" on the Mississippi. Later, the lead was transformed into ingots, or "pigs." Raw lead chunks were smelted in crude furnaces (some can still be found in the region) and molded into pigs, which were then sent downriver. Keelboats, barges, and eventually steamboats were used in the transportation process. From the port of New Orleans, the mineral was shipped to armies and nations around the world.

It would not be an exaggeration to say that once Austin's empire crumbled, there was no local or perhaps even state official to challenge Smith T's power in the mining region. In addition, the national government had not yet established a federal agent to supervise the mines and to ensure that leases were carried out in a proper fashion. This situation allowed the new lead king to continue to act with virtual impunity in the district. A number of prominent figures in the region had called for a supervisory agent since the days of Governor Meriwether Lewis. They believed that a government mining official could contain the squatting on federal lands containing lead and could also stop the intimidation of small miners and the claims jumping by "unscrupulous manipulators." In August 1824 the long-awaited mining agent finally arrived.[2] By that time, however, the mineral area had matured somewhat from its rugged pioneer ways, and order had been established. It is doubtful, therefore, that these new federal developments perturbed John Smith T much at all.

In the first years of the nineteenth century, however, just about every facet of mining posed a problem for him. The biggest obstacle in those days was, of course, Moses Austin. Austin, always the innovator, had early on realized the potential for integrating the lead industry. Taking his cue from John N. Maclot, who in 1809 had erected the first shot tower west of Pittsburgh, Austin expanded his operation. Maclot's tower was in the southeastern part of a small Mississippi River town, Herculaneum, located in today's Jefferson County, Missouri. Austin, who along with Samuel Hammond had laid out the little town at the mouth of Joachim Creek in 1808, placed his own shot towers on these same high Mississippi bluffs in 1810. Austin had named the town Herculaneum because the surrounding limestone strata were so eroded

2. Ibid., 32.

that they resembled seats in the amphitheater of the ancient buried city near Naples, Italy.[3]

Although the small river town grew slowly during the first decades of the new century (it had only two hundred residents in 1821), the shot towers proved to be an invaluable source of profit and power for Austin. Realizing that he must try to match Austin step for step, Smith T also decided to locate a lead shipping point on the river and to manufacture shot in towers on the bluffs. In addition, he added, according to some accounts, a gunpowder mill. The mill put him in a position to reap additional profits on the demand for ammunition by pioneers and the army.[4] Due to the labor-intensive nature of these operations and the back-breaking work involved, both Austin and Smith T employed black slaves to do the manual labor. It was the decision to diversify his lead mining operation that required Smith T to build his own road, Selma Road, from the mines near Shibboleth to the river. Hence, the origins of Selma Hall.

Smith T set out to find a suitable site for his shot towers. Not far from present-day Crystal City he located a mammoth bluff overhanging the Mississippi River. He reputedly called it the "Cliffs of Selma" because it reminded him of a place described in Ossian's poem "Fingal." If the story can be believed, it would suggest that Smith T was indeed well read and a gentleman of some good breeding. The beauty of these cliffs, some four hundred feet high, was enhanced by their white limestone color. Smith T often referred to them as the "White Cliffs of Selma."

The immediate problem he faced after deciding to locate his shot towers near Selma was the fact that the land and landing was already owned by the James White family. The situation was soon solved. As a gentleman skilled in claims jumping, Smith T made a quick investigation of the Whites' title to the property and, finding that it was improperly executed, laid claim to it. The Whites, suffice it to say, were not amused. Nevertheless, they relinquished the property without a bitter struggle. Smith T's violent reputation no doubt preceded him and worked to his advantage. All in all, Smith T may have amassed close to ten thousand acres of land in the river bottom. The absence of

---

3. Eleanor Koch Rehm, *Jefferson County: Its Settlers, Origin and Development*, 1.
4. George Penn Smith, Jr., "John Smith T," 5.

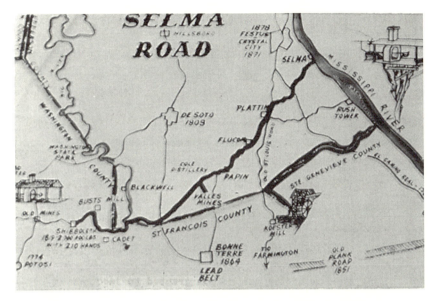

Map of the Selma Road, which stretched forty miles from the lead mines to the Mississippi River. The road was a significant infrastructural feat for the early 1800s.

violence no doubt left possible the irony that would occur some fifteen years later. Smith T's daughter, Ann, after the loss of her first husband, married James M. White of the same family whose lands he had earlier "stolen."[5]

The road to Selma Hall was also part of a larger issue relating to transportation and communication networks during the early 1800s. The importance placed on roads and communications was established very early in the state's history. On July 9, 1806, the Legislature of the Territory of Louisiana passed its first act concerning public roads and highways. It allowed for twelve or more freeholders and inhabitants of a district to petition the courts for the establishment of a public road. Commissioners were then chosen from the counties that the road would cross. These commissioners then chose a chairman and appointed a surveyor and other appropriate personnel to survey and then mark out the route. After completion of this task, the surveyor took the notes he

5. Interview, Frank Magre, April 2, 1992, Crystal City, Mo. Local historians believe Smith T purchased this land around 1805. See the *Heritage News,* issue 4, July 1993.

had written in a field book and made a plat (map), with copies going to designated public officials.

The procedure of course was complicated in these early days by the absence of any federal land survey and the wide variation in the field notes. In addition, courses and distances from one point to another were often imprecise and led to confusion and to further litigation. Some surveyors measured distances in poles (rods) and some in chains. These distances, by whichever measurement, were then converted to miles. Besides measurement problems, individuals such as Smith T with the temerity to build a road had to contend with conflicting claims to land ownership and contentious owners of right-of-ways who sometimes demanded exorbitant sums of money for their land or for the damages incurred to property.

In laying out the forty-mile Selma Road, Smith T, like other builders such as Austin, tried to use preexisting Indian trails when possible. The Indians no doubt followed the paths first charted by the wild animals of the area.[6] Since these early trails were often confusing and indistinct, the early settlers marked their passage by making notches on the trees to keep from getting lost. The notch trails of the territorial days soon became a casualty of progress after Missouri became a state. As the flatboats and barges were replaced by steamboats, there developed a voracious appetite for wood to fuel the new technology, and soon the distinctively notched trees along the trails were gone as the mining region's forests became denuded.

The notched trees and their brethren in the forests succumbed not only to the needs of steamboats but also to demographics. As more people moved into the region, there was an increased demand for wood to heat the lead furnaces and to warm the homes of the people. Men armed with axes and an order for cordwood could now make a living by harvesting timber. By the time of the railroads, the baldness of the Potosi–Ste. Genevieve area was apparent to all.[7] Unfortunately, the roads built by men such as John Smith T indirectly contributed to the ecological problems of the mining region.

Another shortcoming of these early earthen highways was that they did not conform to the classic theories of geometry. For example, they

6. Magre, "Tracing the Old Selma Trail," 1.
7. Ruby M. Robins, ed., "The Missouri Reader: Americans in the Valley," 263; Schoolcraft, *A View of the Lead Mines of Missouri*, 52–53.

seldom adhered to the time-honored dictum that a straight line is the best and shortest distance between two points. Roads often followed traces (paths) along river or creek bottoms but then wound up to higher ground in circular fashion so as not to make a direct, rapid ascent. This allowed for less physical strain on men and animals. Roads sometimes were diverted to intersect with a spring. Although modern engineers might be puzzled by their strange configurations, roads like Selma Road had a logic all their own.

In time, the small trails first used by wild animals, then by Indians and white men with horses or mules, began to widen to accommodate carts and wagons. These heavier pieces of equipment were pulled by oxen. In the dry months, the carts and wagons used a smaller-rimmed wheel with less traction. During the dry season the wagons normally had very high wheels in the back and low ones in the front. The drovers called them the fair-weather wagons. During the winter and spring months when rainfall was more plentiful, the carts used a wider wheel to plow through the mud and snow. The wagon drivers also replaced the smaller front wheels with larger, heavy ones. Even today the ruts from these old caravans provide a silent reminder of bygone days when the mining area was the most dynamic economic region in the territory.

Besides the elements, roads such as Selma Road had to accommodate themselves to creeks and rivers. Other than the constant danger from thieves and highwaymen, water crossings were the most serious threat posed on the long trip. The heavy ore wagons had a tendency to sink in the mud and loose gravel of most waterways. Therefore, Selma Road, like most others, was charted so that crossings were at riverbeds composed of solid, flat rock. This allowed the fording of rivers at all times except during high water. Later, Smith T erected some coarse wooden bridges, which eliminated the problem of soft earth beyond the creek and river floors.

Most of the maps of early roads, including Selma Road, were not given to great accuracy. Rather, they provided a general picture of the route as opposed to a measured plat. Streams, rivers, springs, hills, and other assorted geographical features dot these early sketches.[8] One of the local historians who clearly understood what the roads of the period were like was Frank Magre. He wrote:

8. The author is indebted to Cathy Atwood, "State Road Maps and the State Road System."

In the late 1700s and early 1800s most of this part of the country
was a roadless wilderness. Even the celebrated El Camino Real was
little more than a rugged pathway hacked out of the countryside.
Deeply mired in mud during the spring thaws and periods of heavy
rains, twisting torturously around huge boulders and fallen trees,
fording streams only when the rivers ran low enough to permit
passage, or when gallant swimming beasts could make it across the
swollen water courses in reckless gambles with fate. Travel was no
sinecure or picnic.[9]

Perhaps no other local issue divided the various economic elites of
the mining region as much as the building and maintenance of roads.
An example of the volatility of this issue is reflected in a September 4,
1813, letter sent by Territorial Governor William Clark to some of the
more prominent figures in what would become Washington County.
Clark addressed the letter to some of Smith T's competitors and potential competitors in the mining business. Included in this list were
Samuel Perry, Lionel Browne, John Andrews, Martin Ruggles, and
John Hawkins. Specifically, the governor made it known that government funds, although somewhat scarce, would be made available for
road building and internal improvements in the region.[10] Petitions were
quickly sent to the local commissioners to secure the money.

What concerned Smith T about Clark's letter was the omission of
his name. The oversight, if that was the case, may have been due to
his frequent absences from the territory. Nevertheless, since he and the
governor were not on opposite factional sides, it appeared odd that
Clark would not include at least one or more of Smith T's numerous
business associates. Perhaps Clark had begun to distance himself from
Smith T for political reasons but did not want to dramatize the issue.
Particularly threatening to the colonel and his mining interests was
a notice published on January 3, 1814, by John Brickey. This public
document announced that Moses Austin had been appointed as one
of the road commissioners. William Perry, also a Smith T rival, was
appointed at roughly the same time as the surveyor. One of the first
projects to receive these public monies was a new road from Austin's
Mine à Breton that would link up with new lead diggings in the mineral

9. Magre, "Tracing the Old Selma Trail," 4.
10. William Clark to Lionel Browne et al., September 4, 1813, Washington County
Court Records, 1810–1813, Box 1, Folder 2, MSA.

area. Since the new mines and the lead diggers would have access to Austin's smelting operations, it would effectively shut out Smith T.[11]

Roads linking both the smelting operations to new digs and the ore to the shot towers on the Mississippi were thus important aspects of the vertical integration of the mining economies. But politics greased the wheels of travel as surely as did profits. Austin, for example, seemed to be the political catalyst behind the establishment of Washington County in 1813. By creating a new county out of the immense Ste. Genevieve County, Austin perhaps believed that he would separate himself from some of the more hostile French settlers closer to the Mississippi. He may have surmised that a new county with new officials might be more susceptible to his influence, especially in the areas of roads and surveys. It generally held true to form that road commissioners supported those petitions which emanated from their political allies. Road money was a powerful tool in shaping the political and economic destiny of a developing territory. More than once Smith T confronted hostile commissioners and lost out to his most bitter foes. On one occasion, for example, he and his brother Reuben, along with William H. Ashley, proposed that funds be expended to improve roads from Potosi (near Shibboleth) to Jackson, Missouri. Although the self-serving idea had some merit, the petition got nowhere.[12]

Consequently, Smith T had little recourse except to build and to maintain his own roads, especially the most important of them all, the one to the White Cliffs of Selma. The task was formidable indeed, given the forty-mile distance from the mines to the river. Shibboleth was the starting point for the road. Local historians believed that an earlier version of a road probably existed before 1810 when Smith T put the finishing touches to it. In fact, the old Selma Road was the only primary artery linking numerous smaller roads into one transportation system. The Valles Mines, for example, were linked by a short road to the main line. According to Frank Magre, "Until the railroad came to Valles Mines most of the mined lead . . . undoubtedly was funneled into the

11. Notice, John Brickey, January 3, 1814, Box 1, Folder 1; Petition, Moses Austin et al., July 7, 1814, Box 1, Folder 1, ibid.

12. Notice, Circuit Court, May 1816 Term, Ste. Genevieve County, vol. 1, pt. 2, 1812–1820, and Stephen Austin to James Bryan, February 11, 1817, both in Austin Papers. William H. Ashley et al. to John Brickey, n.d., Box 1, Folder 1, Washington County Court Records, MSA.

Selma Trail, thus adding significantly to the tonnage rolling along the old road."[13] Across the forty-mile trek, a variety of farm roads, trails, and paths intersected and followed the Selma Road for a short distance. Sometimes even the main road would split, only to merge again a few miles down the way.

A major logistical obstacle for road builders was cutting the trees and clearing the stumps that always posed a danger to the large, cumbersome wagons. Travel was expedited on part of the road, however, by the terrain and the flora. Prairies, indigenous to the area, dotted the landscape and lowered the costs of land clearing. The twisting road also did not have to traverse any high mountains or marshy terrain. Although the road crossed some hills, the ridges actually served as an alternate route, especially in months of snow and rain. The Selma Road was often a series of connecting routes, all focused toward the Mississippi. The durability of the road was attested to by the fact that soldiers used it during the Civil War.

The main purpose of the road was quite obviously the transportation of lead. Nonetheless, it served a variety of other functions as well. Travelers moving from the mining region to the river and vice versa found it to be a most expeditious route. The road was also used to ship a number of farm products destined for export down the river. Hides, furs, whiskey, and other assorted products likewise found a water outlet by means of the Selma Road. On the return trip, many wagons were full of grain, flour, and other grocery items. Even though no exact figure can be found to pinpoint the profit margin on this movement of goods, it would appear that Smith T used the road like any other toll road of that day and age. In time, the Selma Road, because it was nearly ten miles shorter than Austin's road, became the most widely traveled road in that section of the territory. The Selma Road, suffice it to say, contributed to the wealth of Smith T by diversifying his income as well as by allowing him to vertically and horizontally integrate his lead empire.

In all likelihood, the Selma Road opened sometime around 1811. During its heyday, it must have been a busy thoroughfare with horses, mules, and the mightiest of the beasts of burden, the sturdy oxen, traveling in both directions. Early French settlers had hauled the heavy lead

13. Magre, "Tracing the Old Selma Trail," 18.

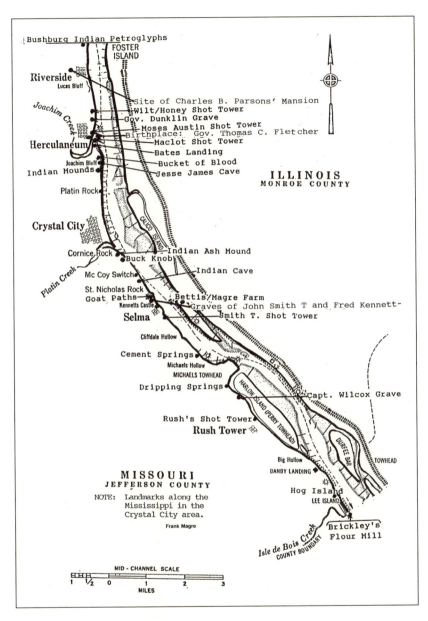

Bushburg Indian Petroglyphs
FOSTER ISLAND
Riverside
Lucas Bluff
Joachim Creek
Site of Charles B. Parsons' Mansion
Wilt/Honey Shot Tower
Gov. Dunklin Grave
Moses Austin Shot Tower
Birthplace: Gov. Thomas C. Fletcher
Herculaneum
Maclot Shot Tower
Bates Landing
Joachim Bluff
Indian Mounds
Bucket of Blood
Jesse James Cave
Platin Rock
CALICO ISLAND
Crystal City
Cornice Rock
Buck Knob
Platin Creek
Mc Coy Switch
St. Nicholas Rock
Goat Paths
Kennetts Castle
Selma
Bettis/Magre Farm
Indian Ash Mound
Indian Cave
Graves of John Smith T and Fred Kennett
Smith T. Shot Tower
Cliffdale Hollow
Cement Springs
Michaels Hollow
MICHAELS TOWHEAD
Dripping Springs
HARLOW ISLAND (PERRY TOWHEAD)
Capt. Wilcox Grave
Rush's Shot Tower
Rush Tower
DURFEE BAR
TOWHEAD
Big Hollow
DANBY LANDING
MISSOURI
JEFFERSON COUNTY
Hog Island
LEE ISLAND
NOTE: Landmarks along the Mississippi in the Crystal City area.
Frank Magre
Isle de Bois Creek
COUNTY BOUNDARY
Brickley's Flour Mill
MID - CHANNEL SCALE
1 ½ 0   1   2   3
MILES
ILLINOIS
MONROE COUNTY

Activities along the Mississippi in Jefferson County, Missouri. Smith T's operations and Kennett Castle are in the central part of the county. Moses Austin's shot tower is near Herculaneum.

ore in ox-drawn wooden carts called "charettes." The later American version of these carts was the "ox bow," in which more weight was placed on the neck and shoulder of the oxen, rather than the head-beam hitches that placed more stress on the animal's head and horns.[14] These sturdy wagons were not a thing of beauty. Nor were they swift. In the best of months, when the paths were dry and hard, the ox-drawn carts could seldom make twenty miles a day. The going was not only tedious and slow but also dangerous.

The ore carts and freighters generally traveled in caravans for mutual protection against outlaws and thieves, who preyed on the unsuspected and isolated. Drovers, if they could not make it to one of the inns, often slept in their covered wagons.[15] The men usually brought their food and other sleeping provisions with them. Water was another matter, especially during the hot and dry summer months of the haul. Drinking water for both men and animals was obtained from springs and wells gushing through the porous limestone rock. These springs were often not directly on the route. Thus, extra time was lost, especially during the hot summer months, going to and from the sources of water. Since the haul took two days or more, Smith T provided a tavern and sleeping inn at a halfway point along the road.

As the road snaked its way across the countryside, it intersected with a number of lesser routes from the mines to the banks of the Mississippi. The road to Mine La Motte, for example, crossed its path. This afforded other miners the opportunity to take advantage (for a fee) of the much better road. Selma Road was quite obviously the artery supplying the flow of resources to Shibboleth, the heart of Smith T's operation. During the years just before statehood, Smith T employed more than two hundred men at Shibboleth.[16]

Exact costs of transporting the lead along the forty-mile road cannot be estimated. One analyst has placed the amount at approximately seventy-five cents per one hundred pounds.[17] This figure, however, may not include the capitalization of wagons, materials, and animals, nor the possible expenditures in lodgings, stores, and taverns on the trail. It would be safe to conclude that very few Missourians at this juncture

14. Higginbotham, *John Smith T*, 8–9.
15. Magre, "Tracing the Old Selma Trail," 9.
16. Ibid.
17. Howard C. Litton, *History of Jefferson County, Missouri*, 20, 147.

in the territory's history had either the means or the determination to turn such a risky proposition into a reality.

By the early 1820s, Smith T was indeed the new lead king of Missouri. It has been estimated by local historians of the mining region that from 1824 to 1854, nearly eighty-six million pounds of lead and shot were shipped from Selma and two other depots at Plattin Rock and Rush Tower.[18] Other local historians have determined that from Selma alone, approximately seventy million pounds of lead were shipped downriver from 1834 to 1854.

At the end of the journey eastward near the shot tower, Smith T provided sustenance for the weary travelers, both animal and human. Stores, a tavern, livery stables, grain and hay storage, a blacksmith shop, a repair shop for broken harnesses and wagons, and an inn were all part of the bustling operation. At the Selma landing, where the shot was loaded on boats headed downriver, a post office was established around 1827 with Luther Kennett as the postmaster. In addition, there were warehouses, scales, loading facilities, and a weighing station.[19] Near the landing but jutting out into the Mississippi was an island, appropriately called Smith Island. Over the years the backwaters filled it in, and the island became part of the mainland. Many people over the course of time have mistakenly identified Smith Island as the site of the famous duel in 1856 between B. Gratz Brown and Thomas Reynolds. This duel, however, was fought on another island not far from Selma Hall.

Today, the old Selma Road, like its once-famous architect, has lapsed into "almost complete obliteration." Occasionally, as one travels across the area, some small patch of the road may still be marked, but modern farming techniques, highway construction, and new methods of mining have changed the face of the landscape forever. Consequently, the perils of modernization have placed the visual accomplishments of John Smith T's mine-to-smelter route in ultimate jeopardy.[20] The memory of Selma has thus been preserved not by the road but by its by-product: the mansion, Selma Hall.

The beauty and grandeur of the White Cliffs of Selma may have tempted Smith T to construct a home overlooking the river that

18. Ibid.
19. Magre, "Tracing the Old Selma Trail," 3.
20. Ibid., 5.

Drawing of Shibboleth, Smith T's home. The structure, remarkable for its time, was dismantled in the early twentieth century.

provided him so much profit and adventure. He did not succumb to the temptation, however, largely because he had already built a fine frontier home at Mine Shibboleth. Although the house was not comparable to the style and elegance of his descendants' mansion at Selma Hall, it was for its day and age rivaled and most likely surpassed only by Austin's Durham Hall.

Shibboleth was a large, two-story, federal-style brick home replete with fireplaces, a long porch, and a winding staircase. According to Henry Brackenridge, Smith T's earlier home had been a double log or dog trot cabin. In this style, typical of prominent frontiersmen, two large cabins were joined by a passage under the same roof. One side had a parlor, a dining room, and a bedroom; the other side had rooms to accommodate strangers. In addition, he observed other detached buildings that served as a kitchen and offices.[21] Brackenridge left the Missouri territory before the construction of the permanent brick home. For its day and age, Shibboleth certainly reflected the power and status befitting one of Missouri's most prominent citizens. Unfortunately, this domicile, the first leg of the run to Selma Hall, has not withstood the ravages of time. Extensive repairs were needed on the house, and no one seemed willing to defray the costs. Furthermore,

21. Brackenridge, *Recollections,* 216–22. Also see "John Smith T: A Missouri Swashbuckler," Collection no. 3524, Robert M. Snyder, Jr., Papers, 4–6, WHMC.

few people at the time recognized the significance of the house or the utility of historic preservation. The house, still in the possession of the family, stood until sometime shortly before World War II.

Shibboleth, like virtually everything surrounding Smith T's life, was also shrouded in myth, legend, and lore. In the early twentieth century, a certain "Boss" Courtois and his family moved into the home. The folklore of the region told of the house being haunted, although no one ever linked the ghost or ghosts to Smith T or his immediate family. Whether these far-fetched tales had any direct bearing on Shibboleth's deteriorating condition cannot be certain. Nevertheless, the Courtois family, despite the apparitions or because of them—again no one knows for sure—began to dismantle Smith T's home brick by brick sometime in the early 1940s. The bricks were then cleaned and shipped to St. Louis for sale.[22] Even before the deterioration of Shibboleth, however, Selma Hall had risen among the rugged white cliffs of the Mississippi.

Selma Hall was no doubt the by-product of the Selma Road. Each in their day was an engineering marvel. The road greatly enhanced Smith T's economic fortunes: it allowed Smith T to compete on a more or less equal footing with Austin, and it also demonstrated how political factionalism played a part in most economic issues of the day. But roads were only a part of the larger political issues. Even the struggle with Austin was only a prelude to a bigger prize, namely, the Spanish Southwest. To gain it, Smith T allied himself with some very undependable men. The result proved nearly fatal.

22. Jefferson County Heritage Society, "Prologue, Tour of Selma Hall," unpublished paper, October 24, 1984.

4. Burr and Thwarted Ambition

Even before his struggle with Austin for supremacy in the mineral area had been won, John Smith T had set his sights on the one prize that would always elude his grasp: an empire in the Southwest. His notoriety and daring served a purpose beyond intimidating potential rivals. Fearless men follow fearless leaders. An attack upon the Spanish frontier (most likely in the Texas–New Mexico Territory) was not for the faint of heart. Pioneer swashbucklers might fight and die, but they must first believe in and be inspired by their leaders. Violent action was one quality highly prized by these men. Smith T no doubt understood this fact and unabashedly promoted his own reputation for violence.

The self-promotion of a violent persona was successful beyond Smith T's own lifetime. Over the next century and a half it was accepted at face value by modern historians as well. Richard Clokey, William Ashley's biographer, wrote of Smith T as a "master of the dueling skills which would later take the lives of fifteen men." Clokey was no doubt influenced by Floyd C. Shoemaker, who likewise called Smith T a "savage fighter" and credited him with the same number of kills. Perry McCandless in his *History of Missouri* also made note of the same lethal figure. David Gracy, Austin's biographer, said that the colonel "never ducked a challenge and never lost a duel." "When aroused," he maintained, "he was one of the most dangerous men in the history of the state." Early-twentieth-century historian Robert S. Douglass echoed the same view. Smith T, he elaborated, was "a man of terrible passions." And finally, William Foley, in 1989, wrote that although Smith T "hardly looked the part of a dreaded gunslinger," the "appearance was deceiving."[1]

1. Clokey, *William A. Ashley,* 16. State Historical Society of Missouri, *This Week in Missouri History, April 30–May 6, 1933.* Perry McCandless, *A History of Missouri, Vol. II,*

Certainly, Missouri in the early 1800s was no place for the meek. Its male inhabitants, wrote nineteenth-century historian Firmin Rozier, were bold, brave men filled with a spirit of adventure and gambling, and none represented "the chivalry of the times" more completely than John Smith T. He was a man, reported Rozier, who "stood unrivaled for skill, undaunted courage and great coolness in those terrible conflicts with his enemies."[2]

All were not so chivalrous. River pirates such as Samuel Mason and Big and Little Harpe plied their trade on the great rivers of the territory, while land pirates preyed upon unsuspecting merchants and trappers who made their way on shore and upstream against the currents of the same mighty rivers. On these waters, "Colonel" Fluger, a river pirate from New Hampshire, dueled one of his lieutenants, a certain Nine-Eyes, in a quarrel relating to the latter's amorous overtures toward Fluger's wife, Pluggy. The affair ended with both men being hit harmlessly in the rear anatomy. Each deemed honor satisfied and finished off a bottle of whiskey to commemorate their good fortune and poor aim. James Hall, a contemporary of Smith T, called the boatmen "proverbially lawless and dissolute." They were men, he wrote, who indulged "without restraint, in every species of debauchery, outrage, and mischief." The general state of society in territorial Missouri was so "savage" that many an enlightened soul moved back East. When you crossed the Mississippi, Rev. Timothy Flint asserted, you "travel beyond the Sabbath." Henry R. Schoolcraft agreed. Missouri, he wrote, was beyond "the pale of civilized society." Even General James Wilkinson admitted that "pettifoggers" swarmed like "locusts" in the territory and "fugitive countrymen" wore their "political morality as loosely" as they did "their cloaths." Here, too, keelboatmen such as Mike Fink and pioneers such as Daniel Boone shot, fought, and drank their way into folk history.[3]

1820–1860, 90. Gracy, *Moses Austin,* 100. Douglass, *History of Southeast Missouri,* 60. Foley, *Genesis,* 163.

2. Firmin Rozier, *Rozier's History of the Early Settlement of the Mississippi Valley,* 312–13.

3. Henry R. Schoolcraft, *Journal of a Tour into the Interior of Missouri and Arkansaw, 1818–1819,* 44. Estwick Evans, *A Pedestrious Tour, 1818,* in Reuben Gold Thwaites, ed., *Early Western Travels 1748–1846,* vol. 8, 308–10. Hereafter cited as *EWT.* For material on Mason, see chap. 1 in ibid. Hall, *Letters from the West,* 265–82; Hall, *Sketches,* vol. 2, 87, 72. Leland D. Baldwin, *The Keelboat Age on Western Waters,* 118. The story of the duel between Fluger and Nine-Eyes was first told in "Col. Plug—The Last of the

John Smith T did not shrink from such a hostile environment. Rather, the violence and turmoil worked to his advantage. In fact, it was during the mineral wars that a series of stories and myths concerning his dauntless courage emerged. Although he had yet to fight a duel in the Missouri Territory and perhaps had never gone to the field of honor, his marksmanship and apparent willingness to target a human body made few men brave his wrath. Smith T's enemies became increasingly intimidated by the stories, both real and manufactured, of his fury. Even Moses Austin fell prey to the myth when he recoiled in horror at the prospect of Smith T's almost demonic capabilities. This "monster," as he confessed to Rufus Easton, seemed incapable of being stopped. To Austin, he had become a "god of Darkness" who had assumed almost mythic proportions in a land of raw and rugged individualism.[4] The myths and legends (first established in Tennessee and later embellished during the conflict with Austin) played an indispensable role in promoting the Smith T style of leadership.

Part of the Smith T mystique lay in a demeanor of dress, style, and manners that defied conventional frontier stereotypes. Although his actions transcended appearance, literary visualizations became the essence of his persona. With his Virginia gentry upbringing and William and Mary College education, his grace and manners (at least when sober) personified that of a southern gentleman. Yet his bearing was decidedly that of a wilderness aristocrat. According to one of his legal advisers, John Darby, he had "a Daniel Boone aspect about him."[5] He was usually attired in an elegant buckskin hunting shirt, heavily fringed and ornamented, with doeskin pants and fine polished boots. While this manner of dress was not uncommon for some polished gentlemen (August Chouteau wore a fancy Indian buckskin coat decorated with Indian quill work), it certainly added to his frontier verve.

In addition, the man was a walking arsenal, and his home an armory. Although accounts vary, it was likely that he carried two pistols under a belt in his hunting shirt, two derringers in side pockets, a dirk

Boat Wreckers," *Western Monthly Review* 3 (January 1830): 355–57. For his views on violence, see Flint, *Recollections,* 175–83. General James Wilkinson to Secretary of State James Madison, July 28, 1805, in *Territorial Papers,* vol. 13, 173–74. "Mike Fink, The Last of the Boatmen," *Western Monthly Review* 3 (July 1829): 16–18.

4. Moses Austin to Rufus Easton, August 14, 1805, Easton Papers, MHS.
5. Darby, *Personal Recollections,* 92–93.

resembling a bowie knife, and a rifle, appropriately named "Hark from the Tombs." Two slaves, one a trusted companion named Dave, were gunsmiths. Theirs was a full-time job making and repairing pistols and rifles. His weapons were considered the finest in the western country. In time they became icons of his age. His own left-handed dueling pistol, specially made for him, was, according to a Wilkes County, Georgia, historian, "the most accurate weapon in the West." Reportedly, Thomas H. Benton used a pistol made at Shibboleth, Smith T's home, to kill Charles Lucas in a duel on Bloody Island. Another prominent Missourian felled by a pistol made by the same gunsmith was Dr. Walter Fenwick. The Ste. Genevieve physician died in 1811 in a duel at the hands of Thomas T. Crittenden.[6]

Throughout these early territorial days, Smith T's reputation as a duelist and his status as a folk hero were enhanced by word of his numerous affairs of honor back in Tennessee. Austin unwittingly added to the myths and legends of his adversary's violent past. Smith T had sued Austin for accusing him of murder, and in the course of the trial, John Andrews testified that he overheard Austin say that the colonel had once stabbed a man to death in Tennessee and "had to fly or fled his country for it." It appears that Andrews knew both men rather well as he also testified that Smith T had repeatedly called Austin "a damned rascal, damned scoundrel, and a damned Yankee." Furthermore, he added that Smith T had been trying to figure out how much money Austin owed and gleefully believed that it was so much "that he will have to flee the country" because he could not pay it all off.[7]

Smith T and his attorney, however, continued to hammer away at the slanderous remarks of Austin. Catherine Miller on October 3, 1811, testified that she heard Austin say that Colonel Smith was "a very arbitrary man in disposition and conduct." Austin, taking the high road of patriotism, proclaimed that he opposed Smith T because he had aligned himself in a conspiracy against the United States with Aaron Burr. Mrs. Miller went on to add that, according to the defendant, for the most trivial insult "Smith T would take his pistol or dirk and make

---

6. Gardner, *Lead King*, 112; State Historical Society of Missouri, *This Week in Missouri History, April 30–May 6, 1933*. Janet H. Standard, *Wilkes County Scrapbook*, vol. A, 55. Higginbotham, *John Smith T*, 48.
7. Moses Austin to Rufus Easton, August 14, 1805, Easton Papers, MHS. Testimony, John Andrews, General Court, 1811 Term, Record Group 1, Box 3, MSA.

use of them." Austin, she claimed, had accused Smith T of killing or wounding many men in his time and in fact could be called "nothing else but a murderer."[8] Four other depositions in essence repeated the claims set forth by Miller. All referred to incidents that had occurred in Tennessee.

Austin nevertheless put up a spirited defense. Less than two weeks before the testimony of Catherine Miller, the defense called a certain A. McCoy. He testified that while in Tennessee some years previously, he happened across a "Negro" washing a bloody shirt. McCoy inquired as to the nature of the accident and the hapless victim. The man replied that the shirt belonged to a local mayor by the name of Hays. He had been stabbed the night before by John Smith. The defense maintained that this was in fact the colonel before he added the infamous T to his name. According to McCoy's deposition, this killing resulted in Smith T's flight from Tennessee to avoid prosecution.[9]

Although his peers found it rather difficult to defend Smith T as the essence of propriety, no one could provide any warrants for his arrest in Tennessee. In point of fact, Smith T had remained constantly involved in a variety of land transactions and other enterprises in the Volunteer State. No effort had ever been made to arrest him, even though he was highly visible in Tennessee. Smith T's lawyer made it quite clear that he had continually moved back and forth from one state to another with impunity. The jury no doubt agreed. Smith T won the suit against Austin, but it remains unclear whether he ever received any monetary compensation.

In any event, the court proceedings reinforced his image as a very dangerous man. The trial and its aftermath were two of the many ways that historical facts were transmuted into folklore. In all probability, Smith T realized that some strategic advantage could be gained by this reputation, for he no doubt embellished his crimsoned past to win political influence and to give an aura of invincibility to his claims jumping. Frederick Bates, a secretary and acting governor of the territory, cited twenty land grants claimed by Smith T in a seven-year period. One of these was a ten-thousand-arpent tract dating to 1797. This land was in addition to thousands of acres purchased legally, which included

8. Testimony, Catherine Miller, ibid.
9. Testimony, A. McCoy, ibid.

mineral deposits, mill sites, and salt springs. In exasperation and dismay, Bates remarked that the man must have a "mineral-mania."[10]

By 1806, Smith T's meteoric rise to power was evidenced by his extensive landholdings and business enterprises, his judicial and military functions, his good political connections, and his social standing in the community. What remained was an "extended sphere of action" to immortalize his fame and deeds. That sphere was the Spanish Southwest. But the man to whom he mistakenly hitched his star was General James Wilkinson. Within a year this alliance proved to be a grave error.

The reversals of fortune, so serious as to have debilitated many a lesser man, began in 1806, the year of Smith T's greatest influence. First, it was a sour year for business enterprises. The partnership with Ashley and Browne had, by the end of the year, proved to be far less profitable than expected. It would dissolve within another two years. Another business venture collapsed the following year: the commercial partnership between Smith T and entrepreneurs Robert Wescott and Thomas Riddick. The dissolution of this partnership resulted in a series of lawsuits against Smith T that lasted roughly ten years.[11] Second, Austin proved to be a resilient and determined foe. The colonel's assault on Durham Hall in an effort to commandeer his three-pounder had failed, as had his efforts to dislodge Austin from Mine à Breton.

Without the quasi-military power available to dislodge Austin by force, Smith T resorted to a variety of legal tactics to harass his adversary. Because of his political and military offices, he was well positioned to use these to his advantage. On August 25, 1806, his attorney, John Scott, filed suit against Austin for trespassing. Scott argued that Austin along with his servants, horses, carts, wagons, and passengers had crossed Smith T's properties and had promised to pay one hundred

10. See the material in chap. 2 on the St. Vrain grant. Documents 1833–34-35, John Smith T to John Scott, Probate File no. 905, Washington County Courthouse, Potosi, Mo.; Lewis Linn Affidavit, August 5, 1837, ibid.; Deed Record Book A, Washington County Courthouse, Potosi, Mo., 28, 55, 354. Hereafter cited as Deed Record Book. Book B, ibid., 12, 38, 114, 136, 151, 277, 278. State Historical Society of Missouri, *This Week in Missouri History, April 30–May 6, 1933.*

11. Court Document, October 14, 1807, Washington County Court Papers, Box 1, Folder 7, Washington County Courthouse, Potosi, Mo. The agreement between Smith T and Wescott and Riddick can also be found in the General Court Records of the Territory of Louisiana. Some of the more pertinent documents regarding the lawsuits include Summons, John Brickey to Lionel Browne, April 28, 1815, ibid.; Court Order, John Brickey to Lionel Browne, June 16, 1815, ibid.

dollars for the services rendered. The suit went on to say that Austin, "intending to deceive and defraud" the colonel, had never intended to make monetary restitution. The case was tried by Jean Baptiste Valle, acting as first justice of the Court of Common Pleas in Ste. Genevieve. Valle, in all probability sympathetic to Smith T's side in the mineral war, ordered the sheriff in the customary language of the day "that you take Moses Austin if he may be found within your bailiwick and him safely keep so that you have his body before our justices of our Court of Common Pleas" on the second Tuesday of September 1806. Austin responded to the charges through his attorney, William C. Carr. Carr denied the charges against his client and claimed that he had met all his financial obligations. Carr further maintained that Smith T had already sued Austin twice in different courts to collect the debt. The case was continued until March 1807, when Austin showed receipts of one hundred bars of lead weighing more than two tons that had been paid to Smith T. Scott argued that the receipts should not be used as evidence in the case. The court said otherwise, and in the end awarded the plaintiff $69.93.[12]

The entire episode illustrated the sometimes petty and quarrelsome side of the mineral war. It also dispelled the notion that men of action and daring such as Austin and Smith T solved all their disputes at the barrel's end of a gun. On the contrary, both men, as well as other moguls of early territorial days, were very litigious. It was not that they shared any deep and abiding respect for law as much as they used legal redress when it was expedient to accomplish their objectives. A cursory examination of Missouri State Supreme Court records indicated that more than fifty cases pertaining to Smith T alone reached the court. This figure, rather staggering in and of itself, was only a small fraction of the litigation that reached the lower courts. And this was just for Missouri! These figures were greatly enhanced by numerous cases in other states and territories.[13]

Another, and potentially more devastating, setback to Smith T's fortunes during the year 1807 pertained to his complicity in the Burr conspiracy. Long before Manifest Destiny had been formalized into the lexicon of expansion, Americans had already begun the relentless march

12. Award, General Court, May Term, 1807, MSA.
13. Index Files, Missouri State Supreme Court, 1806–1957, MHS.

toward a transcontinental empire. Western horizons had lured farmers, trappers, traders, and adventurers since colonial days, but the process accelerated after independence from Britain. Nationalism played an important role in the ideology of expansion, but it generally took a back seat to self-aggrandizement. Sometimes, however, the two forces converged under the guise of filibustering. This was a propitious time for hostile incursions as the United States in the early 1800s was very close to going to war with Spain.[14]

The prospects of filibustering had lured Smith T to Missouri. Wilkinson, who sparked the dream, now came close to snuffing it out. One must remember that in the twisted world of swashbuckling and filibustering, it was always the safest course of action to never let the right hand know what the left hand was doing. And no one played the game better than Wilkinson. According to historian Bernard De Voto, the general was "the master of treachery." He went on to add:

> He was now involved in so much deceit, fraud, betrayal, espionage, and treason that he could never follow a premeditated course for very long but must extemporize as occasion might permit—but something surely could be made of confusion, anger, and frustration in Louisiana.[15]

Whatever the general's earlier intentions for Missouri had been, the Louisiana Purchase ruled out the necessity of a filibustering expedition into the territory. But the treaty's ink was only about two years dry before Wilkinson began to probe the Spanish frontier once again for weak spots. In July 1805 he sent Zebulon Pike on an exploratory mission up the Mississippi, but this was merely a prelude to Pike's second mission a year later to explore the Southwest. Accompanying Pike on this latter assignment was the general's son, James, and his personal agent, Dr. John H. Robinson. After entering disputed territory, James

14. Charles C. Griffin, *The United States and the Disruption of the Spanish Empire 1810–1822;* Walter LaFeber, "Foreign Policies of a New Nation: Franklin, Madison, and the 'Dream of a New Land to Fulfill with People in Self-Control,' 1750–1804," in William A. Williams, ed., *From Colony to Empire: Essays in the History of American Foreign Relations,* 10–37; Richard W. Van Alstyne, "The American Empire Makes Its Bow on the World Stage 1803–1845," in ibid., 40–70. Charles R. Wilson and William Ferris, eds., *Encyclopedia of Southern Culture,* 1504. Robert W. Wilhelmy, "Senator John Smith and the Aaron Burr Conspiracy," 39–49.

15. De Voto, *The Course of Empire,* 427.

General James Wilkinson, Missouri's first territorial governor, who worked closely with Smith T during the Burr conspiracy. Courtesy of State Historical Society of Missouri, Columbia.

returned to safety, and Robinson went to Santa Fe and informed the Spanish of Pike's whereabouts. Pike was subsequently arrested, taken first to Santa Fe and then to Chihuahua. Spanish authorities, probably led on by Wilkinson, had good reason to believe that Pike was in league with Aaron Burr.[16] He was released nearly a year later on the Sabine River, the border at the time between Spain and the United States.

It was not unlike the general to instigate a mission with possible adverse consequences toward Spain and then inform the same authorities as to the whereabouts of the party he had sent to spy against them. As a case in point, earlier in February 1804 he had told Spanish authorities that Lewis and Clark were on the Missouri River and further suggested that they intercept the expedition and force it to turn back or be subject to arrest.[17]

In his memoirs, sanitized and published posthumously by his son, Wilkinson gave no clue as to his spying for Spain or his complicity in

16. General James Wilkinson to Zebulon Pike, July 30, 1805, in *Territorial Papers,* vol. 13, 185. Goodspeed, *The Province and the States,* 361; Dale Van Every, *The Final Challenge: The American Frontier 1804–1845* (New York: William Morrow and Co., 1964), 74.

17. De Voto, *The Course of Empire,* 432.

the Burr affair. Most fittingly, Wilkinson and Burr had served together in the Revolution's Quebec campaign under Benedict Arnold. In all probability, Wilkinson, a seasoned and patient veteran of games of intrigue, saw Burr as a man in too much of a hurry. Wilkinson had carefully placed some of his men in key positions of power: Joseph Browne (Burr's brother-in-law), territorial secretary; James L. Donaldson, registrar of land titles; Henry Dodge, sheriff of the Ste. Genevieve district; Dr. Andrew Steele, court of common pleas in St. Louis; and Major Robert Wescott, commandant of the St. Louis militia. Wescott had married Browne's daughter and thus was related to Burr. Of course, Smith T was a vital part of the plan. All the while, Wilkinson had friends in the territory writing to public figures in Washington and excoriating his enemies. Singled out for special attack were William Carr, Rufus Easton, Seth Hunt, and Judge Lucas—the latter referred to as "second to no man in asperity and imprudence."[18]

But as word got out of Burr's plans, other prominent Missourians such as Easton and Lucas, commandant of the St. Louis district Colonel Samuel Hammond, Auguste Chouteau, Major James Bruff, who was in charge of a troop detachment in upper Louisiana, and Major Timothy Kibby of the St. Charles militia all opposed any overtures from Wilkinson. Wilkinson decided to abandon the scheme at approximately this point. Burr was a loose cannon, an adventurer who could not be controlled. By this time Burr's political capital was running short. He was an outcast in the Republican Party, and "fraudulent rumors" had spread throughout the Ohio Valley concerning Burr's true motives. Jefferson's supporters undoubtedly were at work trying to discredit the vice president. There were also giant egos involved. Neither Burr nor Wilkinson could trust the other. Wilkinson decided the time was not propitious for an invasion of Spanish lands. Shortly afterward he turned Burr in and the plan collapsed.[19]

Exactly what Burr and Wilkinson had concocted remains somewhat of a mystery even today. Filibustering resembled Byzantine diplomacy

18. Ibid., 428; James Neal Primm, *Lion of the Valley: St. Louis, Missouri*, 83–84. John Bledsoe to Attorney General John Breckenridge, February 3, 1806, in *Territorial Papers*, vol. 13, 430–31.

19. Clarence E. Carter, "The Burr-Wilkinson Intrigue in St. Louis," 450–52. Burke Papers, 8; Foley and Rice, *The First Chouteaus*, 128–29; Wilhelmy, "Senator John Smith," 45.

as much as military logic. No one could absolutely trust another. Thus, the plans and the expeditions themselves were often subject to radical and frequent change. It is most likely that Burr and Wilkinson hoped to probe Spanish defenses in the Southwest and to find a point of weakness that could be militarily exploited. How far south and west they intended to go would depend largely upon the amount of resistance they met. Filibustering was not an exact military science.

Nevertheless, it is remarkable that many prominent westerners supported filibustering, believing it was not unpatriotic, and enlisted in one way or another in Burr's scheme. One such individual was Andrew Jackson. Jackson had known Smith T as early as the turn of the nineteenth century and believed him to be a political ally. No doubt Smith T would have agreed with Jackson's 1806 assessment that Burr "would eventually prove to be the Saviour of this western country." Besides sharing the same thirst for action, Smith T and Jackson also engaged in land transactions as well as tobacco and salt sales. In 1805, Smith T purchased more than fifty-two hundred dollars' worth of supplies from the Tennessee partnership of Jackson and Hutchings. Jackson, however, did not authorize the shipment of provisions to Burr. Nor did he become personally involved in the expedition. Although the editors of the Andrew Jackson Papers believed that the goods ultimately reached a Smith T store in either Missouri or Illinois, it is also possible that the supplies were actually stockpiled on the Cumberland River in preparation for the anticipated expedition down the Mississippi.[20]

After the aborted campaign, Smith T fell upon hard times. Stripped of his official positions in the Missouri Territory and politically disgraced, he could not or would not repay his debts to Jackson. It was not until 1808, after he was sued in a Ste. Genevieve court by Jackson, that he made restitution.[21] Although the legal battles ended the close

20. Petition, Tennessee State Senate, October 7, 1803, in Sam B. Smith and Harriet C. Owsley, eds., *The Papers of Andrew Jackson, 1770–1803*, vol. 1, 374. Hereafter cited as *Jackson Papers*. David Campbell to Andrew Jackson, January 25, 1802, ibid., 274. Andrew Jackson to Cuthbert Banks, April, 1806, ibid., vol. 2, 537. John Smith T to Andrew Jackson, July 30, 1804, ibid., vol. 1, 29; James Irvin to Andrew Jackson, February 9, 1805, ibid., vol. 2, 48–49; Memorandum of Payment, February 24, 1805, Calendar, 1804–1813, ibid., vol. 2, 529; Promissory Note, February 24, 1805, ibid., vol 2. See footnote in the text of the papers, ibid., vol. 2, 198.

21. Bill of Complaint in *Jackson and Hutchings v. John Smith T*, June Term, 1806, Ste. Genevieve Territorial Court, and Memorandum of Account of John Smith T with Jackson and Hutchings, April 19, 1808, both in ibid., vol. 2, 539, 551.

personal relationship between the two men, such litigation, especially in the trans-Appalachian West, was not all that uncommon or unusual. Nor did it preclude Jackson from taking an interest in the affairs of Smith T in the years to follow. As for the reasons why the supplies and materials purchased from Jackson never reached their ultimate destination in the Southwest, one must again return to the main players in the filibustering drama.

Exactly what the main conspirators had in mind may never be fully known. Some believed that Wilkinson and Burr planned to separate the western states into an independent confederation south of the Ohio River. This plan may have been floated to the government of Spain, since it would have deflected filibustering energies away from their lands. Other possible targets, perhaps secretly suggested to the British, included Texas and West Florida, both under Spanish control. Some believed that Burr in particular sought nothing less than all of the Spanish Southwest. In any event, as Burr made his way down the Ohio River from Blennerhasset Island, the Jefferson administration by early autumn 1806 became determined to stop him. Burr was first arrested at Frankfort, Kentucky, by U.S. District Attorney Joseph Davies, but Henry Clay defended him and within two weeks he was again on his way. Next, Burr received boats and supplies from Jackson at Smithland. Shortly afterward, he sent a message via a Sergeant Dunbaugh for the Missourians to join his party.[22]

Upon receiving the message from Dunbaugh, Smith T, Henry Dodge, Andrew Steele, and Robert Wescott set out from Ste. Genevieve with a small fleet of canoes and boats loaded with lead, munitions, men, and supplies. They floated down the Mississippi until they arrived at New Madrid, whereupon they received news that the president had declared the entire affair illegal and had issued warrants for the arrest of the conspirators. Smith T abandoned his plans and sought to distance himself from the affair. He sold the boats and provisions and proceeded at once on horseback to Ste. Genevieve.[23] A second chance at a Spanish filibuster had been thwarted.

22. Cunningham, Jr., *In Pursuit of Reason*, 288. Barbé Marbois, *The History of Louisiana*, 363–64; Hall, *Sketches*, 49–50. Burke Papers, 9–11.

23. Walter B. Stevens, *Missouri: The Center State 1821–1915*, vol. 2, 689; Firmin A. Rozier, "Address of Firmin A. Rozier delivered before the Missouri Historical Society," November 13, 1879, Ste. Genevieve Papers, MHS, 1–3. Hereafter cited as Rozier,

The actual turn of events in these last days of the Burr expedition can only be surmised. However improbable the scheme may have been, it was Wilkinson who laid it to rest. In his memoirs, the general revealed nothing of his complicity in the Burr affair. In all probability, he perceived Burr as a man too vainglorious to control. Wilkinson had patiently and carefully placed many of his people including Smith T in control of key posts in Missouri. But Burr impetuously threatened to undo his careful designs. In any event, Wilkinson, who was by now on the Sabine River, decided it was time for another betrayal. He had received Burr's "cipher letter" but since only he had the key to the code, he believed he could implicate Burr in the conspiracy while he himself remained immune from prosecution.

Wilkinson may also have reckoned that if Burr attacked Spanish territory and provoked a war, there was always the chance that he could snatch fortune from defeat by leading American troops into victory. In any event, on October 22, 1806, he sent a young trusted officer, Thomas A. Smith, to Washington to see President Jefferson. Wilkinson liberally rewarded the young lieutenant for his services, which were performed with the utmost caution. Contained in Smith's boot was a secret letter and other messages denouncing Burr as a traitor. Smith journeyed to Washington under the guise of resigning his commission. Wilkinson's letter, however, referred to him as an "admirable young officer" and requested Jefferson to not accept the resignation. On November 25, 1806, Smith arrived at the White House with the dispatches and delivered them to the president. In addition, he spoke candidly with the chief executive about the conspiracy. Since Wilkinson had not sworn him to secrecy, Smith revealed his perception of the affairs in the West, which corroborated Wilkinson's account.[24]

Jefferson of course had heard of Burr's activities from a variety of sources, but Wilkinson's letter along with Smith's firsthand accounts galvanized the president into action. On November 2, 1806, Jefferson issued his famous proclamation denouncing Burr as a traitor, ordering

"Address." Darby, *Personal Recollections,* 88–89; *St. Louis Globe-Democrat* (weekly), September 25, 1887.

24. Parmet and Hecht, *Aaron Burr: Portrait,* 263. Dumas Malone, *Jefferson the President: Second Term, 1805–1809,* 247–49; Cunningham, Jr., *In Pursuit of Reason,* 288–89.

his arrest, and demanding that all filibustering activities associated with the former vice president be immediately halted.[25] The presidential order had a chilling effect that extended from the capital to the frontier. The U.S. Senate quickly began proceedings against its own members suspected of being Burrites. One such Senator who was expelled was John Smith of Ohio. In later days, he and John Smith T would often be confused for the other as each continued his filibustering activities. Besides congressional hearings, court martial proceedings were instituted against high-ranking military personnel, including Wilkinson. In addition, would-be filibusterers as far west as Smith T in Missouri faced the wrath of the president.

Although Thomas Smith's role in these affairs of state should not be over-dramatized, he did play a small but important part in this chapter of the history of filibustering. It is also ironic that this trusted lieutenant of Wilkinson was John Smith T's younger brother. Indeed, history had played a cruel hoax on two frontier brothers, each involved in his separate way with the machinations of Wilkinson. The episode undoubtedly contributed to the bitter rift between them, which lasted nearly twenty years. The deep personal wound inflicted through what Smith T viewed as a treacherous act by his brother never completely healed. The Thomas Smith family was not all that enthralled with Smith T either. Cynthia Berry (White) Smith, the wife of Thomas, reportedly told family members that Jack "should have been hung" for all the grief that he inflicted.[26]

An illustration of how slow and fragile the healing process really was between the brothers occurred a few years before Smith T's death. By this time the tales of his adventures and mayhem had become legendary. His mere presence had become enough to cut a wide swath in bars and dining rooms across the state of Missouri. Only the most intrepid dared to drink or to eat uninvited at his table. One such individual, a general by the name of Street, dared to brave this unwritten but very prudent rule. In a display aimed at convincing his colleagues that he feared no man, even John Smith T, he strode uninvited to the table where the old colonel was dining alone. Hoping to ingratiate himself, he introduced

25. Samuel H. Wandell and Meade Minnigerode, *Aaron Burr: A Biography Written, in Large Part, from Original and Hitherto Unused Material,* vol. 2, 137.
26. George Smith, "John Smith T.," 2.

himself as a friend of General Thomas Smith. "Colonel Jack," as he was later called, was not impressed. He pulled a loaded pistol from his belt and placed it on the table. He then informed his uninvited guest of the numerous differences that separated him from his brother. The intimation was clear—an intrusion into the personal life of John Smith T under the pretext of professing friendship toward his brother jeopardized one's health and safety.[27] This animosity was conditioned in part by the fact that Thomas escaped unscathed from the Burr-Wilkinson affair, his patriotism never questioned. Thomas Smith would eventually rise to the rank of general, retire to what would become Saline County, Missouri, and end his life prosperous and respected. Smith T, on the other hand, would spend the better part of the next decade endeavoring to erase the stigma of Burrism.

No doubt Jefferson (correctly assessing the motives of his former vice president) had every right to rein in the activities of Burr and the other conspirators. Again, few would quarrel with his judgment that foreign policy was, after all, the purview of the executive branch of government. But visions of empire and expansion were as old as the nation itself and were espoused by notables as diverse as Aaron Burr, Alexander Hamilton, Henry Clay, and Andrew Jackson. Even Jefferson himself had remarked in 1805 that Spain "has met our advances with jealousy, secret malice and ill faith." It was perhaps the timing and the leadership of the filibustering expedition that made the president, according to Andrew Jackson, "run like a cotton tail rabbit" from the attack against Spain.[28]

The Spanish Southwest was the logical outlet for American expansion. Burr's expedition was therefore a "direct successor" of other historic filibusters. What made this one suspect was not Burr's means but his end, which envisioned a personal fiefdom unassimilated into the American course of empire. But Jefferson's inclination to find the middle echelons of the expedition guilty by their association with Burr demonstrated little knowledge or understanding of the nature of filibustering. Frontier people had always had a restless and adventurous spirit and unquenchable drive to go west. Laws and proclamations contrary to that continental motion, even if logical and coherent, had little effect upon these people. Foreign powers and their Indian allies only delayed,

27. Darby, *Personal Recollections,* 93–94.
28. Wandell and Minnigerode, *Aaron Burr: A Biography,* 3, 116.

but did not deter, this inevitable march. It was not so much a matter of right and wrong as it was a force of human nature that no official sanction could contain.

It should also be noted that in the early nineteenth century American nationalism was in its infancy.[29] "The Star Spangled Banner," Old Ironsides, slogans such as "We have met the enemy, and they are ours," the military heroism of Oliver Perry, and Jackson's victory at New Orleans were still nearly a decade in the future. Few Americans, then or later, condemned *hidalgos* such as Moses Austin who at least on paper forsook one religion for another and swore allegiance to a foreign power for land, lead, and power.

Perhaps no one personified the shifting loyalties and enterprising zeal of the westerner like George Rogers Clark, the most famous frontier Revolutionary War hero. Clark had fallen on hard times and had begun to drink heavily. As his fortunes declined, so too did his loyalty to his country. A man who scorned authority and whose allegiances were mainly to himself, he had offered, for example, to become a Spanish subject in order to found a colony. He likewise volunteered for French citizenship in order to command a military contingent planning to capture New Orleans. Later he envisioned a march on Santa Fe to wrest the Southwest from Spain.[30]

Smith T, like other western men of action, had little regard for boundaries or nationalities. Flags, edicts, and governments would come and go, political allegiances would be sworn, and religious loyalty oaths would be taken, but all would be rendered intelligible by the denouement of American expansion. Smith T believed that if he were out in front of his country's policies, eventually they would catch up with him. In addition, private citizens with military expertise had oftentimes raised and led volunteer forces in time of war. Their "sacrifices" usually conferred upon them the status of folk hero.[31] Although war with Spain had not yet broken out, it seemed only a matter of time. For westerners, a call to arms, whether by the government or by the men who would bear the brunt of battle, seemed of little concern.

29. Albert K. Weinberg, *Manifest Destiny: A Study of Nationalist Expansionism in American History*, chap. 1; Van Every, *The Final Challenge*, 154–55.

30. Van Every, *The Final Challenge*, 35; Burke Papers, 7–8.

31. Thomas Shackelford, "Early Recollections of Missouri," paper read before the Missouri Historical Society, *Missouri Historical Society Collection* 2, no. 2 (April 1903): 2; Wilhelmy, "Senator John Smith," 45.

All of these arguments, no matter how logical to the western mind, fell on deaf ears at the White House. Shortly after his proclamation, Jefferson began a systematic scourge of Burr's associates. As previously noted, the president's wrath extended all the way to the Missouri frontier. Andrew Steele quickly fled to Florida, where he could engage in other clandestine activities. Robert Wescott returned to St. Louis to face an indictment. Later a jury acquitted him. Smith T and Dodge returned on horseback to Ste. Genevieve to a grand jury indictment of treason. Dodge, who later became a U.S. Senator from Wisconsin, promptly rolled up his sleeves and whipped nine of the jurors. Three others fled before his flying fists.[32] Smith T returned directly home.

Since Sheriff Dodge was already under indictment, it now fell on the hapless shoulders of the coroner, Otto Schrader, to arrest Smith T. Schrader was a former aide-de-camp to the Austrian Archduke Charles.[33] He was no coward. He had fought in a major battle against Napoleon, but he had never seen the likes of a John Smith T. He approached the colonel's home just as the latter prepared to eat his evening's meal. Opening the front door, Schrader, as legend has it, was warned by Smith T:

> I know what you have come for; you have come with a writ to arrest me. If you attempt it you are a dead man. It was a great outrage to arrest me. I am as good a friend of the United States as there is in this territory. Mr. Schrader, dinner is just ready. Get down and come in and take dinner, but mark, if you attempt to move a finger or make a motion to arrest me, you are a dead man.[34]

Such hospitality the coroner could hardly refuse! Smith T pulled up a chair to the table and with pistols on the table, cocked and pointed directly at his would-be custodian, proceeded to entertain his unrequited guest with polite conversation and culinary delights. After dinner, the colonel rode, armed and ready, into Ste. Genevieve. But he was not a prisoner. Nor would he ever be, as charges were never filed against him.

32. Louis Pelzer, *Henry Dodge*, 37–41.
33. English, *Pioneer Lawyer and Jurist*, 61.
34. *St. Louis Globe-Democrat* (weekly), September 25, 1887; Darby, *Personal Recollections*, 88–89.

As the Burr conspiracy unfurled, President Jefferson removed Wilkinson as territorial governor and Browne as territorial secretary. Frederick Bates was appointed as the new territorial secretary and as acting governor. Bates, on May 1, 1807, stripped Smith T of his public offices, including his commission as lieutenant-colonel of the militia, judge of the Court of Common Pleas and Quarter Sessions, and commissioner of rates and levies. He charged that Smith T had resisted a public officer and prevented the execution of a warrant. Bates allowed Dodge to remain as sheriff, as he perceived him to be "an innocent pawn," "misled" by the wily colonel. Smith T continued to profess his innocence of all charges of treason and maintained that filibustering should be construed as an act of patriotism.[35] Bates was unimpressed. Already the acting governor was at work on another plan to stifle Smith T's power even further.

In a letter dated May 6, 1807, Bates defended his actions to Jefferson. John Smith T, he told the president, was an "unprincipled" man whose complicity in the Burr conspiracy covered him and others with "mortification and dishonor." The colonel, he wrote, "of whom so much has been said, on various occasions" had been removed from all his offices. "He was accused of traitorous participation, and when the warrant of Judge Schrader issued for his arrest, he would not suffer it to be executed." As for the sheriff, Henry Dodge, Bates believed him to be an innocent man and

> misled by Col. Smith, and that, when liberated from the official control which that rash and impatient man [Smith T] has imperceptible gained over him, he will repay confidence, by a prompt and honorable discharge of duty.[36]

Bates's words were prescient. Within a few years, Dodge would side with the acting governor's schemes to weaken Smith T's hold on the lead district. As such, Dodge would become a new and dangerous foe. Since both men were always armed and seldom, if ever, backed down from a fight or challenge, the potential for a violent confrontation

35. Rozier, "Address," 1–3; Foley, *Genesis*, 190; State Historical Society of Missouri, *This Week in Missouri History, April 30–May 6, 1933.*

36. Frederick Bates to Thomas Jefferson, May 6, 1807, in *Territorial Papers*, vol. 14, 121.

Frederick Bates. After the Burr conspiracy Bates, as provisional governor, stripped Smith T of his judicial and military appointments in the Missouri Territory. A few years later Smith T twice challenged Bates to duels. Courtesy of State Historical Society of Missouri, Columbia.

remained more than a remote possibility. It would remain so until Dodge left for Wisconsin. In exasperation at this alliance and smarting from the perceived insults dating back to 1807, Smith T challenged Bates to a duel in 1811.

One Smith T biographer has intimated that Bates's motives were not all that dutiful. One of the sisters of Austin's wife had married into the Bates family and her nephews had business dealings at Mine à Breton. These blood connections, wrote Higginbotham, "show" how Austin and Bates conspired "for their mutual advantage" and "often to the disadvantage" of other settlers such as John Smith T. Higginbotham may very well have been right. At the time that Bates dismissed Smith T, the acting governor wrote to Moses Austin that the large lead miners "will enrich themselves beyond visions of fancy or the dreams of avarice." Bates, who praised Austin's "purity of character," confided to him that he too intended to purchase land and slaves and use them to work the mines during slack farming seasons.[37] Within weeks

37. Higginbotham, *John Smith T*, 46. Burke Papers, 9. Frederick Bates to Moses Austin, September 12, 1807, Austin Papers, vol. 1, pt. 1, 1765–1812.

of these events, Bates wrote to newly appointed Governor Meriwether Lewis and accused Smith T of being a Burrite.

In all likelihood, Smith T's professions of patriotism never completely wiped clean the stigma of Burrism. Nor did he ever regain the civil, judicial, and military power taken from him by Bates. Nevertheless, his immense landholdings bequeathed an inordinate amount of economic influence. Furthermore, tales of his fierce competitive nature and his many desperate encounters added immeasurably to his social stature. His dismissal by Bates, for example, set off a storm of protest by colleagues on the Ste. Genevieve Court of Common Pleas, who threatened to tie up most business transactions by resigning en masse. Also, a number of militia officers resigned their commands when they learned of the revocation of Smith T's commission. Some of the more notable resignations included Captains William H. Ashley, Henry Dodge, and Robert Wescott.[38]

The reversals of fortune in the wake of the Burr affair in Missouri were compounded by setbacks in Tennessee as well. Smith T, it will be remembered, had helped establish the town of Kingston near Southwest Point in Knox County. In 1792, Governor William Blount had sent General John Sevier to Southwest Point to establish a fort there. This wilderness outpost served as the magnet to draw the early settlers to the region.[39] Smith T had been appointed as one of the commissioners to lay out and regulate the town. This official position placed him in a unique position to buy choice pieces of property in that vicinity and to speculate on a land boom that he expected would soon come. No sooner had plans been drawn for the town than Smith T petitioned the legislature to establish a new county, Roane, out of part of Knox. His was the very first signature on the September 30, 1801, petition and indicated his stature in the community. The petition cited as its reason for the change the "insurmountable inconvenience" and "great" distances to the Knox County Court.

An additional boon to Smith T's speculative plans in the area was the fact that under the terms of the Treaty of Tellico with the Cherokees,

38. Shackelford, "Early Recollections," 2. Frederick Bates to William H. Ashley, June 13, 1807, in Thomas M. Marshall, ed., *The Life and Papers of Frederick Bates,* vol. 1, 141; Higginbotham, *John Smith T,* 15; Foley, *Genesis,* 190.

39. Wells, *Roane County,* 10.

the Tennessee legislature stipulated that Kingston would become the capital of the state. Involved as he was in the Burr imbroglio, he could not personally take complete charge of the lobbying efforts. During this period other powerful special interests in Knoxville not tainted with Burrism swayed the legislature. Therefore, to honor their treaty commitments, the legislators, on Monday, September 21, 1807, met for one day at Kingston and then promptly moved to Knoxville. Smith T had suffered another major setback.[40]

One might logically surmise that the redoubtable colonel would either fade quietly into obscurity or meet an uninvited bullet from one of his numerous adversaries. Such was not the case. Much of his subsequent career remains shrouded in mystery and myth, in part because no collection of his manuscripts, letters, or public documents has ever been found. The breakneck speed with which he led his life was evidenced by the large number of acres purchased or sold but never properly deeded or paid in full.[41] His whirlwind life was also evidenced by the absence of a last will and testament. This latter problem kept his estate in litigation well into the 1850s. A man of action and few words, it was perhaps only fitting that merely a few terse letters written in the last years of his life to his brother, Thomas, survived in Thomas's excellent manuscript collection. Nor for that matter did the colonel correspond regularly with other prominent men in Missouri. Few letters written by his own hand can be located in other manuscript collections. Nevertheless, some facts can be gleaned from the few available records.

During the next quarter century, Smith T staked out claims, less dubious than his earlier mineral escapades, as a most enterprising frontier capitalist. His relentless quest for wealth was not confined to Missouri. He continued to watch over properties acquired in Georgia while he bought and sold vast amounts of land in Tennessee. His land agents and attorneys such as John Brown and Thomas N. Clark were quite busy in Roane County, for example, where on a 1,018-acre tract, six land entries alone were made from August through September 1807. This bevy of activity was not confined to land transactions. Listed in 1806 under the

---

40. Thornton, *Pioneers of Roane County,* xi–xiii.
41. W. I. White to Thomas Smith, July 25, 1821, Thomas Smith Papers, Collection no. 1029, Folder 21, WHMC.

heading of "A List of Taxes Collected on Suits at Law . . . ," were nine suits either filed against him or by him in Roane County. In addition, he would lead filibustering expeditions into the Wisconsin Territory and the Texas frontier. His life would embrace American commercial and territorial expansion from the northeast corner of Georgia to the upper Mississippi River and all the way to the southwest fringes of the Rio Grande. By life's end he would become, as one biographer so aptly stated, "the prototype of the American go-getter."[42]

42. Land Entry Book, Book A, 1807–1808, Roane County, Tennessee State Library and Archives, Nashville, 37, 46, 50, 51, 69, 103; Thornton, *Pioneers of Roane County*, 24–25. Burke Papers, 2.

5. *Rebounding from Dishonor and Disaster*

After his fall from official grace in 1807, John Smith T intensified his efforts to replace Moses Austin as the kingmaker of the lead district. He faced a formidable task in light of Austin's special relationship with acting governor Frederick Bates. Although Bates did not restore Austin to his former official responsibilities, the two worked hand in glove to discredit the "Burrites" and give every possible advantage to their own political faction. In St. Louis, the *Missouri Gazette* joined the attack and called for the removal of Smith T's supporter, General Wilkinson.[1]

Another obstacle in Smith T's path was the animosity of Judge John B. C. Lucas and the Board of Land Commissioners. Lucas, for reasons both personal and philosophical, had been a thorn in the side of large Spanish land grant claimants since his appointment to the commission by Jefferson in 1805. Arriving as he did after the Spanish grants, Lucas stood to profit more from keeping the land out of the hands of those he referred to as the "nabobs." His sense of republicanism also led him to side with "the industrious and poor actual settler" who would be "in a desperate situation" if Congress conferred land titles to the large speculators. Smith T held claims to enormous amounts of land and to mines, but the manner in which he had acquired them made him vulnerable to litigation and political intrigue. Austin, for example, now moved against Mine à Renault, which Smith T had claimed in 1806.[2]

1. *Missouri Gazette,* August 17 and 24, 1808, October 26, 1809.
2. J. B. C. Lucas to Charles Lucas, November 12, 1807, Lucas Collection. J. B. C. Lucas to William H. Crawford, November 9, 1820, in Lucas, *Letters,* 33. Bates

In March 1807, President Jefferson named Meriwether Lewis as territorial governor and William Clark as Indian agent and brigadier general of the territorial militia. The composition of the land commissioners board also took a turn for the worse when Jefferson removed one of its pro-Wilkinson members, James Donalson. His replacement was Frederick Bates. Bates remained as territorial secretary but was also recorder of land titles. He was especially powerful since Lewis paid little attention to land claims or local politics, concerning himself mainly with Indian affairs. He did not even arrive in the territory until March 1808. When Lewis did inquire into the nature and causes of the mineral feud, he was thwarted by Bates.[3] Bates and Lewis openly quarreled over the land and lead questions, and the issues were still unresolved when Lewis left the territory and mysteriously died, probably by his own hand, in Tennessee in September 1809. Later, Benjamin Howard was named governor, but he too was oftentimes absent from Missouri and distracted from the domestic issues that plagued the mining region. During much of this time, Smith T's dreaded foe, Bates, continued to serve as acting governor.

In February 1808, Bates and Austin felt powerful enough to launch their counterattack. Bates leased Smith T's Mine à Renault to two agents, Michael Hart and William Mathers. Bates maintained, as he would in other rulings he made against Smith T, that the colonel's claims were not "old" ones located specifically by tract. The acting governor further maintained that Smith T had not acted in accordance with U.S. law and had not properly recorded these lands under its provisions.[4] These, of course, were the same arguments made before Wilkinson by Seth Hunt and others less than three years earlier. At that time, for reasons previously discussed, they fell on deaf ears. Now, however, a more sympathetic listener could hardly have been found.

Mine à Renault was located about six miles from Austin's tract. Strategically, it was an important site, and it also appeared to be a

---

Document, December 20, 1807, Fordyce Collection. These documents revealed dozens of certificates for land claims of Smith T, totaling more than three thousand arpents of land. Some are also claims of Reuben. Gracy, *Moses Austin: His Life,* 129.

3. Foley, *History,* 119. Foley, *Genesis,* 181–82, 203–7. Higginbotham, *John Smith T,* 5–6.

4. Frederick Bates to John Smith T, February 24, 1808, in Marshall, ed., *The Life and Papers of Frederick Bates,* vol. 1, 303.

very rich mine. Consequently, Smith T sent three men by the names of Harvey, Campbell, and Cheatham to work it. Bates now widened the mineral war by allowing Austin and his lieutenant, Hunt, to claim it. They in turn sent Hart and Mathers, extremely hardened veterans of the lead conflicts, to the mine. Smith T wrote to Bates that these actions were "truly vexatious" to the law. Even if they were eventually removed, they and their associates were "poor" and therefore "in case of damages compensation cannot be had." Smith T realized Bates's ploy. "Under you," he wrote, "those men mean to cover themselves, befriend Hunt and perplex me." Furthermore, he added, he had contended with "all the difficulties the administration can throw in my way" and regretted his "misfortune of living under a Territorial Government where unheard, I am censured, and untried, found guilty." Bates, of course, was unmoved. The tactic seemed to have worked, and he would use it again, to more devastating effects, against Smith T's most important concession, the St. Vrain grant. In the meantime, however, the colonel took matters into his own hands. Arming a small but hardened group of his own men, he returned to Mine à Renault and retook it by force. According to Firmin Rozier, Smith T "stood unrivaled" for his skill and "undaunted courage" in these "terrible conflicts with his enemies."[5] The incident revealed just how fragile the law was and how violent the mining district had become.

Ironically, Frederick was not the only Bates with whom Smith T had to contend. In the 1820s he filed a petition against the United States through his attorney, Thomas Hart Benton, requesting the government uphold his claim to twenty-five hundred arpents purchased in 1804 from Camille De Lassus. The land was situated in St. Francois County, Missouri, on the Grand and Flat Rivers. In 1825 the petition was filed with Edward Bates, U.S. District Attorney for Missouri. Benton argued that the United States should grant the claim under the terms of the 1803 Louisiana Treaty with France. Bates took the petition under advisement, but, like Frederick, he was ill-disposed toward it.[6]

5. Burke Papers, 8. John Smith T to Frederick Bates, February 14, 1808, in Marshall, ed., *The Life and Papers of Frederick Bates,* vol. 1, 284; Higginbotham, *John Smith T,* 11. Rozier, *Rozier's History,* 313.

6. Petition, *John Smith T v. U.S.A.,* April 6, 1825, Litigation File, Ste. Genevieve Circuit Court, File 13, Ste. Genevieve, Missouri. Hereafter cited as SGCC.

During the first years after his dismissal from office, Smith T divided his time between his holdings east of the Mississippi and those in Missouri. In 1807, for example, he purchased a slave family consisting of Lidda and two children, Sarah and Cloe, from a Lenox County, Tennessee, farmer, John Dudley, for $625. What was interesting about the transaction was that it was witnessed by both his brothers, Thomas and Reuben. Apparently, John and Thomas had not become completely irreconcilable over the Wilkinson-Burr conspiracy.[7]

Smith T and Joseph Browne also continued to maintain their business arrangement, although it produced more litigation than pecuniary reward. By now Smith T's brother Reuben had become a full-fledged associate and acted for him while he tended to his far-flung business enterprises. The conflict with Austin had yet to subside, and Smith T kept his rifle, "Hark from the Tombs," always close by. Among his new and less sanguinary strategies for acquiring more land claims and lead mines was a carrot-and-stick approach toward the district miners. He would issue a public declaration that all persons opposed to his new claims, for example at Mine Liberty, would not be permitted to dig at Mine Shibboleth or on other mineral claims owned by him. This tactic, which oftentimes had the desired effect, forced many of the miners to take sides in the ongoing struggle with Austin. Like Smith T, Austin was not standing idly by. In March 1809 he further diversified his operation by opening a new shot tower in Herculaneum.[8]

Avarice, combined with mutual distrust, led both men to purchase land, household goods, estates, mining claims, and other material possessions at breakneck speed. Many of these acquisitions appeared to have been procured not only for their intrinsic value but also as a means of depriving the other of needed resources. Records of the Ste. Genevieve Court of Common Pleas and later the circuit court reveal more than fifty separate purchases made during these years by Smith T alone. According to Rev. Francis Yealy, a priest and historian of the region, Smith T exhibited the "characteristic virtues and vices of the

7. Recorder of Deeds, Land Record Transcribed, vol. 1, Book A, August 18, 1807, ibid., 73.

8. Court of Common Pleas, Fee Book, 1807–1808, March 1808, Ste. Genevieve District, Louisiana Territory, MHS. The Fee Book can also be located in the MSA. Gardner, *Lead King*, 112–17. Document, September 12, 1812, Alexander Craighead Papers, MHS; *John Smith T v. Henry Elliott*, and *John Smith T v. Ebenezer Armstrong*, December 1806, Folder 26, SGCC; *Missouri Gazette*, March 8, 1809.

old robber barons." Both lead moguls employed lease arrangements whereby miners agreed to pay approximately 10 percent of the value of all minerals removed. Smith T often would loan the money for the goods and merchandise necessary to begin a stake. At other times he would provide the products from the purchases made at numerous estate sales. Loans and leases made in this fashion resulted in endless litigation. Some of these loans were for as little as one dollar and some were to illiterates who borrowed money with only an "X" for their signature. In many cases he recovered part of the money owed him by taking cattle, goods, slaves, household furnishings, and in some cases barrels of whiskey. On other occasions he sued miners for damages that occurred while digging on his property. His reputation for being "very quick on the trigger" and a deadly shot usually gave added weight to his point of law.[9] In these early days, John Scott, later a judge and U.S. Congressman, represented him. Later, Smith T was represented by Rufus Easton, a territorial representative and former associate of Austin.

During the years prior to the War of 1812, many of the loans and leases that Smith T had made in the first years after the Louisiana Purchase began to pay off handsomely. In April 1805, for example, he loaned a certain John Price five hundred dollars. Nearly three years later, on February 8, 1808, after the value of the land had considerably increased, he was able to receive five hundred acres in return for the bad debt. Reuben Smith also parlayed loans into land, although the records do not indicate whether he was acting completely on his own or for his brother. The same day that his brother took the Price property, Reuben acquired eight hundred acres from James and Nicolas Keith. An even better deal for Smith T was the acquisition of eight hundred arpents in an area called the Murphy settlement from John Capehart for only ninety dollars, and a choice 120-acre piece of property in the "big field" from De Lassus for less than a dollar per acre.[10]

---

9. Francis J. Yealy, *Sainte Genevieve: The Story of Missouri's Oldest Settlement,* 92. *John Smith T v. John Hinkson,* October 1811, and *John Smith T v. Joseph Brewer and William Dial,* July 1809, Folder 30, Folder 33, SGCC. This latter debt was for one thousand dollars. Note, October 1811, Folder 584; Litigation File, *John Smith T v. Jesse Blackwell,* July 1809, File 29; *John Smith T v. James Keeth,* June 1810, Folder 33; Litigation File, *John Smith T v. Abraham Parker,* March 1810, File 34, all in SGCC. George Smith, "John Smith T," 2.

10. Deed Records, Book A, February 8, 1808, SGCC, 226, 218, 222.

The year 1809 also witnessed the dissolution of the Smith T, Joseph Browne, and William H. Ashley partnership. Two years before, Browne had signed a handwritten note pledging to pay the colonel $729.58 in ten days. When Browne failed to pay, Smith T had him arrested and Ashley posted his bail. It was the final act of what just a few years before appeared to be a promising business arrangement. In March 1809 Smith T sued for the full amount plus $200 in damages.[11] Before the suit could be settled, Browne died, and the case was carried forward into 1811 against the estate. This early difficulty, including the arrest of the elderly Browne, contributed to a long-standing family quarrel that culminated in 1819 with a deadly duel between Smith T and Browne's son, Lionel.

Despite all the litigation, accusations, dismissals, and factional animosities, Smith T remained one of the most celebrated characters in the Missouri Territory. His standing in the community was confirmed on October 10, 1809, when he was selected by some of the large Missouri land claimants to represent them before the U.S. Congress at their next session. In addition, he was named to a committee to consider second-class government for the territory. His name, as late as 1812, would appear next to Henry Dodge on the petition presented to Congress.[12]

As a member of the land claimants committee, Smith T urged the national government to remove Judge Lucas as land commissioner.[13] Smith T's opponents, however, fought back. In a territorial article they claimed that a self-styled clique had met without consulting the people of Missouri and therefore his appointment as an "agent" to Congress was invalid. His opponents further maintained that Smith T had become "the GREAT instrument to tear down" Judge Lucas's standing in the community. Furthermore, Smith T's critics contended that his and other large "10,000 or 20,000 acre claims" could not be mixed with small bona fide claims. Finally, the article asked the readers and the small claimants to remember that "the very name and nature of colonel Smith's own claims will render all he could do for you *suspicious.*"[14]

11. Litigation File, *John Smith T v. Joseph Browne*, March 1809, File 34, SGCC.
12. Petition to Congress from Inhabitants of the Territory, April 22, 1812, in *Territorial Papers*, vol. 14, 473.
13. *Missouri Gazette*, October 12, 1809. The paper only reported that he had been appointed to the position while his detractors maintained that he had usurped the job. Also see Rozier, "Address," 1–3. Rozier intimated that Smith T was elected.
14. "A Land Claimant," *Missouri Gazette*, October 16, 1809, in *Territorial Papers*, vol. 14, 328–30.

Smith T's opponents had a logical argument, since no one knew the exact procedure used to select the land claimants. The *Territorial Papers* referred to this three-man committee as delegates chosen "by the good people at Upper Louisiana," but did not spell out who constituted these "good people." The papers did state that only land claimed before October 1, 1800, had been confirmed. Furthermore, the papers suggested that the representatives to Congress had argued that land claimed up to and on December 20, 1803, had not yet been confirmed but should nevertheless be granted. They contended that since the "Treaty of Il Defonco [*sic*]," which transferred the Louisiana Territory from Spain to France, was made in secret, the land claimants had acted in good faith and should be allowed to keep title to their lands.[15]

On October 26, 1809, "A 'Corrector' to the People of the Louisiana Territory" appeared in the *Missouri Gazette*. Its purpose was to restore the good name of Smith T. It held that the people of St. Louis had voted for the general committee and that Smith T had been chosen "agent by a majority of votes." It was "sufficient," said the "Corrector," that "the general committee confided in him, *'vox populi, vox dei.'* [The voice of the people is the voice of God]."[16] Legend has it that Smith T went to Washington and accredited himself well with Congress. Unfortunately, there are no papers or manuscript collections to corroborate the claims.

No doubt these, as well as other matters pertaining to Judge Lucas and the territorial status of Missouri, occupied Smith T's time in Washington. His motives, however, were not completely altruistic as the sojourns afforded an opportunity to argue not only the propriety of his Missouri lead claims but also his unbelievable title through the Yazoo schemes to the northern half of Alabama.[17] Smith T's manners and temperament during these visits to the nation's capital must have been uncharacteristically mild and even-handed. One amusing but unreliable reference to his time spent in Washington came from an 1887 *Globe-*

15. "Representation to Congress by Committee of Inhabitants," October 10, 1809, in ibid., 324–27.

16. *Missouri Gazette,* October 26, 1809; "Corrector," in *Territorial Papers,* vol. 14, 337.

17. Burke Papers, 12–13.

Democrat article. The paper had tried to perpetuate his legend. It obliquely praised him when it wrote:

> he considerately refrained from killing anyone, and even found it impossible to scrape up a duel with any of the fire-eaters that abounded there.[18]

Smith T's political popularity among the mining folk mirrored his equally high social rank in the community. For example, in October 1809, E. Fenwick sent a challenge to a duel by way of J. M. Neil to an "ignominious muckworm," A. C. Dunn. Dunn rejected the challenge and sent an oral apology back to Fenwick via Neil. The problem was that the messenger was a stranger in the area and therefore his social rank might be called into question. Fenwick let it be known through the *Missouri Gazette* that Colonel Smith T would vouch for his standing as a gentleman.[19] The matter was closed.

Not all, however, was going well in 1809. Factional tensions were still running high and the land commissioners, Judge Lucas, Frederick Bates, and Clement Penrose were beginning to hand down a series of adverse decisions. Smith T's claim to the land previously owned by Seth Hunt, for example, had gone before the commission on July 19, 1806, but it was not until October 9, 1809, that the group ruled on the claim. Predictably, in this case and scores of others presented, the commission voted unanimously against them. At the same time, Lucas was covering his political bases in Washington. On October 19, 1809, he wrote to his close friend, Secretary of the Treasury Albert Gallatin, that Smith T would be in Washington that winter as an "agent" of the large claimants. He identified his adversary as "one of the principal Cooperators" along with Zachariah Cox in the Yazoo land fraud. He was, noted Lucas, "one of my most active enemies." By December of that year, Lucas had made the connection between Wilkinson and Smith T and was openly stating it. In a letter to William Eustis, Lucas stated that Wilkinson had known that the large land claimants had obtained their titles fraudulently. Perhaps, he wrote, Wilkinson had hoped to gain some popular support. The other reason, of course, and

18. *St. Louis Globe-Democrat* (weekly), September 25, 1887.
19. *Missouri Gazette*, October 12, 1809.

this directly implicated Smith T, was that the Burrites had hatched "a deep laid scheme to secure on his side the physical strength of the Territory, for some future important occasion."[20] The charge, no doubt true, was never proven in any public tribunal. But in the years immediately following the ill-fated Burr expedition, it was enough to give Smith T considerable worry.

By 1810, the continuing struggle with Austin was also beginning to take its toll. On June 29 of the previous year, Smith T had sent Austin a letter suggesting that some type of compromise be reached. Austin promptly responded on July 1. Although expressing exasperation at the many abuses suffered at the hands of Smith T, he nevertheless believed that the "misunderstanding" between them could be rectified. The specific proposal almost had the trappings of a verbal, nonlethal duel about it. Austin suggested that each protagonist name two gentlemen friends to investigate the "wrongs" committed by each party. Each side would therefore be confronted with the "unmerited justice" they had done.

Smith T did not adequately respond to Austin's proposal, and the parties never met on this particular field of honorable inquiry. Yet the suggestion was instructive in and of itself as it showed that informal avenues for personal redress were still operative in territorial days. Austin's recourse to other than legal means to settle disputes did not mean that Smith T had escaped other litigation. Throughout 1810, many more legal suits were filed and won against the partnership that at this time was called John Smith T and Company. One particularly troublesome problem was Smith T's inability to deliver on his contractual obligations. Mining operations such as the Falconer Company paid in advance approximately five dollars per hundredweight for the colonel's minerals. John Smith T and Company often did not deliver a sufficient quantity. A suit by Christian Fender over mining contracts was one of many legal actions brought by his creditors. It called for the county clerk, Thomas Oliver, to command Sheriff Henry Dodge "to take the said John Smith if he be found within your bailiwick and him safely keep so that you have his body before the same judges." This

20. *American State Papers, Public Lands,* vol. 2, 389. In all fairness to Judge Lucas, he also voted against the claims of his own son, Charles. See ibid., 416. John B. C. Lucas to Albert Gallatin, October 19, 1809, John B. C. Lucas to William Eustis, December 1809, both in *Territorial Papers,* vol. 14, 335, 354.

was, of course, to suffer the ultimate insult. Although Smith T paid the debt and damages of more than $250, records do not indicate whether or not Dodge carried out the summons.[21]

Besides mining contracts, other legal problems bedeviled Smith T in 1810. Ironically, the piece of land that involved Smith T in the most litigation to prove valid ownership was the St. Vrain grant. This ten-thousand-arpent tract had been purchased by James (or Jacque) St. Vrain from the Baron de Carondelet. St. Vrain in turn sold it to Smith T in August 1806 for five thousand dollars. The first down payment of twenty-five hundred dollars was to be made by the sale of three slaves, six or seven horses, and the remainder in unspecified merchandise "all which at the estimation of two honest men at cash price." The other half of the bill was to be paid in one year "in money or in lead at cash price." If payment was not made on time, the contract called for fines that would bear interest for a term of three years.[22] Three years after the alleged failure of Smith T to meet his second payment, St. Vrain sued. The crux of the problem was a clause in the contract that rendered it null and void if the board of land commissioners rejected the validity of the claim. In 1810, the matter had not been resolved. In fact, it would not be settled until 1836, and Smith T did not satisfactorily settle the account with St. Vrain. The suit put him in a quandary. On the one hand, he was deeply involved in litigation trying to prove the claim's validity. On the other hand, he was not honoring the terms of the contract because he had yet to gain a complete title. Although the circumstances of this legal imbroglio were unique in terms of their scope and consequences, it was only one of many legal battles fought by Smith T.

In all fairness to the colonel, his attention may have been diverted by the absence of his brother Reuben, who spent much of 1810 in a Spanish prison mine in Chihuahua, Mexico. Although rumor had it that Smith T traveled alone to Mexico and freed his brother, it was more likely that his efforts were confined to petitioning Congress and

21. Gardner, *Lead King*, 119–20. *Falconer and Co. v. John Smith T and Co.*, August 1810, Folder 33; Recorder of Deeds, Land Record Transcribed, vol. 1, Book B, November 20, 1810, 247; Land Record Book, Book B, November 1810, 95–97; all in SGCC.

22. For the complete description and terms of this agreement, see Deed Records, Book A, August 16, 1806, 106, Ste. Genevieve Court House.

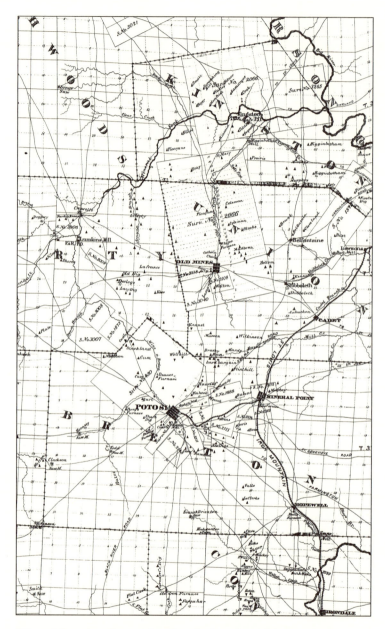

Map of the mineral area, showing the location of the most important mines, including Smith's Shibboleth. Courtesy of State Historical Society of Missouri, Columbia.

planning expeditions in the event his lobbying activities failed. In any event, there was some slippage in the efficiency of his vast operations in Missouri, but there was no abridgment in the myths and folklore that surrounded Reuben's release from prison and the part Smith T played in it.

More than any single event, the mystery surrounding this Mexican adventure reserved Smith T a place in the annals of Missouri folklore. It began, like so many of his multifarious ventures, with his customary penchant for intruding into the affairs of others. By this time, his entrepreneurial ambitions had led him not only down the Mississippi and eastward toward Tennessee but into the Southwest as well. Although he may not have been the first businessman to envision the potential profits of the Southwest trade, his activities in 1809 predated many of the other traders who would someday make the Santa Fe Trail a historical landmark.

In all likelihood, the trading mission began more as a profit-seeking enterprise than as a filibustering scheme. The plan envisioned Reuben leading a small group of Missouri traders to Santa Fe. While in the city they would exchange frontier goods for finished products. One man who figured largely in the idea was the Reverend James Maxwell. This Irish Catholic priest from Ste. Genevieve was known for his love of politics, racehorses, and land speculation. He had been brought to Louisiana by the King of Spain around 1796 to deal with the arrival of the Americans. Later, he became a member of the pro-Wilkinson, French Creole faction arrayed against Moses Austin. These connections made him a natural ally of Smith T. Like the colonel, Maxwell had visions of an empire. He envisioned an Irish immigrant settlement with himself, no doubt, as the taskmaster. In 1799 he had obtained from De Lassus a 130,000-arpent claim mainly between the Black and Current Rivers in today's Reynolds and Shannon Counties. Like Smith T, his efforts to obtain validation of title to the land were never successful. Later, with no compunction as to separation of church and state, the priest represented Ste. Genevieve, along with John Scott, in the Council of Nine in the General Assembly of the territorial government in 1812.[23]

23. Burke Papers, 12; Yealy, *Sainte Genevieve*, 72, 95–97; Rozier, *Rozier's History*, 129.

As Smith T put together his trade team sometime around November 20, 1809, he believed that a letter of introduction from Maxwell might better pave the way for the mission. Besides Reuben, other members of the trade mission included Joseph McLanahan, a former sheriff in St. Louis under the Wilkinson regime, James Patterson, "scion" of a prominent Tennessee political family, and Manuel Blanco, a Spanish-speaking guide from the lead mining region. They were accompanied by three slaves.

The expedition was, as the colonel surely knew, a calculated gamble that put his trusted younger brother, Reuben, in serious jeopardy. Spanish memories, for one thing, were not that short-lived. They could not have so quickly forgotten that only three years earlier Smith T had been the focal point of the Missouri connection in the Burr conspiracy. For another, they had good reason to doubt the reliability of Smith T's ally and mentor, James Wilkinson. Spanish colonial archives indicate that Spanish agents before and throughout the period of Smith T's trade mission were watching their American spy closely for any kind of double-cross.[24]

Although in the pay of the Spanish government as Spy No. 13, Wilkinson could also play the part of an agent provocateur. Only two years before Reuben's mission, Wilkinson had sent Zebulon Pike into the same territory in order, the Spanish believed, to "reconnoiter" it. The following year Pike observed that twenty thousand U.S. troops could produce a revolution in Mexico and wrest the area from Spain. Spanish officials were constantly warned to expect an invasion of thousands of western riflemen against Mexico.[25] Quite obviously this intrusion, ostensibly for commercial reasons, was the first of its kind since Pike's mission. Because it was concocted by a known filibuster such as Smith T, the trading party could easily be construed as part of an overall imperial design directed against the Spanish Southwest.

---

24. Colonial Archives of Texas, Spanish and Mexican Periods, 1717–1836, Bexar Archives, General Manuscript Series, Roll 35, September 1, 1806–April 30, 1807, through Roll 41, April 16, 1809–June 30, 1809, in Barker Library. Hereafter cited as Colonial Archives of Texas.

25. Marques de Casa Yrujo to Pedro Cevallos, July 21, 1807. Original no. 887, in Donald Jackson, ed., *The Journal of Zebulon Montgomery Pike*, 253–54. Zebulon Pike, "Pike's Observations on New Spain," April 12, 1808, in ibid., 95–96. For some of the early adventurers who later fought in the revolution, see Military Muster Rolls, Texas Revolution, Collection no. 1535, Barker Library.

Filibustering at this time, however, was not confined solely to the Southwest. Plans for revolutions in East and West Florida were also being made. George Matthews of Georgia, a neighbor of the Smith family, John McKee, who had followed Smith T to the lead country, and Dr. Andrew Steele, who had left the Smith T–Dodge expedition at New Madrid in 1806, were all engaged in a variety of clandestine activities. Smith T's other brother, now Colonel Thomas Smith, had been ordered to the Georgia border, "where he winked at privateering against the British and filibustered aid" to Americans in East Florida.[26] Spanish spies were no doubt aware of this sibling connection.

Another factor that prejudiced Smith T's commercial venture was the chaotic state of affairs in New Spain. In 1808, Napoleon launched an invasion of the Iberian peninsula. This set in motion the abdication of King Ferdinand VII of Spain. Shortly afterward, Napoleon replaced the Spanish monarch with his brother, Joseph. Soon revolutionary agents were at work throughout the former Bourbon empire declaring their independence from the hated French. The French, in the meantime, worked with the revolutionaries in hopes of gaining economic advantages vis-à-vis the United States and other hemispheric powers. Meanwhile, Great Britain, ever anxious to undermine Napoleon, threw her support to the Spanish loyalists. This latter group remained committed to Ferdinand. Since Britain and the United States were increasingly at loggerheads, this rapprochement increased loyalists' suspicions of the Americans. American envoys in Europe also suspected that once Britain gained a foothold in the Spanish colonies she would use this leverage to squeeze out American commercial interests in the region.[27]

The times were especially vexing for the loyalist government in Mexico, whose leaders believed that New Mexico and Texas were the keys to fortifying and retaining their empire in the north. News of Reuben's

---

26. John Rydjord, *Foreign Interest in the Independence of New Spain: An Introduction to the War for Independence,* chap. 13.

27. President and Vice-President of Venezuela to James Monroe, April 25, 1810, U.S. Department of State, *Correspondence Relating to the Filibustering Expedition against the Spanish Government of Mexico, 1811–1816,* Record Group 59, National Archives, Washington, D.C. Hereafter cited as DS, *Correspondence.* Dispatch, Robert Smith, Secretary of State, to General John Armstrong, Minister to France, April 27, 1809, in William R. Manning, ed., *Diplomatic Correspondence of the United States Concerning the Independence of the Latin-American Nations,* vol. 1, 3. Hereafter cited as Manning, *Diplomatic Correspondence.* Dispatch, Jonathan Russell, Chargé d' Affaires, London, to James Monroe, Secretary of State, February 3, 1812, ibid., vol. 3, 1432.

mission quickly reached the highest echelons of Spanish power. Don Luis de Onís, the Spanish minister to the United States, warned the viceroy of Mexico City about the venture. He reportedly said that the so-called commercial enterprise had "the makings of revolution." Onís reasoned that the trade mission was provocative, if for no other reasons than that it would describe Spanish territory and publicize her potential wealth. Onís further suggested that it would only encourage more Americans to head for the Southwest. To many observers, both foreign and American, Reuben's trade mission had "overtones of a political nature." The *Louisiana Gazette,* edited by Joseph Charless, an ardent opponent of Smith T, could only say that "we presume their object are mercantile." A leading historian on filibustering also believed the group's ultimate objective was to prepare a military force to march on Mexico.[28]

The demise of the Bourbons not only gave rise to questions of independence or continued allegiance to some form of European control but also prompted ideas of popular sovereignty and individual rights in the colonies. Joseph McLanahan and Reuben Smith later referred to this "spirit of change" sweeping away "many of the glooms on the continent of America."[29] Spanish authorities therefore sought to contain any and all sources of trouble. They most especially desired to isolate Mexico from the contagions of freedom and revolution spread by American filibusterers who posed as traders. Intrigue was the order of the day as French and British agents carried out their imperial designs while Spanish and Mexican factions challenged each other's legitimate rights to rule the unsettled country. The most serious of these official government intrigues involved the United States.

The advent of the Madison administration in March 1809 signaled a surge of filibustering activity directed against Spain's New World colonies. The architect of many of these activities was none other than Secretary of State James Monroe. Unlike some revolutionary leaders who saw the American mission of expansion in ideological terms,

28. Julia K. Garrett, *Green Flag over Texas: A Story of the Last Years of Spain in Texas,* 25. W. A. Goff, "Reuben Smith," in Le Roy R. Hafen, ed., *The Mountain Men and the Fur Trade of the Far West,* vol. 7, 262. *Louisiana Gazette,* December 28, 1809. Harris G. Warren, *The Sword Was Their Passport: A History of American Filibustering in the Mexican Revolution,* 25.

29. Joseph McLanahan et al. to Governor Benjamin Howard, June 18, 1812, Mary Louise Dalton Papers, MHS.

Monroe's sights were clearly set on the ground. That ground, however, just happened to be Spanish soil in North America. In 1805, after becoming minister to the court at Madrid, he had encountered first-hand Spanish despotism. His negotiations were deemed a failure when he could not purchase West Florida and Texas. Later, in discussions with Napoleon over Louisiana, Monroe gained further insights into the world of diplomatic intrigue. At the helm of the Department of State, he quickly became a Machiavellian of the first degree. The secretary often operated clandestinely and used both special U.S. agents and unofficial spies and filibusterers to carry out his expansionist plans.[30] Although Monroe took pains to keep himself officially distant from the fray, the Spanish minister Onís knew better. Any and all American trade and scientific or exploratory activities that touched Spanish soil were going to be viewed with a jaundiced eye. Reuben's mission fell within the purview of these suspicions.

Spain no doubt had cause to fear for her empire as the lure of filibustering in the western country had not faded with the failure of Burr. Another cause for alarm was the inability of the United States and Spain to reach an agreement satisfactory to Washington on the exact location of the Louisiana boundary. At approximately the same time that Burr's expedition set off on its abortive mission, the United States and Spain negotiated a demilitarized neutral zone between the Sabine River and the Arroyo Hondo. This tenuous document would continue in effect until the 1819 Transcontinental Treaty. Nevertheless, during the dozen or so years of its existence, many filibusterers including John Smith T would violate both the spirit and the letter of this agreement. For example, another Missourian—Dr. James H. Robinson, who had accompanied the earlier Pike expedition—was busily engaged in revolutionary activities on the border. Wilkinson, now stationed in New Orleans, still "kept company with visions of empire." Lieutenant Augustus Magee, stationed on the border near Natchitoches, Louisiana,

---

30. Griffin, *The United States and the Disruption of the Spanish Empire*, 22–23. Harry Ammon, *James Monroe: The Quest for National Identity*, viii; Stuart G. Brown, ed., *The Autobiography of James Monroe*, 210–11. Anonymous letter to James Monroe, November 10, 1810, and José Álvarez de Toledo to James Monroe, January 14, 1812, both in DS, *Correspondence*. Also see William Shaler to James Monroe, May 2, 1812, U.S. Department of State, *Correspondence from Special Agents, 1810–1815*, vol. 2, National Archives, Record Group 59, Washington, D.C. Hereafter cited as DS, *Special Agents*.

and under the command of Pike, would soon leave the U.S. Army to coordinate anti-Spanish activities. Although Napoleon's brother was the nominal king of Spain, Ferdinand VII still held part of Spain and claimed the Spanish colonies. On April 14, 1810, the viceroy in Mexico City issued strict orders to impede French and American revolutionary agents in Texas whose designs were to stir up "disorder and create anarchy."[31] This order merely bolstered suspicions that Reuben and the others in his party were spies.

In light of these and many other intrigues, it was not unexpected that Spain would become increasingly cruel to her uninvited American guests. In late February 1810, as Smith T's trade mission reached the headwaters of the Red River, its members were promptly arrested by troops of the Spanish commandant, Don Nemesio Salcedo. The Spanish authorities did not treat the group as respectfully as Captain Pike's earlier assemblage had been treated. The six *extranjeros* were referred to as "vermin" and marched on the *Jornada del Muerto* (Journey of Death) to the Spanish mines of Chihuahua, a place of slow execution for many of the unfortunates trapped in its confines. Since no writ of habeas corpus existed in Spanish judicial tribunals, Americans such as Reuben Smith could be "seized and harassed" with impunity. It was just the kind of treatment that prompted the *Louisiana Gazette,* on hearing of the arrest of Smith and the others, to warn, "Yet a little while and a day of terrible retribution will arrive."[32]

The arrests piqued the interest of many prominent figures. Andrew Jackson, for example, made inquiries into the nature and whereabouts

31. Pamphlet, "Mexican Imprints Relating to Texas," Manuel Cordéro, Governor of Texas, 1805–1810, in La Real Audiencia de Mexico, Governadora del Reyno de Nueva España, 1820, Collection no. 673, Barker Library. Hereafter cited as La Real Audiencia. Félix D. Almaráz, Jr., *Tragic Cavalier: Governor Manuel Salcedo of Texas, 1808–1813,* chaps. 2–3. Burke Papers, 14. No evidence has been found that Wilkinson, at this point, had any direct contact, written or otherwise, with Smith T. La Real Audiencia, *Spain, Laws,* April 14, 1810.

32. Louise Barry, ed., *The Beginning of the West: Annals of the Kansas Gateway to the American West,* 62; W. B. Douglas, ed., "Note," in Thomas James, *Three Years among the Indians and Mexicans,* 288; Goff, "Reuben Smith," 263–66. Antonio Menchaca, *Memoirs,* 35–50. The author took an active role in Mexican independence and later worked with Sam Houston and Jim Bowie. Also see Bennett Lay, *The Lives of Ellis P. Bean,* 62–95. Both books document the harsh treatment of American prisoners in Spanish prison mines in Chihuahua. Josiah Gregg, *Commerce of the Prairies or the Journal of a Santa Fe Trader,* vol. 1, 2d ed., 133. For the early history of the Santa Fe trade see Douglas, ed., "Note," 101–4. *Louisiana Gazette,* October 4, 1810.

of the party, while at roughly the same time, Territorial Governor Benjamin Howard related the seizure and detention of the men to Secretary of State James Monroe. Monroe in turn instructed Governor William Claiborne in New Orleans to request that Nemesio Salcedo release the prisoners. Like Howard, Monroe believed the men to be innocent and noted that several congressmen "have interested themselves warmly on behalf of the sufferers." By this point, Don Nemesio was well versed in dealing with American importunities. Ellis Bean, for example, had been arrested in the same area in 1801. President Jefferson had pleaded his case for years until his eventual release. There was little cause, therefore, for hope of an early release for Reuben and his party.[33]

The following spring proved just as vexing as it witnessed the continued incarceration and suffering of the trading party, providing an ample pretext for retaliation.[34] The *Louisiana Gazette* on March 14, 1811, reported that three hundred men (it did not say under whose command, but it was likely to have been headed by Major John Scott and Joseph Walker) were expected to rendezvous at the mouth of the Canadian forks of the Arkansas River within a week and a half to effect the release of the men and to bring back what gold they could conveniently seize. If this course of action proved impossible then it was assumed, reported the paper, that the rescue party would be "joining the revolutionary party" and promoting more destruction. The newspaper nevertheless cautioned against such expeditions, calling them "mischievous" and "illicit." The government agreed with the *Gazette*'s assessment and informed the leaders of the organization that they faced arrest and prosecution if they continued their plan. The group disbanded without much fanfare.

By the time of the *Gazette*'s admonition against filibustering raids into Spanish lands, it was within reason to suspect that John Smith T had already left on his own for the wilds of Mexico to rescue his brother. The colonel, "discontented with the timid efforts of the government" to effect his brother's release, may have surmised that his

---

33. Secretary of State James Monroe to Governor Benjamin Howard, December 11, 1810, in *Territorial Papers*, vol. 14, 427; Robert Smith to Andrew Jackson, November 10, 1810, Jackson Papers, vol. 2, 561. Jackson's earlier letter to Smith is not published. Ellis P. Bean, *Memoir of Col. Ellis P. Bean: Written by Himself, about the Year 1816*, 9–21.

34. John Aphelian to Thomas A. Smith, February 15, 1818, Smith Papers.

former association with Burr prejudiced the Madison administration against the family. Although no direct information can be found that the administration tried to distance itself from the affair, Monroe did write to Governor Howard on September 3, 1812, to warn him that another Smith mission to Spanish territory went against official policy as it would probably be "of an unfriendly nature."[35] Whether Smith T journeyed to Chihuahua and actually effected Reuben's release is subject to conjecture. In any event, it was the stuff of myth and legend. A common theme that gives rise to legend is a hero's journey across hostile and forbidden lands and against implacable enemies to achieve a noble and selfless deed. The author most responsible for magnifying this and many other stories of John Smith T was his friend and attorney John Darby, later the mayor of St. Louis. Darby maintained that Smith T set out "solitary and alone," encountering many perils along the route, before he accomplished his mission. Darby added:

> [with] Courage, self-reliance, and determination possessed by few men, he encountered perils, dangers, and difficulties at almost every step, all of which he met without flinching, and with a bravery and daring unsurpassed, and encountering savages and wild animals nearly the whole way.[36]

Firmin Rozier, another friend and contemporary of Smith T, maintained that his "roving disposition" led him to Chihuahua "to aid to revolutionize Mexico, traversing a wild, vast country, surrounded by dangers." Truth may often be stranger than fiction, but seldom is it as entertaining. Such is the case of Smith T and the Mexican adventure. While it is perhaps true that he rode to the Southwest in search of his brother, it is far less certain that he played a direct role in his release. Those who maintained he actually freed his brother point to circumstantial evidence at best. They have argued that he supplied Father Miguel Hidalgo's forces with money to buy arms to support the revolution. One family member maintained that he loaded his saddlebags with twenty-dollar gold pieces that he dispensed to the revolutionaries. This tactic supposedly diverted Salcedo's attention long enough for Smith T to effect Reuben's rescue. Furthermore, it has

35. Goff, "Reuben Smith," 268, 271, 276.
36. Darby, *Personal Recollections,* 94–95.

been noted that years later, after he married, Reuben named his two sons Thomas McLanahan Smith, after his trading partner, and Francis Hidalgo Smith, after the priest who abetted his release. These same sources also point to a January 29, 1829, letter written by Smith T to his brother Thomas to support the captivity and release story. In that letter, Smith T contemplated a trading venture down the Santa Fe Trail and needed five thousand dollars' worth of goods on credit. While in that country, he believed the time propitious to apply to the Mexican government for compensation for services and money he had advanced in support of the patriots. He presented no other details as to the merits of his case.[37]

Smith T never issued a formal request for compensation. Nor did he make the commercial trip to Mexico, which he hoped would improve his financial fortunes. As for the Mexican government, its finances remained as disorganized as its politics. And, in the interim, it had replaced Spain as the target of American adventures. Thus, the Mexicans saw no utility in rewarding one of the earlier filibusterers or encouraging new ones. Smith T was never paid. In his mind, the Mexican government owed him money as well as gratitude. Since his letter to his brother did not elaborate as to the nature of the debt, we are left mainly with conjecture as to the true course of events.

What is certain, then and now, was the westerners' distaste, exemplified by men such as John Smith T, for Spanish injustice and inefficiency. Westerners loved freedom but were intolerant of Spanish institutions. Spain, on the other hand, realized the "class of neighbors" with which she had to contend and therefore tried to stem the flow of inhabitants to her lands by fear and intimidation.[38] From his early days in Spanish Missouri, to the Burr conspiracy, to his activities on the Santa Fe Trail, to the imprisonment of Reuben, and through his efforts to revolutionize Mexico, a constant object of Smith T's aversion was this Iberian relic of colonialism obstructing the march of American individualism. Smith T was never one to pass up an opportunity to enhance his reputation for

---

37. Rozier, *Rozier's History*, 314. George Smith, "John Smith T," 10. Burke Papers, 14–16; Higginbotham, *John Smith T*, 39. John Smith T to Thomas A. Smith, January 29, 1829, Smith Papers.

38. Excellent primary material on Spain's attitudes and policies toward the American frontier and expansionist tendencies can be found in Elena Sánchez-Fabrés Mirat, ed., *Situación Histórica de las Floridas (1783–1819)*, 289–316. Rydjord, *Foreign Interest in the Independence of New Spain*, 206–8.

fearlessness or to embellish the myths and legends that were beginning to circulate around him. If he did not make the early journey as his chroniclers suggested, then he made no effort to correct the impression that he did.

Nevertheless, some facts persist that lend credence to the tale of the rescue journey to Texas. In the first place, as Hidalgo's struggle became increasingly desperate, he instructed his lieutenants to elicit overt American military support for the revolution by promising that once the independence movement succeeded he would transfer Texas to the United States. Dangling this kind of expansionist bait before American eyes would most surely entice the likes of Smith T. It would also explain why in 1813 Smith T could pledge five hundred filibusterers under his authority for another incursion into Texas. If he had actually been in that country only a year or so before, then he would have been knowledgeable enough to commit such a sizable force. His knowledge of Texas would also help to explain why hundreds of adventurers felt confident enough to serve under his command.

In addition, it should also be noted that in a revolutionary setting such as prevailed in the Southwest at this time, official and nonofficial information was sketchy to say the least. In a letter to Secretary of War William Eustis, Indian agent John Sibley reported from Natchitoches that a number of Americans were fighting alongside General Ignácio Rayon, a Hidalgo subordinate. Sibley further wrote that one such officer was a brother of Colonel Thomas H. Smith. He identified this Texas officer as Reuben Smith, a colonel of artillery. He also had reason to believe that Reuben had been "lately killed in Battle."[39] Sibley, of course, was mistaken on one minor point. The one brother referred to as Thomas was not Thomas H. but Thomas A. Smith. More important, however, was that Smith T's brother Reuben could not have been fighting with General Rayon, as he was still in late 1811 a prisoner in Chihuahua. In addition, no one before or since the days of the filibusterers referred to Reuben as a colonel. That title was held by Smith T.

On the other hand, the timing of Sibley's letter (December 31, 1811) makes it highly implausible that Smith T could have been in Texas

---

39. John Sibley to William Eustis, December 31, 1811, in "Dr. John Sibley and the Louisiana-Texas Frontier, 1803–1814," 404–5. Hereafter cited as Sibley, "Letters."

very long, as he had launched another brief filibustering expedition in June of that year against the Indians controlling the Dubuque and Galena lead mines on the Mississippi River in Iowa.[40] This expedition of well over a hundred adventurers under his command met stern Indian resistance and sustained nearly 50 percent casualties. The band returned crestfallen to St. Louis. Redoubtable as he was, it would have been quite a feat, even for Smith T, to have set out so soon on another even more perilous journey.

There is, however, a more compelling reason to doubt Smith T's presence in Texas this early. It concerns one of his numerous invitations to prominent frontier political leaders to meet him on the field of honor. One such challenge occurred on December 22, 1811, when he requested a personal interview with the acting governor of the territory, Frederick Bates. Two days later, after receiving an unsatisfactory reply, he issued another and even more forceful challenge.[41] Bates again refused to duel the man reported to be the finest shot in the western country. From the correspondence between them at this time, it would appear that Smith T could not have left for Texas until well into 1812. Sibley's letter and the identity of the Smith who fought with the Mexican revolutionaries both cast doubt as to Smith T's actual whereabouts.

Upon their return to Missouri nearly two and one-half years after their arrest, McLanahan, Reuben Smith, and the others wrote to Governor Benjamin Howard on June 18, 1812, to give their version of the mishap. Their ill-fated journey, they maintained, had been for "geographical and commercial information" but met with only "suffering and privation" at the hands of the authorities. Finally, "in poverty and rags," they were released. They made no mention of any rescue mission by Smith T or any other American party. This may have been a deliberate omission on their part if any of them with or without the support of Smith T envisioned another foray onto Spanish lands. Their letter went on to state that they believed the people of Mexico to be kindly

40. Judge John B. C. Lucas to Albert Gallatin, June 13, 1811, and Richard Wash to Thomas Jefferson, June 10, 1811, both in *Territorial Papers,* vol. 14, 454, 455–56.

41. Challenge, John Smith T to Frederick Bates, December 22, 1811; Reply, Frederick Bates to John Smith T, December 22, 1811; Challenge, John Smith T to Frederick Bates, December 24, 1811; Reply, Frederick Bates to John Smith T, December 30, 1811; all in Frederick Bates Papers, MHS. Also see Marshall, ed., *The Life and Papers of Frederick Bates,* vol. 2, 210–11.

disposed toward Americans, with only the government inclined toward hostility. Furthermore, their humiliation was, in greater measure, an insult to U.S. sovereignty. Finally, the traders voiced their desire to make another journey on the Santa Fe Trail, but not without the full support and protection of the government. The letter from the trading party appears consistent with U.S. Department of State special agent William Shaler's assessment. On May 2, 1812, he wrote to Monroe about the party's release after nearly three years of "cruelty peculiar to Spaniards." He attributed their liberation to the "precarious situation of Salcedo in his government," but did not elaborate. He further reported to Monroe that Reuben and the others believed Mexico was ripe for revolution and that five hundred men could easily do the job. Knowing the character of these men, he stated, it was very likely that they would soon be back in the country "in arms."[42]

Although Reuben, his health broken from the prison ordeal, never returned to Spanish territory as a filibusterer, his brother most certainly did. His later adventures and misadventures on the other side of the Sabine River, documented through State Department archives, were, however, never as dramatic as the earlier lore surrounding Reuben's rescue. It was this first Mexican episode, regardless of its historical validity, that became the basis of a powerful tale and the building block of Smith T's persona. Since folklore was an essential raw material in the process of building a people's self-identification on the frontier, the stories of his adventures overshadowed reality and launched him into fame and status. He would need it in the trying years that were to follow.

---

42. McLanahan, Smith et al. to Benjamin Howard, June 18, 1812, in Douglas, ed., "Note," 289–92. William Shaler to James Monroe, May 2, 1812, vol. 2, DS, *Special Agents.*

6. Years of Tumult

John Smith T was always a stormy petrel on the Missouri frontier. Hence, the lead, land, and wealth offered by his adopted land never fully satisfied his enterprising temperament. On the one hand, he was pulled back to the lands of Tennessee and Georgia from whence he had come. On the other, he was pushed toward the vistas of new frontiers and the excitement of new filibustering adventures that seemed to be the only drink to quench his restless spirit. Like the proverbial prodigal son, he would always return to Missouri. But in his absence his enterprises, even left in the trusted hands of his brother Reuben, usually suffered.[1] It appeared to matter little to this man who lived by the adage "A man's reach should exceed his grasp or what's a heaven for?"

Although few years in Smith T's life were not filled with controversy and danger, the years from 1811 to 1813 were exceedingly vexatious. Early in 1811, he expanded his holdings in the St. Charles area with the purchase of the Julian Dubuque estate.[2] Although the Dubuque property in Missouri was of some monetary value, it appeared that the ulterior motive for the purchase was to obtain some semblance of a claim to the so-called Spanish mines in Iowa. Reportedly, these were the richest mines on the upper Mississippi River for not only lead but also copper. Around 1786, Julian Dubuque had traveled northward and had begun negotiations with the tribes along the river. Two years later he obtained a 140,000-acre tract from the Indians. He lived and traded among these people until his death.[3]

1. His filibustering also affected his land litigations in Tennessee. See Legislative Material, 1813, Record Group 60, Folder 16, TSLA.
2. *Missouri Gazette,* June 6, 1811.
3. Perkins, *Annals of the West,* 677.

When Dubuque died in 1810, Auguste Chouteau of St. Louis had become the administrator of his estate. To settle the accounts of the estate, the courts had ordered that some of his land and claims be sold to meet debt payments. Smith T, along with a new partner, Fergus Moorhead, enthusiastically made the purchase for fifty-nine hundred dollars.[4]

A major problem with Dubuque's Spanish mines in Iowa, but one which Smith T believed solvable, was that the mines already had an owner. For some time the lead mines near Dubuque and Galena had been worked by Indian tribes.[5] Historically, the tribes had derived considerable income from these enterprises and consequently had no desire to give them up. With the purchase of the claims, therefore, Smith T bought himself a war. For a claims jumper the likes of the colonel, however, the temptation was far too great to resist. His concept of private property rights did not extend to Indian property. The title to these lands and minerals gave him some legal groundwork for his assault on the mines, but more than any other factor, it offered a convenient rationale to carry out a series of attacks on the one people he despised even more than the Spanish. From his early days on the eastern frontiers and throughout the remainder of his life, he remained an adversary of the Indians. Consequently, he had no compunction in attacking their diggings.[6]

Few details of the Iowa excursion have survived, but Smith T probably first received a license from the territorial government to trade with the Indians on the Mississippi north of the mouth of the Missouri River.[7] The license, along with Dubuque's titles, served as the pretext for the invasion. Perhaps territorial officials never intended to give him the liberties he would take with the license, but two factors mutually influenced their decision. First, he was one of the largest manufacturers of shot in the western country. Second, war with the British and the Indians seemed certain. What better man to corner the lead and to deprive the enemy of this valuable resource? Consequently, the possible riches and military importance of the Iowa mines worked to the mutual advantage of both the government and the entrepreneur. Whether he was a point man in a larger imperial design

4. *Missouri Gazette,* September 19, 1811.
5. Amos Stoddard, *Sketches, Historical and Descriptive, of Louisiana,* 398.
6. John Smith T to Thomas Smith, January 29, 1829, Thomas Smith Papers, Collection no. 1029, Folder 33, WHMC.
7. Higginbotham, *John Smith T,* 16.

or merely a reckless filibusterer acting on his own instincts cannot be fully determined.

To get official support for the plan, Smith T enlisted the aid of Thomas F. Riddick, the clerk of the St. Louis Board of Commissioners. Riddick's close friend, Frederick Bates, according to Judge Lucas, appeared "though cautiously to countenance the expedition."[8] Ostensibly, it would appear that the filibustering scheme had made for some strange bedfellows if Bates and Smith T could reconcile their differences and agree on any plan of action. Yet upon deeper examination, an entirely different reason may have motivated Bates. Within a week after the departure of the flotilla against the Indians on June 16, 1811, Bates leased Smith T's Mine Shibboleth to Henry Dodge, Nicholas Wilson, and Alexander Craighead.[9] A year later, he made a continuation of the same lease. Although Smith T did not realize it at the time, he was now engaged in a war on two very different fronts.

In the meantime, Smith T and Moorhead marshaled an army of around 150 men. The volunteers were armed with both weapons to fight the Indians and tools to mine the lead. The force was divided into two groups. Smith T headed the first group and departed with it. Before leaving St. Louis they hoisted the American colors on their boat, fired some occasional "blunder buss's," and paraded around the grounds in military fashion. Judge Lucas, who disapproved of the expedition and the men leading it, believed that all of these manly displays were designed to impress the territorial inhabitants of the quasi-official authority of the undertaking.[10]

On June 20, 1811, Richard Wash, then residing in St. Louis, wrote to Thomas Jefferson at Monticello and enthusiastically endorsed the mission. He spoke of Smith T and Moorhead as "gentlemen of capital and great enterprise" and identified the lead mines to be taken about forty miles "this side of the Prairie de Chien." Trying to convince the former president of Smith T's propriety and the efficacy of his filibustering activities might have been a difficult task. Yet Wash believed that within six months the Iowa mines would have eight hundred to a thousand men "engaged in raising mineral."[11]

8. Judge John B. C. Lucas to Secretary of the Treasury Albert Gallatin, June 13, 1811, in *Territorial Papers,* vol. 14, 454.
9. Edward Tiffin to Frederick Bates, July 25, 1814, in ibid., 779.
10. John B. C. Lucas to Albert Gallatin, June 13, 1811, in ibid., 453–55.
11. Richard Wash to Thomas Jefferson, June 20, 1811, in ibid., 455–56.

Wash's optimism, like the colonel's, proved to be unrealistic. Smith T's men were undoubtedly skilled in both fighting and mining as many were seasoned veterans from the earlier mineral wars. The plan of attack, however, was poorly conceived and even more poorly carried out. Understandably, this disastrous enterprise has been one of the least publicized aspects of Smith T's checkered career. It was also the one episode that gave rise to few if any of the Smith T folktales or legends. Some accounts maintained that after a series of bloody battles that cost him fully half of his men, he retreated back to Missouri. Lieutenant Colonel Daniel Bissell, at Fort Belle Fontaine near St. Louis, confirmed the gloomy news to Secretary of War William Eustis. Bissell believed that the Indians had killed a number of the miners at the Dubuque site and feared more attacks. Bissell had received previous reports from Captain Horatio Stark, the commanding officer at Fort Madison, a far outpost on the upper Mississippi. Stark had written that the "melancholy intelligence" had it that "all" the Americans at the mines had been killed and "butchered in a most horrid manner" by "Puants or Winebago" Indians. From the mines, reported Stark, the Indians were going upriver killing every American they could find.[12] The Dubuque attack was especially unfortunate because it stirred up the forces of the Prophet, a Shawnee who was the spiritual leader of his people and a brother of the famous and dreaded warrior Tecumseh. Together, these siblings rallied many of the tribes to their cause of ridding the Indian lands of whites.

The attacks and the resulting debacle no doubt damaged Smith T's image of invincibility. But the greatest national disservice the raids created was to provoke the possibility of further Indian reprisals against unsuspecting pioneers on the northern edges of the frontier. It was a very delicate time in international affairs, especially with the British and their native allies, and the swashbuckling forays undoubtedly exacerbated matters.[13]

Ironically, John's brother Thomas A. Smith was the only family member to benefit indirectly from the disaster. A few years after Smith T

12. *St. Louis Globe-Democrat* (weekly), September 25, 1887; Frank Magre, "Notes on John Smith T," no. 23, Magre Collection. Dispatch, Lieutenant Colonel Daniel Bissell to Secretary of War William Eustis, January 12, 1812; Dispatch, Bissell to Governor Benjamin Howard, January 12, 1812; Dispatch, Captain Starks to Lieutenant Colonel Daniel Bissell, January 6, 1812; all in *Territorial Papers,* vol. 14, 504, 506.

13. For details on frontier conditions, see Benjamin Howard to William Eustis, January 13, 1812, in *Territorial Papers,* vol. 14, 505.

had stirred up the northern frontier, his brother was sent to the same region to pacify it. In August of 1815, Andrew Jackson had assigned Thomas the command of federal troops in the Missouri and Illinois Territories. Thomas had recently been promoted to colonel of a rifle regiment. On November 5, 1815, he dispatched a letter to General Jackson informing him that he traveled up the Mississippi River to "Demoine" and had prepared to receive the surrender of the Indians in that region.[14] His success in this and other delicate missions would soon earn him the rank of brigadier general.

After the military operations it fell to Governor Benjamin Howard and General William Clark to assure the region's Indians that no reprisals or future hostile expeditions by filibusterers such as Smith T would be tolerated. The warnings were heeded. The colonel never again invaded the Indian mines of Iowa, but the incursion left him enmeshed in litigation for years to come. If he planned no further invasions, then it also appeared that he had no intention of making good the debts incurred. He and Moorhead were hit with a series of lawsuits in the territorial courts. Included in these suits were claims represented by Auguste Chouteau, administrator of the Dubuque estate. These estate claims would continue against him for several years. By the October 1812 term of the Superior Court and throughout the May and October 1813 terms, Smith T was not sued in this court at all. In fact, it was not until 1814 that his name, along with Rufus Easton, Edmund Roberts, and Edward Cheatham, appeared in court documents, and in this instance they were the plaintiffs.[15] The absence of litigation involving Smith T from late 1812 through 1815 was likely due to his many absences from the territory.

The colonel's most immediate concern when he returned from the filibustering raid against the Indians was the disposition of his and Reuben's properties. He would soon be engaged in fighting his brother's battles on the home front as well as on the Spanish frontier. The Smiths' nemesis was once again Frederick Bates. With Smith T

14. Dispatch, Thomas A. Smith to Andrew Jackson, November 5, 1815, in Harold D. Moser et al., eds., *The Papers of Andrew Jackson*, vol. 3, 390–91.
15. John Bradbury, "Travels, 1809," in *EWT*, 253. In 1812, the territory made the transition from the Territory of Louisiana to the Territory of Missouri. Cases were no longer referred to as "General Court Cases" but as "Superior Court Cases." Case nos. 24, 37, 44, 48, and 51, Box 16, May Term 1812, Territorial Court Cases, 1804–1820, MSA. Case no. 14, Box 19, October Term 1816, ibid. Case no. 27, Box 18, May Term 1814, ibid.

safely up the Mississippi, Bates began to forfeit the brothers' properties under the rather dubious justification that the Spanish land grant titles by which the Smiths held claim to these lands were illegal.[16]

Bates had always contended that Smith T had not gone through the proper procedures for validating many of the properties he had acquired in the period after the Louisiana Purchase. The truth is that in the turbulent years in which Wilkinson served as governor, Smith T may have believed that his claims were secure. He may also have reasoned that to follow different methods than the ones he used to obtain the concessions would be an admission on his part of improper, illegal, or careless procedures. In any event, he began the process of validating these claims only after his dismissal from public office by Bates. It was a very unpropitious time to do so.

The situation as it stood in early 1812 was certainly confusing. Realizing that Bates would use every means available to strip him of his mining claims, Smith T had, as early as December 29, 1807, begun to claim the following tracts of land under the St. Vrain grant: 1,000 arpents at New Diggings, about two and one-half miles from Mine à Breton; 300 arpents each at Mine à Robina, Doggett's Mines, and the branch above the Renault Mines; 200 arpents at McKee's Discovery; 50 arpents near Big River; and 800 arpents on the St. Francois River in the Murphy's Settlement. Smith T also claimed tracts that he had purchased in 1805–1806 on the Old Mines concession of approximately 1,920 arpents.[17] These claims were made in written correspondence to Bates. Bates, however, had not favorably replied.

Smith T therefore should not have been all that surprised to find out upon his return from Iowa that Bates had made a preemptive strike against his properties. Several years earlier, for example, on February 14, 1808, he had written to Bates complaining that two men by the names of Hart and Mathers had been given a lease from Bates and had "taken possession of my land" at Mine à Renault. The colonel believed it would be "truly vexatious" to sue these "poor" men "from whom in case of damages compensation cannot be had." After making his

16. A good description of the land claims dispute that puts the issue in perspective is found in U.S. Senate, *Journal of the Senate of the United States of America,* 19th Cong., 2d sess., 283.

17. Higginbotham, *John Smith T,* 10. A description of Smith T's mines can also be found in Schoolcraft, *A View of the Lead Mines of Missouri,* chap. 2.

case as to the validity of his claims, he complained of "the difficulties" the administration had placed in his way and believed that he was as entitled to equal protection under the law "as the squatter on he knows not whose lands" he settles. If these impediments to justice continued, he wrote, then he "must regret my misfortune of living under a Territorial Government where unheard, I am censured, and untried, found guilty." Ten days later, Bates responded by reiterating his contention that Smith T's was not "an old claim." He pledged that no rights were being violated and that the colonel was "under the guardianship of the laws" of the United States.[18]

Matters of course had not been resolved in the period from 1808 to 1811 as the wealth of lawsuits and violence in the mining district continued to run its course. But Smith T's protracted absence from the territory in the summer of 1811 galvanized his opponents into action. On June 20, 1811, Bates, who now referred to himself as the Land Recorder, wrote to Secretary of Treasury Albert Gallatin that "an accidental concurrence of circumstances has enabled me to gain possession, without employment of force, of a lead mine, which promises to be abundantly richer than any yet discovered in Louisiana." The land, he further wrote, belonged to Reuben Smith. He had "located" a thousand acres in the summer of 1801 on the St. Vrain grant "before his departure for Mexico."[19] It was interesting that Bates did not mention that Reuben not only had departed for Mexico but also had not yet returned from a Spanish dungeon. This fact, Bates might have revealed, would explain why the "employment of force" was not necessary. Bates also did not reveal that these rich mines would be leased to his friends and that he too hoped to share eventually in the wealth of these properties. According to W. A. Goff, biographer of Reuben, "Mr. Bates was passing up no opportunity to plague the Smiths, especially when such action resulted in a profit for himself." To the acting governor, according to Goff, "the Smiths were fair game especially in their absence."[20] Later that same year, Reuben's 1805 Grand River claim was also denied. This land was located in the Ste. Genevieve district and contained approximately eight hundred arpents. This forfeiture also went to the allies of Bates.

18. Higginbotham, *John Smith T,* 11–12.
19. Goff, "Reuben Smith," 274.
20. Ibid., 274–75.

Smith T immediately challenged Bates's fait accompli on his return from the Iowa excursion. It was surely a bitter pill to swallow, particularly coming on the heels of the disaster on the Mississippi and the exasperating confinement of Reuben in Chihuahua. His first means of redress was to challenge in the courts the new proprietors of Mine Shibboleth. These men were Nicholas Wilson, Alexander Craighead, and his former friend, Henry Dodge. A writ was brought against the tenants, but the earliest he could get his petition on the territorial court docket was the May 1812 term.[21] In the meantime, Bates allowed the tenants to lease the mines rent-free. His reasoning, although somewhat specious, was that if the Smith court challenge was successful, then the government would have to repay the tenants. He did not mention that in the meantime Dodge and the others could be extracting sizable amounts of lead without paying any compensation to the government or the previous owner.[22]

Another Smith T legal maneuver, designed in part to give substance to his claim of possession, was to begin deeding small amounts of the St. Vrain grant to other prominent members of the community. This tactic would also cause further litigation and confuse the entire issue even more. On December 23, 1811, for example, Smith T deeded three hundred arpents of land to former Moses Austin ally Rufus Easton. The sale price was five hundred dollars.[23]

The crux of Bates's argument against Smith T's claims was an old one. Smith T had derived his grant from St. Vrain Lassus, who on November 16, 1795, applied to the governor of Louisiana, the Baron de Carondelet, for ten thousand acres to be located on lead mines and salt springs. On February 10, 1796, the Spanish government granted the claim. Since it was a floating concession, no warrant of survey was made "nor any attempts made to take up land during the continuance of the Spanish authorities." Smith T, after acquiring the grant, made no legal attempt until 1807 to record it with the U.S. government. Regardless of the fact that Smith T operated the mines for some time, according

21. Suits, Case nos. 23 and 45, Box 16, May Term 1812, Territorial Court Cases, 1804–1820, MSA.

22. Frederick Bates to Edward Tiffin, November 12, 1813, in *Territorial Papers,* vol. 14, 708–9.

23. Deed, Smith T to Rufus Easton, December 23, 1811, Recorder of Deeds, Book B, SGCC, 165–67.

Henry Dodge, an ally
of Smith T during the
Burr conspiracy but later
a mortal enemy of the
colonel. Courtesy of State
Historical Society of Missouri,
Columbia.

to Bates, this neglect rendered the claim invalid.[24] Edward Tiffin, commissioner of the General Land Office in Washington, agreed with Bates. Smith T, on the other hand, could with considerable justification maintain that even squatters were given greater consideration to their titles than what was being shown to him.

Legal challenges were not the colonel's only recourse. No doubt his resentment toward Bates existed since at least May 1, 1807, when, as acting governor, his old enemy branded him a traitor and removed him from all public offices in the territory. Bitter memories, compounded by these new intrusions, provoked a challenge to a duel. On December 22, 1811, he sent his invitation by way of Dr. Bernard Farrar. "Wrong and injustice commenced on your part towards me with our acquaintance," the note read. Furthermore, these "practices of oppression and

24. This grant can be found in Deed, James St. Vrain to John Smith T, August 16, 1806, Recorder of Deeds, Book A, Ste. Genevieve County Court Records, 106.

injustice" had continued, he went on to say, and required "prompt satisfaction."[25]

No doubt Smith T had ample complaint for the actions taken against him. Nevertheless, it was a course of action that in all likelihood he would have taken in any event if and when the opportunity had presented itself. In the no-holds-barred world of dubious claims, speculative greed, and mine jumping there were few if any legal or extralegal rules that were considered unfair. Smith T for his part had unsuccessfully used his St. Vrain claim in 1806, for example, to try and wrest Mine à Breton from Austin. His attention had been diverted that year only because he found sizable lead deposits at a site called New Diggings. He, like other territorial elites hell-bent on gaining wealth and power by any means, disregarded the law whenever it was convenient to do so. For example, he continued to hold by force of arms Mine à Renault throughout 1806–1808, long after Bates leased it to William Mather and Michael Hart.[26] In this case, as in the events of 1811, Smith T believed in the validity of his claims and did not intend to give them up without a fight.

The invitation for a "personal interview" with Bates was made out of more than mere exasperation and resentment. To Smith T the *code duello* was a metaphor of civility that harkened back to the days of chivalry. Wronged by a protagonist whose actions impugned both his honesty and honor, the challenge expressed the gentleman's ideology of violence. Honor, according to men of the code, was self-ascriptive; that is, it was defined by the individual within the context of personal and class conduct. Bates had crossed that line.

But words such as "honor" were more than mere rhetorical camouflage masking a personal feud. Heroic language was more than semantic and more than a pretext for violent action. Behind the vocabulary of the duelist lay not only concepts of personal identification but also notions of social order and cohesion that were linked to their general image of the world. In every society these notions are in the custody of the articulate classes whether they collectively be the poets, theologians, lawgivers, philosophers, scientists, educators, or artists. In early

---

25. Challenge, John Smith T to Frederick Bates, December 22, 1811, Bates Papers. Also see Marshall, ed., *The Life and Papers of Frederick Bates*, vol. 2, 210–11.
    26. Gardner, *Lead King*, 117–20.

Missouri, however, the articulate class was a small group of lawyers, editors, and entrepreneurs. These men might challenge each other in combat, but they seldom challenged the violent cultural norms that were the underpinnings of their society.

Unlike many young upwardly mobile and ambitious men who resorted to dueling to enhance their social position, Smith T had already achieved considerable wealth, status, and power in the territory. The duel for him represented civility since it presumed the centrality of personal responsibility for slights and wrongs committed in either public or private conduct. To gentlemen who ascribed to medieval protagonism, combat in the defense of character was as justified as self-defense. Their philosophy was a romantic idealization of courage, leadership, and honor. The protagonist, ever vigilant of his honor, also believed that if he was afraid to defend it on the field of honor, he forfeited his claim to political and social leadership. The protagonist, if he was unwilling to fight his personal battles, was unfit to fight the people's battles. To face a pistol at ten paces was a measure of one's character and leadership.

In the mind of a protagonist such as John Smith T, his challenge, no matter what the outcome, offered vindication of honor. In the first place, there was no dishonor in dying on the dueling field. Second, he would gain considerable satisfaction in shooting Bates and eliminating a troublesome adversary. Finally, even if Bates refused to duel, the colonel had ways to slant the declination in his favor.

Bates replied to the challenge the very same day that he received it. His reply was almost condescending. The note, he said, had given him "much surprise," since he was "unconscious" of any wrongdoing toward the challenger. "Perhaps," he exclaimed, if the charges were more specific then they might have been "more susceptible of explanation."[27] The reply, although courteous, made no apology nor did it affirm or deny the recorder's willingness to duel. If Bates for a moment believed that his note would end the controversy, then he was sadly mistaken.

On Christmas Eve, Dr. Farrar carried a second, more lengthy challenge. It was the essence of protagonism. Smith T first of all wanted

27. Reply, Frederick Bates to John Smith T, December 22, 1811, Bates Papers; Higginbotham, *John Smith T,* 12.

to end any speculation as to why he sought a rencounter. "I pass over the manner in which you removed me" from public office, he wrote. Nevertheless, the note continued, it was "arbitrary" and "had it been to you" [Bates], he continued, it would have been deemed "unjust and oppressive." Then he invoked the golden rule. "Of course, you do not do by others as you would that others should do to you." The note further exclaimed that the challenged party would not have committed "these injuries" if he possessed a conscience ("That monitor which the Supreme Being has placed in the breast of every man").

The challenge was one of Smith T's clearest and finest pieces of writing. Although he believed Bates had "the power," he did not have "the right" to exercise that power in the manner which he did. Still, it was "an official exercise of power" that did not menace property. Property, he continued, was "a principle maintained by the great Charter of our Natural Rights—the right of personal protection of liberty and property is dictated by God to every man even should it be at the hazard of life itself." No doubt Smith T anticipated the distinction Bates would make between public and private duty when he argued that an agent of the government, however much he would like "to shield himself under the cloak of his official character," could not violate the natural principles of law. If he did so, then he "must be, held responsible for his acts and behavior."

The next three paragraphs of the challenge read like a litany of property violations. It was more than a call to arms; rather it was a summation of their years of differences, describing people, places, and events that violated the natural order of business, including the prevention of a ten-thousand-dollar receipt. In many respects the challenge, a work of art in and of itself, was the most remarkable of its kind ever issued in territorial Missouri.

Finally, again in anticipation of a refusal to meet him on the field of honor, Smith T issued the following caveat. To "shrink from this test," he taunted, was tantamount to a confession of guilt and a loss of "manhood." Reminiscent of trial by combat, an institutional practice nearly a thousand years old, the colonel's challenge reminded his foe that a refusal to fight was an admission of guilt. Pistols in the hands of two protagonists, a fatal yardstick of divine ordination, would prove culpability or innocence. It would also give Smith T "honorable satisfaction."[28]

28. Challenge, John Smith T to Frederick Bates, December 24, 1811, Bates Papers.

Bates did not send his second reply until December 30. The tone was somber and to the point. He offered no apologies or explanations other than to say that Smith T's letter was "very extraordinary" but that he owed to "the Government alone, an account of my official conduct."[29] The matter at hand ended here. Smith T issued no more formal challenges to a duel. To do so appeared pointless. He had made his point and in his mind he felt vindicated. Politically, Bates was not adversely affected. He rejected the chivalric code and believed in a different sense of honor. During the following years, Smith T would face other challenges from Bates, Austin, and various rivals, but they would be matters settled on the business field, not the field of honor.[30]

Throughout 1812, Smith T continued to fight for his economic life. For most of the year he was without the assistance of Reuben, who had been a source of much strength in earlier business contentions. Lawsuits continued to be filed against him for past commercial failings, while he was unable in the courts to wrest control of his home and properties at Mine Shibboleth. According to Edward Tiffin, commissioner of the General Land Office in Washington, it was not until November 30, 1812, that Smith T "under a claim of St. Vrain Lassus, entered for the first time this pretended claim with the recorder of land titles." Obviously, Tiffin either sided with the anti–Smith T faction in Missouri and purposely omitted from documentation the colonel's earlier filings, or else he was unaware of Smith T's efforts to document his claims as early as 1807. Also, it was not mentioned at the time that opponents as far back as Seth Hunt had forbidden the surveyor to survey any land claimed by Smith T. To the untrained eye it appeared in 1813, even after Reuben's return from a Spanish prison, that he had bowed to the inevitable. Frederick Bates in November of that year related the good news that Smith T had dismissed the suit against Dodge, Craighead, and Wilson at the last session of the Territorial Supreme Court.[31]

Smith T, however, was not a man to back down easily from the law or from other men. As the animosity and bitterness grew between Smith T and the others, especially his former friend Henry Dodge, who had

29. Reply, Frederick Bates to John Smith T, December 30, 1811, ibid.; Higginbotham, *John Smith T*, 14; Marshall, ed., *The Life and Papers of Frederick Bates*, 211–12.

30. *John Smith T v. Moses Austin and Henry Elliot*, October 1813 Term, Case no. 22, Box 18, Superior Court Cases, MSA.

31. Edward Tiffin to Frederick Bates, July 25, 1814, in *Territorial Papers*, vol. 14, 779. Gardner, *Lead King*, 114. Frederick Bates to Edward Tiffin, November 12, 1813, in *Territorial Papers*, vol. 14, 708–9.

taken Mine Shibboleth, it became all the more likely that it was just a matter of time until a violent encounter occurred. That time appeared to have arrived when Dodge and Smith T accidentally met in John Scott's law office. According to Judge William V. N. Bay, both men were "desperate and fearless" and "armed to the teeth in anticipation of a meeting" that "would result in the death of one or both." Only the quick-thinking Scott, recalled Bay, kept a bloody mayhem from occurring.[32] The two old adversaries, according to Varina Davis, met once again many years later in Galena. In her memoirs of her husband, Jefferson Davis, Varina Davis recounted the Confederate president's story of how Dodge "covered Smith T" with his pistol. Smith T "bowed coolly and said, 'This time you have the advantage of me, general, but the next!' " "The general's eyes flashed," recalled Davis, "as he told it, and he added, 'he came *very* near getting me, sir—*very near!*'"[33]

Throughout the early years of his struggle with Dodge and his cohorts, Smith T employed a variety of legal tactics to stifle his opponents. It was a formidable task, since Dodge had served as both sheriff and U.S. Marshal for the territory. Since no courthouse existed in the Ste. Genevieve area until 1821, the court oftentimes met in the parish house, a tavern, or a private home. In 1814, Dodge moved the sessions to his home. This location obviously gave him additional leverage against his rivals. Smith T, however, was not deterred. On November 19, 1813, he gave his brother Reuben, now a year returned from Mexico, power of attorney to act for him in all business transactions.[34] Next, he began transferring thousands of acres of land to Reuben, including Mine Shibboleth, Bellefontaine, and Mine à Robina. Some of these titles dated back as far as 1797.

These particular actions came roughly three months after much of his property fell under the jurisdictional purview of the new county of Washington. The creation of this county, separated now from Ste. Genevieve County, added another court in which litigation could be waged both by and against Reuben and his infamous brother. Legal battles over Shibboleth and other property would also continue to be fought in higher courts well into the next decade. Smith T, for example, in 1820

32. Bay, *Reminiscences*, 117.
33. Varina Davis, *Jefferson Davis: A Memoir by His Wife*, vol. 1, 151.
34. Pelzer, *Henry Dodge*, 17–18. Publication, John Smith T to the Public, June 30, 1814, Recorder of Deeds Office, Washington County Courthouse.

sued in the Superior Court for three thousand dollars in damages to properties taken from him "with force and arms," which deprived him of mining profits. The attorney representing him in the territorial court in this particular suit, David Barton, was soon to be a U.S. Senator.[35]

During the year 1813, however, and well into the following year, Smith T continued to sell off large tracts of land to Reuben. The apparent reasons for these land transactions were threefold: first, Smith T had already begun to plan his invasion of Texas and needed some cash; second, if he encountered the law during the struggle with Dodge and his partners, he wanted very little property available for legal seizure; and third, without these properties to manage there would be less distractions in Missouri and more time to travel and to plot in Tennessee.[36]

Contrary to their appearance, these actions did not mean that Smith T was willing to submit peacefully to what he believed was the unlawful seizure of Mine Shibboleth. For nearly two years he fought a rearguard action both physically and legally to take it back. Arrayed against him were of course formidable opponents such as Austin, Bates, the Perry family, Lionel Browne, Daniel Dunklin, Dodge, Craighead, and Wilson. On the other hand, Governor William Clark, who had replaced Meriwether Lewis, appeared to be more evenhanded, while U.S. Attorney John Scott openly supported Smith T.[37]

By the summer of 1814, his efforts paid off. Dodge and the others were forced out of the mines. Land commissioner Edward Tiffin, writing to the secretary of the treasury, hoped that Shibboleth could be leased to another party but added that "John Smith's illegal and shameful possession and opposition alone prevents" it from being accomplished. The government, he added, should "see the impropriety of suffering him any longer to commit such trespasses with impunity." Two weeks later, on July 25, 1814, Tiffin wrote to Bates and again called Smith T's seizure of Shibboleth "illegal." He further added that the War Department would soon be "called upon to order out a military

35. *John Smith T v. Declaration in Ejectment Damages,* Superior Court Cases (Northern Court), April Term 1820, Case no. 27, Box 22, MSA.

36. Deeds, John Smith T to Reuben Smith, 1813–1814, Deed Record Book A, Washington County Courthouse, 28.

37. Edward Tiffin to Albert Gallatin, July 11, 1814, in *Territorial Papers,* vol. 14, 778.

force to put him down, and clear him and all other intruders" off the property. Tiffin, with the luxury afforded a bureaucrat safely situated in Washington, then gave Bates the following instructions. "Perhaps it would be well to see him," he suggested, "and inform him of the forthcoming military action."[38]

Meanwhile, in another part of Washington, the capitol to be exact, the territorial representative from Missouri, Edward Hempstead, was supporting the Spanish land claimants. In a March 1814 speech delivered to Congress, Hempstead maintained that "even in a conquered country, individual property is usually held sacred." He went on to add that "a few acres of land to the United States are nothing—but taken away from an individual, may cause distress and ruin."[39]

Although Smith T had for some time physically resisted Dodge and his partners, it was Reuben and a contingent of the colonel's men who in the summer of 1814 sustained the battle for Shibboleth while John was filibustering on the Texas frontier. The July 1814 term of the court of common pleas in Washington County was informed that no warrant could be served against Smith T or his wife, Nancy, because they did not reside in the county at the time.[40]

Throughout the time that Dodge and his cohorts operated Shibboleth, they encountered considerable problems running the mining operation. Miners such as John Westover had taken their lead to Shibboleth to have it smelted. But the new lessees, after agreeing to pay the miners, had reneged on their promise. Many legal complaints were filed against the group and, from the evidence available, it would appear that the proprietors ran a very questionable operation. In one instance, when the court required Daniel Dunklin, an associate of Dodge's group, to come forth with the miners' contracts that he had in his possession, he notified the court that they were lost. Even as they relinquished their mining lease, they sued Smith T and Reuben for trespass and damages amounting to five thousand dollars. The territorial court agreed that the petition had merit, and on February 19, 1814, it notified Sheriff Lionel

38. Ibid., 777. *Joseph Boujie v. John Smith T,* July Term 1814, Box 1, Folder 7, Washington County Courthouse; Notice, Lionel Browne to John Brickey, June 15, 1814, ibid.

39. U.S. Congress, *The Debates and Proceedings of the Congress of the United States,* 13th Cong., 2d sess., March 1814, 1831, 1834.

40. *Joseph Boujie v. John Smith T,* July Term 1814, Box 1, Folder 7, Washington County Courthouse; Notice, Lionel Browne to John Brickey, June 15, 1814, ibid.

Daniel Dunklin. As sheriff of Washington County, Dunklin tried to evict Smith T from Shibboleth. Dunklin did not challenge Smith T when the colonel refused to leave, and so he lived to later serve as the state's governor. Courtesy of State Historical Society of Missouri, Columbia.

Browne to make the brothers post bond of two thousand dollars. In June, as the court continued the case, it summoned Dunklin to appear before it to give testimony for the plaintiffs.[41] Dunklin, who would later serve as sheriff of Washington County and governor of the state, was all too happy to comply, since he was an ardent opponent of Smith T.

The following April the court decided against Smith T despite the pleas of John Scott, his attorney. Damages were assessed at $1,117.07 plus court costs of $32.44. Sheriff Browne was ordered to collect the sum and if it was not paid to put Smith T in custody until further deliberation by the court. The vast amounts of property deeded to Reuben over the previous two years now appeared to pay off. Almost two weeks after the court order, Sheriff Browne told the court, "There being no property of John Smith T. found" and no jail to hold him, he goes at large. It was the same report that Browne made in January of

41. Court Order, John Brickey, Clerk to Dodge, Wilson, and Craighead, October 8, 1814, Box 1, Folder 4, Washington County Courthouse. Testimony of John Brickey, February 8, 1814, Box 1, Folder 4, ibid. Court Notice, Territorial Court to Lionel Browne, February 19, 1814, Box 1, Folder 5, ibid. Summons, John Brickey to Daniel Dunklin, June 28, 1814, Box 1, Folder 5, ibid.

that year when he communicated that the defendant had no property and therefore went "at large."[42] It was perhaps fortunate for Browne, and the other sheriffs who followed him in this job, that no jail existed at the time, because history indicated that Smith T would violently resist arrest no matter who issued the warrant or who came to serve it.

The particular case that prompted the court to act against Smith T revealed a rather feckless side to his character. Documents presented in court showed a May 1813 note for $94.91 with his seal. The note promised to pay this amount plus interest to the estate of one John McArthur within one year. As the time neared, it was apparent that the note would not be paid. Granted, the sum was not that large and Smith T was probably not in the territory to take care of the debt, but the cavalier way he treated many of his debtors was all too typical of the business style of hustlers and hucksters on the frontier.[43]

Although it is difficult to ascertain Smith T's exact whereabouts during 1815, it appears that he returned from his Texas sojourns by the spring of 1815. He immediately faced another summons, this time for charges filed against him by a former business partner, Robert Westcott. The latter demanded repayment of $201 and $400 in damages. Smith T was forced to post a bond of $400 and pledged that either he or Reuben would make full restitution.[44] As the number of cases and the amount of debts continued to mount against him, Smith T appeared in no hurry to satisfy his creditors. He had sold off large tracts of land in Tennessee as well as in Missouri to defray the costs of two misguided filibustering expeditions, and he had fought a series of costly legal and physical battles against, among others, Bates, Austin, and Dodge. In September 1815 the Washington County Court ordered the arrest of Reuben, who still represented his brother, for past judgments. He was

---

42. Court Notice, John Brickey to Lionel Browne, April 10, 1815, Box 1, Folder 5, ibid.; Plea, Andrew Scott to Territorial Court, April 20, 1815, Box 1, Folder 5, ibid. Sheriff's Notice, Lionel Browne to John Brickey, April 22, 1815, Box 1, Folder 5, ibid. Sheriff's Notice, Lionel Browne to John Brickey, January 5, 1815, Box 1, Folder 7, ibid.; Court Order, John Brickey to Lionel Browne, January 5, 1815, Box 1, Folder 7, ibid.

43. Another creditor, Joseph Boujie, alleged that he had been swindled out of 3,502 pounds of lead for services rendered. See Court Order, John Brickey to Lionel Browne, May 13, 1815, Box 1, Folder 7, ibid.

44. Summons, John Brickey to Lionel Browne, April 28, 1815, Box 1, Folder 7, ibid.; Court Order, John Brickey to Lionel Browne, June 16, 1815, Box 1, Folder 7, ibid.; Bond, John Smith T to Washington County Courthouse, April 27, 1815, Box 1, Folder 7, ibid.

to be brought into custody and "safely [kept] so that you [the sheriff] have his body before" the judge at the next session.[45]

During much of this tumultuous period, Reuben of course bore the brunt of his brother's inattention to the details of business. Although a reputable man and competent administrator, Reuben could not be expected to defend his own and Smith T's interests without benefit of the same kind of resources and reputation at the disposal of his brother. The brothers had lost many battles during the years 1812–1815. But they had not, as the coming years would attest, lost the war. By sheer determination they had fought their adversaries in Missouri to a virtual standstill. Even more remarkable, this stalemate was accomplished despite Smith T's prolonged absences from the territory. What most distracted him from the turmoil in Missouri was Texas and the allure of a Southwest fiefdom of immeasurable riches.

45. Court Declaration, John Brickey, September 17, 1815, Box 1, Folder 9, ibid.

7. To Texas—Again?

John Smith T was better at assembling armies than making use of them. His privateers had battled Austin's gang of equally reckless men, but only to a standstill. His filibustering expedition to Iowa had ended in disaster, and his organization to aid Burr had been unceremoniously disbanded before it left Missouri. Undeterred by this unfortunate chain of events, he began preparation in 1813 to undertake once again an adventure to distant lands. Once more, the object of his attention was Texas.

No doubt Smith T was only one of a long line of filibusterers whose ultimate goal was an American transcontinental empire. Long before Manifest Destiny had been formalized into the lexicon of national expansion, men such as Smith T had already begun the marches that would end at the Pacific and the Rio Grande. Nationalism, still in its infancy, played an important part in the ideology of territorial expansion, but it always shared center stage with self-aggrandizement. Sometimes, as in the case of Smith T, the two forces converged under the guise of filibustering.[1]

Earlier setbacks had impeded Smith T's ultimate objective: a southwestern fiefdom in Texas. His brother Reuben's treatment in Chihuahua helped to rationalize his thirst for retribution and reward against the Spanish. No doubt he shared the sentiments of a fellow filibusterer, William D. Robinson, who believed that Spanish policy had long been "a steady, systematic course of injustice and outrage towards the unfortunate Americans."[2]

---

1. Wilson and Ferris, eds., *Encyclopedia of Southern Culture*, 1504. Griffin, *The United States and the Disruption of the Spanish Empire*, 16; LaFeber, "Foreign Policies," 10–37; Van Alstyne, "The American Empire," 40–70. Weinberg, *Manifest Destiny*, chap. 1. For suspicions of Spain, see Francis Paul Prucha, *The Sword of the Republic: The United States Army on the Frontier 1783–1846*, 64–70.
2. Robinson, *Memoirs*, 1; Parmet and Hecht, *Aaron Burr: Portrait*, 234.

Smith T was a man on a mission. The mission, however, was colored by a number of factors. First, the War of 1812 further complicated American diplomatic relations with Spain. As the war went badly for the United States, the Madison administration became more reluctant to jeopardize its tenuous relationship with Spain. If it chose to do so, Spain was in a position to unleash Indian attacks against the U.S. frontier. James Monroe, acting in the capacity of secretary of state, tried his best to control events and forces rather than allowing them to control him. As much as he desired to see revolutions spread through the Floridas, Cuba, and New Spain, Monroe was equally desirous that the remnants of the decaying Spanish empire not fall into French or British hands.[3] Monroe hoped to use revolutionary agents and filibusterers, but only if he could control them. He further hoped that in the process these adventurers would spread republican virtues that were in accord with the principles of government in the United States. If, in the vortex of these upheavals, the nation could avail itself of some valuable territory, then Monroe had no qualms. Two difficult parts of this diplomatic equation were controlling the filibustering ardor of Americans such as John Smith T and manipulating the self-serving interests of Latin American leaders.

The intrigue on the Southwest frontier was complicated by shift-ing alliances, divided loyalties, conflicting policies, and uncontrollable personalities. At the American helm was Monroe. His task was to find Latin American military men who would do Washington's bidding. These leaders must be willing to fight Spain and "free" Texas. They must not, however, harbor any nationalist sentiments for the new state of Mexico. To supervise these "patriots," Monroe relied upon a number of Americans to serve in official and unofficial capacities. The former included U.S. military men, Indian agents, diplomats, and political appointees. Unofficial representatives included former army officers who "volunteered" to serve with the Latin American armies, spies, and filibusterers such as Smith T. Besides these forces, Monroe could also count on American public opinion for aid and comfort. Newspapers, commercial and business organizations, and politicians generally supported expansionist designs in the Southwest.

Southwestern intrigue was not limited to the United States and Spain. France and Great Britain also had spies and revolutionary agents

3. José de Toledo to James Monroe, January 4, 1812, DS, *Correspondence*.

throughout the region. In addition, there were indigenous elements throughout Mexico that desired not only independence but also Mexican suzerainty over Texas. Secretary of State Monroe was no doubt aware of these complexities. Unfortunately, he also believed that he could control these disparate forces and make them work to the United States' advantage.

Unknown to Monroe, his schemes were being undermined from the very beginning. In the first place, the revolutionary forces were badly divided over issues of policy and personality. Monroe also failed to control or to unite the various American filibusterers. Within two years' time this lack of coordination would spell disaster for Smith T and a host of other would-be expansionists.

In 1812, however, the prospects for territorial acquisition seemed bright. Monroe believed it possible to manage José Bernardo Gutiérrez de Lara, a self-styled Mexican patriot who traveled throughout the United States in 1812. From the center of power, Washington, D.C., to Natchitoches, Louisiana, on the far stretches of the frontier, Gutiérrez made his case. His main effort was to convince leaders in the Madison administration, especially Monroe, that he was a reliable ally of the United States. This imprimatur, he believed, would win him the unofficial right to lead an expedition against Spain.[4]

At virtually the same time that Monroe handpicked Gutiérrez, he instructed Dr. James H. Robinson, an unofficial confidant, to relay to the captain general of the Spanish Provinces of New Spain that the United States opposed filibustering expeditions into both Spanish territory and the neutral zone. The neutral zone lay between the Sabine River, which served as the boundary between the two nations, and the Arroyo Hondo, a tributary of the Red River. This virtual no-man's-land had been negotiated by James Wilkinson and Simón Herrera, the governor of Nuevo León. Both governments, according to the agreement, were to police the area and prevent any military buildup.[5]

Monroe was fully aware of how the neutral zone fitted into the overall schemes of the administration. Most filibustering activities, as Monroe stated to Robinson, began in Natchitoches, crossed the Sabine River,

4. José Bernardo Gutiérrez to John Graham, January 28 and April 28, 1812, DS, *Correspondence.*
5. Griffin, *The United States and the Disruption of the Spanish Empire,* 31–32. Garrett, *Green Flag over Texas,* 14–15.

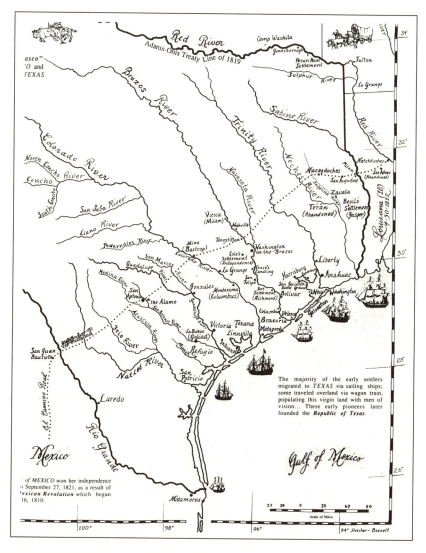

The majority of the early settlers migrated to *TEXAS* via sailing ships; some traveled overland via wagon train, populating this virgin land with men of vision... These early pioneers later founded the *Republic of Texas*.

Map of the contested U.S.–Spanish border and the Camino Real, the revolutionary highway into Texas and down toward Mexico City. This area served as the staging point for Smith T's filibustering expedition into Spanish territory.

and headed toward Nacogdoches, Texas. The road that facilitated this traffic was called the Camino Real. The road came up from Mexico City and then headed toward San Antonio. From the Texas capital it wound its way to Nacogdoches, twenty leagues west of the Sabine River. From here the road led to the American outpost at Natchitoches. The Camino Real, in short, was the revolutionary highway into the heart of Texas. Monroe, an ardent expansionist, still hoped, if possible, to win territory without war. He did not want his timetable for expansion upset by un-controllable filibusterers such as Smith T. Monroe not only feared that premature hostilities might push Spain to cut off commercial relations with the United States but also worried that a filibustering expedition might push Spain into an alliance with Great Britain. Furthermore, Monroe did not believe that the American intruders into the neutral zone could be effectively controlled in such delicate and important times. In short, the integrity of the neutral zone and the Camino Real must be maintained. Monroe thus instructed Robinson to allay Spanish concerns and to control American filibusterers. Both instructions, as it turned out, proved impossible to implement.[6]

Monroe was far too crafty to rely solely upon Robinson or to com-pletely trust Gutiérrez. To counteract these knight-errants, he turned to another individual of "doubtful authority," José Álvarez de Toledo, who in 1811 had acted as a representative of the Latin American delegation to the Spanish Cortes. Most accounts have portrayed him as Cuban by birth. The same year, 1811, he became an agent for Monroe. That November he showed up in Philadelphia and received a small down payment of money. He also held discreet talks with Monroe. After their meeting Toledo hastily informed Don Luis de Onís, the Spanish ambassador to Washington, of Monroe's plans to invade the province of Texas. For a sizable fund, he said, he would betray the Americans and see that the loyalists in Texas destroyed them. Apparently de Onís did not fully trust the Cuban. Toledo left the clandestine meeting with the ambassador without funds sufficient to warrant the betrayal of the Americans. Within a few months Toledo returned to the Spanish border to instigate a revolt in San Antonio.[7] Toledo also had secret

6. Almaráz, *Tragic Cavalier*, 10–11. Arthur P. Whitaker, *The United States and the Independence of Latin America, 1800–1830*, 95–98. James Monroe to James H. Robinson, July 1, 1812, DS, *Correspondence*.

7. Philip C. Brooks, "Spain's Farewell to Louisiana 1803–1821," 35–38; Ike H. Moore, "The Earliest Printing and First Newspaper in Texas," 84–85. José de Toledo to James Monroe, November 16, 1811, DS, *Correspondence*. Harris G. Warren, "José Álvarez de Toledo's Initiation as a Filibuster, 1811–1813," 60–66. Almaráz, *Tragic Cavalier*, 135.

meetings with Gutiérrez in an obvious attempt to undermine or coopt his authority.

Toledo was an extremely poor choice for Monroe. But Monroe was not the only expansionist to be fooled by him. In just over a year after his treacherous dealings with de Onís, Toledo had convinced John Smith T that he possessed the pedigree and character to team up with the Missourian and take the Hispanic borderlands. It would be a fateful and regrettable decision.

Besides Toledo, Monroe turned to William Shaler, a special agent of the State Department, to promote his expansionist activities. This adventurer hailed from Bridgeport, Connecticut. During the first decade of the nineteenth century, Shaler was a sea captain in the Pacific. Later he was assigned as a U.S. agent to Havana, Cuba. In late 1811 he returned home, discussed the possibilities of Texas independence with Monroe, and left in early 1812 for Natchitoches to supervise filibustering activities. Also in Natchitoches in the spring of 1812 was Lieutenant Colonel Zebulon Pike. This former western explorer, who harbored no love for the Spanish, added fuel to the border fire when he ordered American troops into the neutral zone. The Spanish government was furious over this incursion since they believed these troops were on a reconnaissance mission, preparatory to an American invasion.

One gentleman of questionable character who still loomed large on the Louisiana frontier was James Wilkinson. It is most likely that Pike's incursion into the neutral zone was instigated by him. Thomas Jefferson was one American leader who still doubted Wilkinson's true intentions. On January 11, 1812, for example, the former president wrote to Monroe about Wilkinson and his suspicious activities during the Burr conspiracy. The letter closed with this admonition: "As to the rest of his life," Jefferson wrote, "I have left it to his friends and his enemies, to whom it furnishes matter enough for disputation."[8] Obviously, Jefferson still held reservations about the general and his strategic position on the Texas-Louisiana border.

By the following year a war between Spain and the United States seemed possible. Spain, sensing a possible conflict, issued an order on May 24, 1813, that U.S. citizens would no longer be admitted into the interior provinces of Texas. The proclamation, however, did not

---

8. Dumas Malone, ed., *Jefferson and His Time. Vol. 6: The Sage of Monticello,* 110.

deter most Americans. Filibusterers flocked to the border in droves, and Spanish authorities were quite rightly concerned. General Antonio Humbert, a former general in the French Army, arrived to sell his services. General Thomas Adair, an old Burrite, likewise appeared in Natchitoches ready to do battle. Doctor John Sibley, the Indian agent on a border outpost in Louisiana, was also prepared to do his part in the upcoming war, as were Robinson and Shaler. In April 1813 Toledo appeared on the Louisiana-Texas frontier.[9] He too feigned a patriotic fever.

Such a vast array of adventurers certainly piqued the interest of John Smith T. Recovering from the Iowa disaster, he was hardly in a position to quickly assemble a new band of adventurers. Nevertheless, he watched the developments very closely and hoped to join the fray. Although a land buccaneer with some knowledge of Spanish politics, he knew little of the Byzantine world of Mexican filibustering. This lack of understanding of the complexities of southwestern intrigues would contribute greatly to the military setbacks he encountered in 1814.

The events of 1813, however, shaped up in such a way as to jeopardize the possibility of Smith T ever making his presence felt on the Spanish borderlands.[10] By 1813 the Mexican Revolution was in full swing. Gutiérrez, with American backing, had formed the Republican Army—ostensibly to liberate the Spanish Southwest. Robinson and Shaler, under directions from Monroe, became unofficial advisers. To provide more direct military supervision over Gutiérrez, Monroe had secured the services of Augustus William Magee. This Bostonian was a former army officer who had served on the Louisiana frontier under General Wilkinson from 1809 to June 12, 1812. At that time, at the age of only twenty-four, Magee ostensibly resigned his commission and assumed a leadership command in the Gutiérrez expedition. His command's banner was green in deference to Magee's Irish heritage. Despite the green flag, it was imperative in filibustering expeditions such as this to have a man of Spanish heritage nominally in charge. Monroe always believed that such an individual should be controlled

---

9. Rosario Parra Cala, ed., *Documentos Relativos a la Independencia de Norteamérica,* 748. Hereafter cited as *Documentos.* Records of Governor Salcedo, Colonial Archives of Texas, Rolls 52 and 53. Garrett, *Green Flag over Texas,* 25, 201, 187–89.

10. Spanish officials foresaw a problem with Texas as early as the Louisiana Purchase. See *Documentos,* 619.

by an American. This masquerade, the Madison administration hoped, would prevent the British from joining sides with Spain and jeopardizing the revolution.[11] To entice American filibusters the two leaders, Gutiérrez and Magee, offered each man forty dollars per month and a Spanish league of land totaling 4,428 acres for their services. Nearly eight hundred recruits quickly signed up.

Gutiérrez was no neophyte when it came to military matters. As early as 1811 he had attacked the Spanish forces in Texas, but he was driven off. The year 1812 proved to be a different matter due to the assistance of the Americans. In August 1812 the Republican Army of the North (as it was now called) crossed the Sabine and captured Nacogdoches. Within weeks, all the territory from the Sabine to the Guadalupe River was under their control. Texas seemed to be within their reach. In April 1813 the Republican Army, having swelled to fourteen hundred volunteers and four hundred Indian allies, forced the surrender of Governor Manuel Salcedo at San Antonio. Despite protestations from the Americans, Gutiérrez condoned the slaughter and mutilation of the governor and his subordinates. Magee, who might have controlled the bloodletting, had died a few months before Salcedo's surrender and had been replaced by Samuel Kemper of Virginia.[12]

The brutal murder of Salcedo and his officers galvanized Spain into action. They realized that Texas was the key to retaining their entire empire in North America. The Spanish likewise understood that a spirited defense of Texas required an aggressive and strong leader. Spain found such a man in General José Arredondo. As Arredondo prepared to strike against the filibusters, he could not have realized that dissension and division among the Mexicans and Americans would make his task a much easier one.

After the slaughter at San Antonio, Shaler, Robinson, Sibley, and Wilkinson all turned against Gutiérrez. In addition to the needless killings, Gutiérrez had made other moves that distanced him from his American benefactors. Proclaiming himself president of the new republic, he began to rule arbitrarily. Even special trade concessions to the United States were canceled or delayed. Shaler, in fact, wrote

11. James Robinson to James Monroe, July 26, 1813, DS, *Correspondence.*
12. *The Herald Extra* (Alexandria, La.), August 31, 1812. Almaráz, *Tragic Cavalier,* 167–71; William Shaler to James Monroe, January 10, 1813, and James Robinson to James Monroe, April 13, 1813, both in DS, *Special Agents.*

Monroe and told the secretary that he had impressed upon Gutiérrez "the most importance of giving the most liberal arrangement to foreign commerce." When Gutiérrez refused to cooperate, he was unceremoniously dumped by the Americans. Robinson and Shaler even suggested that Gutiérrez had turned to Napoleon for money, arms, and military tacticians. Rumor also had it, according to Robinson, that the British had offered to put down the rebellion in Texas for Spain in return for Cuba and the Floridas. Robinson intimated that Gutiérrez might even go over to the British side. The Americans also believed that England might double-cross the Spanish and try in the future to corner the new Latin American markets after their successful revolutions.[13]

Toledo now became the puppet of choice and would, according to Shaler, "wipe away" the disgrace of Gutiérrez.[14] The trick was to see that he continued to win military victories but not become so strong as to challenge the Americans' tutelage. In a memorandum to Monroe entitled "Present State of the Mexican Revolution," Robinson reported that an army of filibusters who "certainly oppose our claim to territory" were planning to enter Texas and set up an independent state. Robinson may have had Smith T in mind when he penned this caveat. These "evil consequences," he warned, must be avoided. One way to ensure this was to keep a close rein on Toledo so that he could not fall in with privateers. Given Toledo's checkered past and unreliability, American policy-makers wanted him to succeed but not to become too powerful to control.[15]

As events quickly proved, the Americans had little to fear from Toledo's military abilities. Shortly after General Arredondo crossed the Nueces River, Toledo made a tactical error and divided his forces. Part of the army under Henry Perry and Colonel Miguel Menchaca split from the main force and openly quarreled with Toledo. This military

---

13. *Gaceta de Texas,* May 25, 1813; William Shaler to James Monroe, July 14 and April 3, 1813, DS, *Special Agents.* Garrett, *Green Flag over Texas,* 191; Odie B. Faulk, *The Last Years of Spanish Texas 1778–1821,* 33; Warren, "José Álvarez," 67–68; William Shaler to James Monroe, July 20, 1813, DS, *Correspondence.* After Burr's activities, Spanish officials closely watched prominent American figures. See *Documentos,* 635. *El Mexicano,* June 19, 1813. Julia K. Garrett, "The First Newspaper of Texas: *Gaceta de Texas,*" 211–12. Memorandum, Jonathan Russell to James Monroe, February 3, 1812, in Manning, *Diplomatic Correspondence,* vol. 3, 1432.

14. William Shaler to James Monroe, August 7, 1813, DS, *Special Agents.*

15. Memorandum, James Robinson to James Monroe, July 26, 1813, DS, *Correspondence.*

mistake was compounded by an even more demoralizing decision. Toledo ordered his men to fight in segregated units. The Americans, therefore, fought separately from their Mexican and Indian allies. Arredondo, with roughly the same number of men, made quick work of the divided army. Although Toledo had more than fourteen hundred troops, they were routed near San Antonio at the Battle of Medina. Shortly afterward they suffered another defeat at the hands of the loyalists. All in all, the Republican Army lost nearly a thousand men. Toledo fled along the Camino Real and barely outran his pursuers to the border. His tenure as head of the army was one of the greatest political and military disasters in the history of Texas independence. Even Arredondo later admitted that the victories were due in no small part to Toledo's blunders. Shaler, disgusted and worn out, left the Spanish borderlands for an assignment in Ghent, Belgium. Robinson left for Washington and then traveled across Pennsylvania and other eastern states. He printed hundreds of pamphlets encouraging American volunteers to join another army of liberty and revolution.[16]

Toledo also remained active. He headed for Nashville and a rendezvous with Smith T. The colonel may not have been privy to all of Toledo's intrigues, miscalculations, and incompetent activities. Nevertheless, in the winter of 1813–1814 Smith T and Toledo began a series of meetings. Toledo impressed upon Smith T the urgency of immediate action. Toledo obviously wanted to show the Madison administration that he was undeterred in his revolutionary objectives. Furthermore, he wanted to return to Texas before Monroe had time to select a new Latin leader for future expeditions.

Exactly when Smith T first met Toledo may never be known for certain. Nevertheless, by 1813 Smith T had ordered his slaves to step up the production of pistols and rifles. Perhaps at the time only the colonel knew whether these weapons were being made for the Texas incursion. Even Aaron Burr was rumored to have made plans to reenter the fray. In his journal dated February 1, 1809, the former vice president made

---

16. Joaquin de Arredondo, "Joaquin de Arredondo's Report of the Battle of the Medina, August 18, 1813," 200–232. Moore, "The Earliest Printing," 84–85; Faulk, *The Last Years of Spanish Texas,* 34. Garrett, "The First Newspaper of Texas," 228. James Robinson to James Monroe, November 15, 1813; Pamphlet, James Robinson to the People of Pittsburgh, November 19, 1813; Álvarez de Toledo to William Shaler, January 16, 1814; all in DS, *Correspondence.*

reference to a note from a certain Colonel Smith but did not elaborate on its contents. Whether a plot spanning the Atlantic was even possible, historians will probably never know. Nonetheless, men of the West from Andrew Jackson to Henry Clay kept a close watch on activities in Texas. Smith T was no exception. As for the Toledo–Smith T connection, Toledo wrote to Shaler in November 1813 and told him that he and Smith T had met in Nashville and that the colonel had offered five hundred men armed with rifles and bayonets "of a new invention." Unfortunately, he did not elaborate what the new invention was or how it would be used against the royalists. In any event, this regiment would be ready to march under Smith T's command when Toledo gave the order. Toledo told Shaler that he had accepted the offer. At roughly the same time Toledo received word that General Jean Humbert would also defer to the general's command.[17]

By January 1814 Toledo and Smith T were preparing their plan of attack. For Smith T it was a chance to play both nationalist and profiteer. His filibustering could help destroy the remnants of the Spanish empire in North America, deter British and French designs on the territory, and provide him the opportunity to realize his dreams of a southwestern kingdom. Time was now of the essence. Robinson had popularized "the cause" in the North and had more than ten thousand dollars appropriated for arms. He had also recruited General Adair for his expedition, and was only waiting for the ice on the Ohio River to melt before moving men and material downstream and toward Texas. Robinson, knowing that Toledo was working with Smith T, also sent a letter in early January to the general warning him of any precipitous action.[18]

Toledo was not intimidated by Robinson. He still believed he had the blessings of the Department of State and conveyed his optimism to an American army officer, Captain James Luckett. Toledo told the officer of Smith T's negro mechanics making many of the weapons for the expedition and suggested that he had made contact with another U.S. officer, James T. Johnson, who was serving in a front organization

17. Aaron Burr, *The Private Journal of Aaron Burr*, 74–75. Álvarez de Toledo to William Shaler, November 19, 1813, and William Shaler to Álvarez de Toledo, November 8, 1813, both in DS, *Special Agents*.

18. James Robinson to Unknown, January 4, 1814, and James Robinson to Álvarez de Toledo, January 4, 1814, DS, *Correspondence*.

at this time called the Mexican Patriotic Army.[19] Toledo hoped to head this army and quickly descend upon Texas.

Robinson, however, had already launched his invasion plan. With an advance unit of three thousand men, he had by February 1814 reached Natchez. His strategy envisioned an attack across the neutral zone as early as possible. This plan, he anticipated, might preempt a similar attack by Toledo and Smith T later in the spring or early summer. It obviously did not. Toledo, upon hearing of Robinson's movements, hastened to the Sabine River and awaited the arrival of his armies. In late May 1814 he communicated with Monroe's agent that one party of revolutionaries had descended the Colorado and had rendezvoused with Colonel Smith (Toledo did not use T when referring to him). The plans were progressing smoothly and Smith T, according to the general, had meshed in well with the overall operation.[20] As for the colonel, he had left Nashville early that spring with a sizable force and proceeded toward Natchitoches. If he hoped to persuade Robinson to join his force or to abandon his own schemes, he was badly mistaken.

By now Smith T was enmeshed in the diplomatic intrigue of filibustering. By rashly heading toward the border and allying himself with Toledo, he gained the enmity of the State Department, public officials such as Governor Claiborne in New Orleans, and military commanders such as Wilkinson. In addition, powerful expansionist interests in Natchitoches and Natchez turned against Toledo and Smith T. These men included General Humbert, Ellis P. Bean, and the pirate Jean LaFitte. Despite these obstacles, Smith T pushed on. He faced three formidable foes. The first and least apparent was his wily ally, Toledo— a man as unreliable and changeable as a Texas storm. The second foe, of course, was the Spanish military, an army determined to hold Texas at all costs. The third and most immediate problem was Robinson. If Robinson's attack on Texas proved successful, then other filibusterers would likely join his cause. This kind of political setback was even more unpalatable to Smith T than the possibility of defeat on the battlefield.

Toledo and Smith T by now realized that they must discredit Robinson. The junta formed at Natchez by Robinson was composed of "very low" men, Toledo reported. Their object was to set up a government

19. Álvarez de Toledo to Captain James Luckett, April 10, 1814, ibid.
20. Álvarez de Toledo to William Shaler, May 30, 1814, ibid.

in the Mexican provinces separate from the United States. Toledo believed that Robinson's group, if successful, would establish their own commercial company, giving them a special trade monopoly. Sibley, the Indian agent, as well as Anthony Campbell and Dr. William Kennedy, were, according to Toledo, part of this nefarious plot.

To demonstrate his manliness and to show how thoroughly despicable he believed Robinson to be, Toledo took the ultimate plunge and challenged him to a duel.[21] The site more than likely would have been on the east side of the Sabine River. Since the preparations for the duel might take some time to complete—the choice of weapons, the seconds, the surgeons, the terms of engagement, etc.—Toledo must have believed that the challenge would give him time to position his army under Smith T's command on the Sabine and to make ready for the invasion. The situation became even worse for Smith T and Toledo with the defection of General Humbert. This opportunist believed that the most propitious attack against the Spanish would be from the sea. Consequently, he and other filibusterers such as Bean threw in with the pirates of Barataria, led by Lafitte. Barataria was a small island below New Orleans. The pirates on the island were well armed, and many believed their military strength to be more than fifteen hundred men, making them one of the strongest forces in Louisiana.[22] The defection of Humbert dampened the spirits of Toledo and Smith T, but it did not deter them.

Another matter that complicated the various expeditions was the ambivalence of the American officials in New Orleans. Wilkinson was still an unpredictable character who no one seemed to trust. Smith T, because of his earlier connections with the general and Aaron Burr, was probably ambivalent about Wilkinson's presence on the frontier. He could only rely upon the general's opportunistic nature. If the expedition had a chance of success, then he might throw his weight toward it. If it appeared doomed, then he would most likely provide it with a quiet euthanasia. Governor Claiborne, on the other hand, did not take an active role in coordinating the revolutionary activities. By most accounts he mistrusted the filibusterers and doubted their chances of success against the Spanish. As previously mentioned, Shaler had

21. Walter Prescott Webb, ed., *The Handbook of Texas*, 785–86.
22. D. Brackenridge to William Shaler, December 27, 1813, DS, *Correspondence*.

become thoroughly disillusioned with the chain of events and had left for Europe. Monroe, unfortunately, did not replace him with anyone of his diplomatic stature or force of personality. It appeared that Monroe was willing to allow the forces of greed and division to control events rather than to continue to manage the operation.

Without any coordination, the revolutionary plans began to unravel. Bickering and mistrust between the rival factions continued to worsen. In fact, Robinson, angered by Toledo's criticism, reversed roles and challenged the general to the field of honor. This of course was what Toledo had hoped for all along. A meeting of the antagonists and their "mutual friends" at Natchitoches helped to end the affair without bloodshed. Nevertheless, considerable rancor among the various groups still prevailed. At the meeting Robinson produced a letter written by Toledo and addressed to Colonel Reuben Kemper. In it Toledo accused Robinson of being in the pay of the French and hence a traitor. In order to prevent a duel, Toledo conceded his error and retracted it. Still, in order to avoid being branded a liar, Toledo stated that at the time he wrote Kemper, he believed Robinson's actions to be unpatriotic. He further stated that he had no desire to injure Robinson's character.[23]

While the two sides negotiated the affair of honor, Toledo ordered Smith T to proceed southward. The colonel arrived in Natchitoches and immediately began "to inform himself of the state of affairs."[24] Like Toledo, he believed that many Mexican patriots, as well as a number of American filibusters, were suspicious of both Robinson and Humbolt. These "honorable men" Smith T believed would most certainly support his cause if all of the facts were presented to them.

Fearless men will more likely follow a fearless leader, and Smith T certainly had that reputation. The times undoubtedly required such men. The neutral zone and the lands to the west were, as Stephen F. Austin recalled, "a howling wilderness" filled with bandits, Indian bands, adventurers, and pirates along the coast. The revolutions and counterrevolutions had, as Robinson so aptly put it, created "violence and misery almost without parallel in history."[25] This was no land

23. Statement of a Meeting, T. Davenport, Chairman, n.d., ibid.
24. Álvarez de Toledo to William Shaler, May 30, 1814, ibid.
25. Garrett, "The First Newspaper of Texas," 228–32; Memorandum, James Robinson to James Monroe, July 26, 1813, DS, *Correspondence.*

for the faint of heart. And General Arredondo, who had defeated Toledo's army the previous year, made sure that all filibusterers knew the risks of their high-stakes gamble. He issued a declaration that anyone crossing the Sabine, which he now considered to be the legal boundary between Spain and the United States, would be shot if captured. The commandant general's words, Smith T realized, were no idle threat. In fact, many filibusterers believed that suicide rather than surrender was the only feasible alternative in such a situation.[26]

One last problem plagued the would-be expansionists. The American government, most likely influenced by Monroe, believed that the various rival factions could not be coordinated to the degree necessary to pull off a successful invasion. Without an agent like Shaler, Monroe in particular did not trust any of the competing factions enough to allow them free rein in Texas. Toward that end, the Madison administration issued an order for Robinson's arrest. The order arrived at Natchez and was given to Sibley to implement. He was a poor choice to place much confidence in, since he was a party to Robinson's schemes. Sibley wasted eight days before moving against Robinson, and by that time Robinson had moved into the neutral zone.

The government also moved to stop Toledo. The junta at Natchez hurried this arrest order to Governor Claiborne as quickly as possible to prevent the general from reaching Smith T's army. Toledo, however, also had spies among the Americans and escaped before the order could be executed. Although Shaler had left the border and was in the process of reassignment, Toledo hurried off a letter to him and begged that "an active and intelligent agent" be sent to the area "to counteract the machinations" of Toledo's enemies. Toledo reiterated that under his command it was still possible to form a "respectable army."[27]

Putting together that army was the task of Smith T. Certainly his reputation as a man of action served him well on the frontier. Just how many Louisiana men Smith T was able to enlist in the blood sport of filibustering was uncertain. Nevertheless, he felt militarily strong enough to cross the Sabine and to engage either Arredondo's army or Robinson's band of adventurers. His spirits were also bolstered by

26. In 1816 Francisco Xavier Mina led an expedition to Mexico. Suffering from a wound and about to be captured, he committed suicide. See Almaráz, *Tragic Cavalier,* 181.

27. Álvarez de Toledo to William Shaler, May 30, 1814, DS, *Correspondence.*

Toledo's assurances that he had recruited more men and added more "provisions of war," which would be sent immediately to him. All of these developments augured so well for the fortunes of the expedition that even General Humbert and his men decided to throw in once more with Toledo. Toledo, fearing a double cross, refused their request. Nevertheless, Humbert's offer suggested that the combined armies of Toledo and Smith T had the best chance of success in a war with Spain.

Encouraged by these positive signs, Smith T led his army across the Sabine and into the neutral zone. He then continued west along the Camino Real. In all probability he did not know that the American government was in the process of trying to shut down all of the filibustering expeditions, including his own. His scheme of empire with Burr and Wilkinson had been ended unceremoniously by governmental fiat. Ironically, it now appeared that history was to repeat itself. Fate, acting once again through the agency of the government, appeared ready to end his dreams of empire.

Not far from the town of Nacogdoches, Smith T found the campsite of Robinson, who had slipped into Texas after dodging the arrest order. Most likely both old protagonists had warrants outstanding for their arrests. Each man urged the other to cease their hostile activities. On April 10, 1814, Robinson sent a letter to Smith T requesting a meeting for the following day. Smith T refused. This prompted Robinson to send another letter. He referred to a directive dated January 24, 1814, which gave him the authority to proceed to Nacogdoches where volunteers could come and join his expedition. Furthermore, he suggested that he possessed the money and authority to pay the filibusterers of earlier invasions who had not yet been reimbursed. Robinson stated firmly that he was not acting as a foreign agent and that he would do nothing to offend the government of the United States. Finally, he offered the olive branch to Smith T by inviting him to join his command and be subject to his orders.[28]

On the same day as Robinson's "invitation," Smith T responded by saying that he regretted the differences between the two men but that he would take orders only from Toledo. Fearing a trap, Smith T refused to go to Robinson's camp. The following day Robinson again

---

28. John Robinson to John Smith T, April 10, 1814; John Robinson to John Smith T, April 11, 1814; both in ibid.

demanded a face-to-face meeting, citing the Natchez Resolution as the basis for his authority. If these differences were not soon resolved, he wrote, it would most certainly "overthrow the expedition."[29]

Smith T wasted no time in issuing a reply. He no doubt placed little or no credibility in the Natchez Resolution but granted the following concession. "I will," he wrote, "consent that you occupy your stand." If Toledo relinquished his command, he went on to write, he would then communicate that change to Robinson. The note suggested that if Toledo quit, or was arrested, wounded, or killed, then Smith T might take over the entire command. Until he heard from Toledo, Smith T decided to refrain from hostilities against Spain and toward Robinson. "I wish," he concluded, "a union of sentiment and action to take place."[30]

During this war of nerves the opposing armies apparently engaged in serious hostilities. Neither side released exact casualty figures, but the battle concerned Robinson enough that he hurried off another note to Smith T imploring him to come to camp for talks. The note further suggested that although blood had been shed it was still not too late to solve the problems "to our mutual satisfaction." Smith T was unimpressed. He placed the blame for the clash on Robinson's forces. The note indicated that by this time Smith T's patience was at an end. "You would have saved much trouble and have given me satisfaction," he exclaimed, "by a personal interview."[31] Robinson had now been challenged to the field of honor by both Toledo and Smith T. For the colonel, the resort to a duel was the time-honored method of resolving personal difficulties. In this case, killing Robinson held forth the possibility, however remote, that without their leader, Robinson's forces might be persuaded to join Smith T's expedition and continue their struggle against the Spaniards.

The impasse over command soon reached Toledo and the Natchez junta. Both sides seemed to realize that internecine warfare between the rival factions jeopardized the entire Texas operation. In early May 1814 a new front organization called the Committee to Free Mexico, which

29. John Smith T to James Robinson, April 11, 1814; James Robinson to John Smith T, April 12, 1814; both in ibid.

30. John Smith T to James Robinson, April 12, 1814, ibid.

31. James Robinson to John Smith T, April 12, 1814; John Smith T to James Robinson, n.d.; both in ibid.

supported Robinson, pledged safe conduct for Toledo if he would meet with them and resolve the command problem. Sensing that once again the opposing side was attempting to win at the negotiating table what they could not achieve in the field, Toledo refused to meet with them but extended an invitation for them to come see him.[32] Toledo's invitation was rejected the same day that it was sent.

By this time two new twists in this Byzantine game on the Spanish borderlands had occurred. First, in late April, with reconciliation between the hostile camps a virtual impossibility, Smith T launched an attack against Robinson and captured him. The military incursion was typical of Smith T. Never a man given to patience and moderation, his impetuosity once again had gotten the best of him. Unable to receive personal satisfaction on the field of honor, he was determined to receive recompense, if only on the field of battle. As he had done so often in his life, he resorted to violence as the best and, in his mind, the only course of action. Smith T's assault not only ended the command question but also made Robinson's forces too weak to threaten Arredondo.[33] With Robinson and some of his officers in the custody of Smith T, Toledo then hastened to cross the Sabine and join the colonel.

The second twist in the Texas drama took place on May 11, 1814. Acting in the capacity of commander-in-chief of the Republican Army of the North, Toledo issued a proclamation of independence for northern Mexico. "Humanity," the proclamation read, must reject the cruel oppression of Spain that had endured since the days of Cortez and Pizarro. The Spanish empire was engulfed in revolutions and, according to Toledo's document, it was now time for Mexico to be free as well. The general's public statement said that he had been authorized by the chiefs of the revolution to take command of the armies marching against Spain and to establish a provisional government in the north. This government, he added, would eventually replace the entire Spanish structure in Mexico, and Toledo looked forward to the day when he would rule from Mexico City. Finally, the proclamation stated that anyone not obeying his authority would be treated as an enemy of the state.[34]

32. Committee to Free Mexico to Álvarez de Toledo, May 9, 1814; Álvarez de Toledo to Committee to Free Mexico, May 20, 1814; both in ibid.
33. Álvarez de Toledo to William Shaler, May 30, 1814, ibid.
34. Proclamation, Republican Army of the North, May 11, 1814, ibid.

Toledo's proclamation was both premature and quixotic. He had yet to defeat a sizable Spanish army. He had not been able to unite the rival filibustering organizations. He had little or no support from the American government. Nor did he have any real support from the Indian masses who would ultimately determine Mexico's future. In fact, Toledo's main asset was a strong and reckless lieutenant in the person of John Smith T. Yet, in spite of these obstacles (or perhaps because of them), Toledo had declared his intentions to take all of Mexico and free her from her imperial shackles.

Smith T, always a dreamer himself, must have at some point begun to realize that the plot to conquer Texas had become far more complicated than he ever envisioned. He must also have sensed that he too was a pawn in a far greater imperial struggle than what he had originally thought. Once again his hopes of empire had been dashed not by the clash of armies but by a cabal of his fellow Americans. Just as he had been defeated by the intrigues of Burr-Wilkinson, his last Texas venture was doomed by the same kind of conspiratorial forces. As a man of action, Smith T believed that he deserved a better fate.

The immediate problem, however, concerned the disposition of Robinson and his fellow captives. As word filtered back to Natchez and Natchitoches of Robinson's defeat, Toledo faced the possibility of even more retaliation by rival factions. On May 5, 1814, John Nancarrow, a junta member, excoriated Toledo for Smith T's "violent outrage." He demanded the immediate release of Robinson, John Winn, and the others taken prisoner by the colonel. Once again, the junta spokesman placed the blame for the failure to take Texas squarely on the shoulders of Smith T and Toledo.[35]

Toledo, who by now had taken command of the filibusterers, named Smith T's campsite Camp Independence. From this position, well inside what Spain considered to be her rightful territory, Toledo published his grandiose proclamation. The week before its issuance, however, he worked to resolve the question of what to do with the Robinson faction. Writing to the junta, Toledo informed them that the captured leaders had been promised "their liberties" provided they promised to leave Texas and not return. When they refused to take such a pledge, Toledo warned them that they would be held as prisoners until such time as

35. John Nancarrow to Álvarez de Toledo, May 5, 1814, ibid.

they would be tried under military law. This was a position, the general reiterated, that he would support "with my last man."[36] In another letter to the junta, dated the same day, Toledo retreated somewhat and declared that he would turn over his prisoners to the U.S. government if the Madison administration demanded it. This last bit of strategy would of course have implicated the administration in filibustering and would have given Toledo some degree of official recognition.

Negotiations between Toledo and the junta stalled for the better part of the early summer. In the meantime, Toledo negotiated unsuccessfully with other filibustering organizations over the question of a united command structure. As for the Spanish forces under Arredondo, their mission was more political than military. Rather than attacking the divided American factions and possibly giving them some reason for unity, they merely waited for their inevitable self-destruction. By the fall of 1814 the zeal to take Texas was all but gone. Arredondo, for example, made no mention in his memoirs of any major military engagements during this time. In fact, he felt certain enough that American expeditions were no longer a threat that he returned shortly to Mexico City. By 1817, Antonio Mariá Martínez, governor of Texas, could report no major organized filibustering activities.[37] Spanish authorities, even if they had anticipated such disasters, could not have dreamed that their policies could have been so completely successful.

John Smith T had played the high-stakes game of filibustering and had lost. Over the course of a few months, his armed forces began to drift back across the Sabine to the safer confines of American soil. Factionalism, jealousy, miscalculation, egoism, deceit, and even treachery characterized the ignominious Texas expedition. Other American adventurers over the next few years also unsuccessfully tried to complete the task of independence, but John Smith T would not be among them.

In retrospect, it may be possible that the colonel and his men fell prey to one of the craftiest opportunists on the Hispanic borderlands, namely, Álvarez de Toledo. In 1816, for example, Dr. Felia Calleja, Viceroy of New Spain, confirmed that Toledo was in fact an agent of the Spanish government and working for Onís, the Spanish ambassador in Washington. Perhaps the best historian to chronicle filibustering,

36. Álvarez de Toledo to John Nancarrow, May 5, 1814, ibid.
37. Pamphlet, Manuel Cordéro, 1820, La Real Audiencia de Mexico.

Harris G. Warren, revealed Toledo's true nature when he wrote that, after receiving a full pardon from the Spanish king (sometime around 1816), he returned "a repentant subject, back 'to the bosom of his fatherland.'"[38]

It was, ironically, in the midst of this most humiliating of personal defeats that Smith T, at least to many of his most ardent admirers, rescued his fame and reputation. No one in Texas, including the colonel, had been able to assemble the filibusterers under a common flag. But events in a few short months were to change that situation. The man who united the disparate parties, however, was not a filibuster. He was Andrew Jackson. As the soldiers of fortune made their way out of Mexico, word arrived of an impending battle with the British. General Jackson had hastened to the vicinity of New Orleans to confront a veteran British army under the leadership of Sir Edward Pakenham.

According to legend, Smith T contributed indirectly as well as directly to the American cause in the War of 1812. His activities, claim his eulogists, finally wiped clear the stain of Burrism and secured his status as a great American patriot. First, they claimed, there were his mines throughout the mineral area, which produced the lead that his armada of wagons carried to the landings of Selma. Here the process of turning the lead into bullets and balls was facilitated by his shot towers. This argument may be specious, since wartime conditions brought most lead mining activities in the Missouri Territory to a virtual standstill. Without Smith T's business records it is impossible to ascertain what if any activity occurred. Second, his admirers believed he contributed directly to the American victory at the Battle of New Orleans. Vallé Higginbotham quoted family records as indicating how "he put his marksmanship to use as a member of the 'Tennessee Riflemen.'" In order to qualify for membership in this group, she wrote, he gave as his place of residence Davidson County, Tennessee.[39] For the record, the tax rolls of District Number Six in Davidson County indicate that he did pay property taxes throughout these years. Smith T did not, as one would expect, appear on the War of 1812 military rosters from the county because he was a volunteer and not under the military command structure.

38. Dispatch, Felia Calleja to the Spanish Ministry of War, November 10, 1816, ibid.; Warren, "José Álvarez," 82; Moore, "The Earliest Printing," 84–85.
39. Higginbotham, *John Smith T,* 52.

Other relatives of Smith T, such as George Penn Smith, Jr., not only accepted the New Orleans story but embellished it with their own myths. Smith Jr., for example, credited his famous ancestor with developing the battle formation for the volunteer troops, protecting the American army from hostile fire by the use of cotton bales, and conceptualizing the rapid fire sequence that was used with such destructive accuracy at the battle. This tactic, he wrote, "had the effect of a modern repeating rifle." The Smith family genealogy was perhaps best kept by Susan and Guy Richardson. Sometime in the early 1900s the Richardsons completed a family scrapbook entitled The "Book of Doom." This book in at least two places also referred to Smith T's participation in the battle. Others accepting "the tradition" included one of the local historians of Smithland, Kentucky. Such heroics, wrote Mrs. Gabe McCandles, would seem "to fit his temperament and his talents."[40]

The facts surrounding this legend, however, are much more difficult to establish. Nevertheless, some credence must be given to the legend of Smith T and the battle that ushered in a new age of American nationalism. As for the battle itself, many references have been made to the number of filibusterers who joined Jackson's forces. One such individual was Ellis P. Bean. Bean fought intermittently in Texas for nearly two decades. Other filibusterers who joined the American forces were Reuben Kemper and Jean Humbert.[41] The pirate Jean Lafitte also joined the fray.

Undoubtedly, General Jackson needed all the men, no matter how unsavory, he could muster. Generals William Carroll and John Coffee, both from Tennessee, contributed much of the manpower for the New Orleans encounter, but the American forces desperately needed ammunition, flints, artillery, and supplies as well. Some of these necessities were obtained from the Baratarian pirates, but the filibusterers also contributed their share.[42] Smith T quite obviously could have provided

40. Smith, Jr., "John Smith T.," 6. Book of Doom, 138. The other reference to the battle in this book does not have a numbered page.

41. Alexander Walker, *Jackson and New Orleans*, 274–75.

42. Sesquicentennial Celebration Commission, *Battle of New Orleans*, 116. Also see Wilburt S. Brown, *The Amphibious Campaign for West Florida and Louisiana 1814–1815*. Jane Lucas de Grummond, *The Baratarians and the Battle of New Orleans*, ix. The best description of the battle is Charles B. Brooks, *The Siege of New Orleans*. Also see Stanley C. Arthur, *The Story of the Battle of New Orleans*.

some of these military requirements. Jackson's military needs, of course, do not establish a direct causal link to Smith T. Yet there were other pieces of circumstantial evidence that point to a possible connection.

In 1826, as his economic fortunes were waning, Smith T petitioned the U.S. Congress for relief pertaining to military expenses incurred in 1814. A bill for his relief, as well as that of Wilson P. Hunt, was brought before the Senate on December 14, 1826. On January 2 of the following year the Senate referred it to the Committee on Military Affairs. It should be noted, parenthetically, that this committee handled the petitions of veterans of the War of 1812. There was a sense of urgency in Smith T's request, since in March 1827 his bitter foe, Andrew Jackson, would assume the presidency. This would no doubt seal the fate of his relief bill. The petition, on the motion of Senator Thomas H. Benton, reached the floor in late February. This body, acting as the Committee of the Whole, debated the measure and voted twenty-one for the bill and twenty-one against. Voting against the bill was Missouri's senior senator, David Barton. The vice president then cast the deciding vote against the relief bill. The exact nature of this debt, as well as the debate itself, cannot be ascertained from the Senate *Journal,* but the request referred back to the time of the Texas incursion. The expenses would also have coincided with Smith T's possible arrival in New Orleans.[43]

Another bit of information which might help substantiate that Smith T was at the Battle of New Orleans had to do with David S. Deadrick. This young officer from a prominent Nashville family was a trusted aide of General Jackson during these trying times. Later Deadrick married Smith T's only daughter.[44] Although Nashville social circles were small enough for gentlemen, even of such disparate ages, to have known each other, it is possible that the two future in-laws met at the Battle of New Orleans.

Another piece of the historical puzzle can be found in the personal papers of Andrew Jackson. In the early 1800s, one might recall, Smith T and Jackson were close business and political allies. This friendship extended well into the mishaps of the Burr expedition when the two

43. U.S. Senate, *Journal of the Senate of the United States of America,* 19th Cong., 2d sess., 39, 71, 101, 187. *Missouri Republican,* March 8, 1827.
44. *The Tennessean,* March 13 and 20, 1983.

men placed their trust in the former vice president. In an 1806 letter, for example, Jackson believed that Aaron Burr "would eventually prove to be the Saviour of this Western country." Jackson and Smith T fell out shortly after this time, and Smith T ended up owing the future president a sizable amount of money. The litigation continued for a number of years in the Missouri and Tennessee courts. John Coffee, later a hero of the Battle of New Orleans, had at one time been given power of attorney by Jackson to settle the debts of Smith T.[45] Most definitely, Smith T would not have been personally welcomed by Jackson in the last difficult months of 1814. But the need for men and supplies would still have outweighed Jackson's dislike of his former business partner.

Given the personal animosity between Jackson and Smith T, it would be unlikely that Jackson would sing Smith T's praise after the conclusion of the battle. This might explain the lack of notoriety. Also complicating the New Orleans mystery was the number of John Smiths who were present or likely to have been present at the battle site. One John Smith was a young staff officer who in late October 1814 was sent on a mission to Pensacola. He most likely did not return to southern Louisiana until the battle was close at hand. Another John Smith was the ex-Burrite and former senator from Ohio. He too was most probably in the vicinity of the battle. In fact, he died in St. Francisville, Louisiana, on July 30, 1824.[46]

In his personal papers, Jackson on November 14, 1814, commented on the surrender of a town and fort previously held by the British. The surrender was affected by "dismounted volunteers" led by Colonels Williamson and Smith.[47] In a footnote to the text, the editor of the Jackson papers identified the first name of Williamson to be Thomas and the Smith in question to be John. The explanatory note went on to reference this John Smith as the former Ohio senator.

Most definitely Senator John Smith would have relished a fight with the British, but it is very doubtful that in late 1814 and early 1815 he could have turned his dream into reality. Senator Smith had indeed

45. Andrew Jackson to Cuthbert Banks, April 1806; Power of Attorney, Jackson and Hutchings to John Coffee, February 4, 1805; both in Moser et al., eds., *Papers of Andrew Jackson,* vol. 2, 537, 528.

46. U.S. Congress, *Biographical Directory of the United States Congress 1774–1989,* 1832.

47. Andrew Jackson to Willie Blount, November 14, 1814, in Moser et al., eds., *Papers of Andrew Jackson,* vol. 3, 185.

gone to the warmer climate of Louisiana, but not for purposes of filibustering or combat. He had made the venture for health reasons. The *Biographical Directory* put his birth date as 1735. This would have made him nearly eighty years of age when, as a dismounted volunteer, he would have had to storm a fortress. This kind of constancy and intrepidity, suffice it to say, was best left for younger men.

Finally, it should also be noted that omission of the appellation "T" was also common among many of the prominent figures in Tennessee. These men, more so than those on the Missouri frontier, had a tendency to refer to him only as Colonel Smith. General Jackson was no exception. In past references to Smith T, Jackson did not use the T to describe his old associate. The absence of the T was not in and of itself unusual in the general's correspondence.

No definite conclusions concerning Smith T's presence at New Orleans, therefore, can be drawn from the historical records. Certainly, he had motive and opportunity. Like most of the major events of his life, this one too seems destined to remain shrouded in mystery and controversy. Perhaps this is fitting, since it nourishes the myths and legends of the swashbuckler without bringing them into the full light of historical disclosure.

8. *At the Top of His Game*

The return voyage from Texas and the possible excursion to New Orleans to aid Andrew Jackson certainly provided Smith T with time to reflect upon his many misguided activities. In these moments of retrospection he would have had to consider at least four major military undertakings—all of which either ended in failure or brought a mounting toll of injury and death. Earlier in Missouri he had enlisted a veritable army of tough and reckless men to confront the formidable Moses Austin in the Ste. Genevieve mineral wars. Later he had put together a filibustering expedition to serve under Burr and Wilkinson. His next and perhaps most bloody and costly military adventure was the attack against the Indian miners at Dubuque and Galena. Now, in 1815, as he returned from his latest foray into Texas, Smith T must have sensed, with some bitterness, his own limitations and the end of his most ambitious plans.

Whatever doubts may have arisen during the return journey to Missouri must also have been partially allayed by an impressive economic reality. The decade beginning in 1816 saw the emergence of John Smith T as one of the most powerful entrepreneurial figures in Missouri's early history. It was also a time when his unique combination of character traits produced many of the myths and legends that would later surround his life. These events would include, in succession, a near fatal engagement with Daniel Dunklin; his challenges to duels with Samuel Perry and Andrew Jackson; a lethal duel with Lionel Browne; the mysterious deaths of two Tennessee antagonists; the murder of the abolitionist Richard Rose; and a confrontation with Sam Houston.

In the year or so after his return from the Texas frontier, it became ever more apparent that Smith T would use almost every legal maneuver available to him to circumvent the law. In fact, he often considered himself above the law when the judicial process worked to his disadvantage. Lionel Browne, whom he would kill in a duel in 1819, had left the office of Washington County sheriff by the summer of 1816. He was replaced by another nemesis, Daniel Dunklin. In August, Dunklin was instructed by the court to proceed to Mine Shibboleth and to arrest Smith T for failure to pay his legal debts. The filibustering expeditions to Iowa and Texas, along with his numerous dealings in Tennessee, had exacted their economic toll. It should also be remembered that the controversy over Shibboleth, as well as the rest of his St. Vrain claim, had not been fully settled in court. Payment of "legal" debts, therefore, provided his opponents with a rationale for land grabbing.

Dunklin, however, found the scheme to confiscate Smith T's properties and take him into custody theoretically sound but practically impossible. Dunklin reported back that he had found the colonel armed and "in the upper story" of Shibboleth. The sheriff further reported that he left the premises with the warrant unserved. Later, with a larger body of deputies, he returned to Shibboleth, but his would-be prisoner was nowhere to be found.[1] There would be an ironic postscript to this unsuccessful arrest attempt. In 1832, Dunklin successfully ran for governor, and Smith T was one of his opponents. If the governor had seriously tried to apprehend Smith T some sixteen years beforehand, it is probable that one of them would not have lived to see the contest at the ballot box.

A second dangerous situation that developed shortly after the War of 1812 pertained to Smith T's difficulties with John and Samuel Perry. The problems had begun during the years of the mineral wars when the Perry family occasionally sided with Moses Austin and other Smith T competitors. The Perrys were an ambitious and daring group who ranked just under Austin and Smith T in the pecking order of lead moguls. Samuel, perhaps the most reckless of the bunch, would go on to kill J. D. Handy in an 1823 Missouri duel. It was generally recognized in the mining district that Samuel Perry was a dangerous man to cross. He was more, however, than just another brave and daring adventurer. In the late territorial period he served in the Missouri General Assembly and later became one of the delegates to the Missouri Constitutional

1. Daniel Dunklin to John Brickey, August 19, 1816, Box 1, Folder 7, Circuit Court Papers, Washington County Courthouse.

Convention. After statehood, he served in the Missouri Senate. Besides his far-flung mineral enterprises, he was a director of the ill-fated Bank of St. Louis. These political and economic positions put him in a strong position to rival Smith T in the mineral region.[2]

The situation between Smith T and the Perrys reached a low ebb in June 1811 when, according to John Scott, Samuel and John Perry went to the colonel's Liberty Mines and broke into his safe. Scott, who was serving as Smith T's attorney at the time, filed charges against the Perrys for trespassing, breaking into private property, and stealing. The court document went on to list the damages incurred by this unlawful entry and the items stolen. Smith T, through his attorney, asked the court to award him a staggering sum of one hundred thousand dollars.[3] Court documents, however, do not reveal that Smith T received much if any compensation for the alleged incident. Although the complete records may have been lost or destroyed, it appears from the sum of money requested in the lawsuit that the colonel must have been grandstanding. In any event, he was not able to destroy the Perry family financially.

Another of Smith T's troubles during these years was not characterized with such aplomb. According to Harry Burke, the colonel was returning from one of his many forays into the Southwest when he discovered some warm springs in the Arkansas Territory.[4] He decided to claim them with one of his floating grants. He confided his plan to Andrew Jackson, but Old Hickory, believing the springs should be public property, used his influence to have them withdrawn from land open to entry. Smith T was furious and believed that Jackson had betrayed his confidence. According to Burke, Smith T related to John Gillespie, a friend in Illinois, the following sequence of events. Still smarting from the perceived insult, Smith T rode to Nashville to challenge Jackson. The future president, however, was accompanied by his "gang" and meant to do to the colonel what he and his group had done to Thomas Hart Benton—run him out of Tennessee. " ' . . . when

2. Paul Richeson, "The Perrys of Potosi," 15–18, unpublished speech, Brazoria, Texas, June 18, 1977. Located in the State Historical Society of Missouri, Columbia.

3. Complaint, *John Smith T v. Samuel and John Perry*, July 1811, Ste. Genevieve Court Records, Case Number 31, Reel Number 1987089, MSA.

4. Vallé Higginbotham found claims to a salt spring near the White River in Arkansas. Although she did not refer to it as "warm," it may have been the spring in contention since at that time the Arkansas Territory was attached to the New Madrid District. Higginbotham, *John Smith T,* 28.

John Scott, a U.S. Congressman and ally of Smith T in the Ste. Genevieve area. Scott served as one of Smith T's attorneys. Courtesy of State Historical Society of Missouri, Columbia.

not excited,'" Smith T reportedly said, "'Jackson is not destitute of prudence, but if you were to excite him and the earth was a magazine of gunpowder, he would hurl a firebrand and blow the world to atoms to obtain satisfaction.'"[5] Smith T on this occasion beat a hasty retreat back to the confines of Missouri.

It was also during the years immediately preceding statehood that Smith T had his only formal duel in Missouri. His antagonist, Lionel Browne, was a Potosi lawyer, former sheriff, and nephew of Aaron Burr. Browne was born in Westchester County, New York, sometime in the 1780s. In 1805 he had come to Louisiana when his father was appointed secretary of the territory. Besides his official duties as sheriff, he had also represented Washington County in the territorial legislature.[6] Browne's father, Joseph, was Aaron Burr's brother-in-law. Joseph had once been a partner of Smith T, but this past business association carried no weight with the colonel. At the time of the duel Browne was an ally of the rival

5. Burke Papers, 18.

6. Douglass, *History of Southeast Missouri,* vol. 1, 190–91. Magre, "John Smith T., Missouri Pioneer in the Lead Industry" and "Selma Hall, Symbol of Success," Slide Presentation, c. 1980, Frank Magre Collection, 6–7. Hereafter cited as Magre Slide Programs.

anti-junto faction that gave Smith T endless amounts of trouble. From virtually all accounts, Smith T insulted Browne and goaded him into a challenge. Some accounts suggest that the final straw was a series of insults leveled at Browne's sister that forced him, reluctantly, to act. Whatever the exact nature of their problem, it was resolved on the field of honor and cost Browne his life. The antagonists met on an island opposite Herculaneum in 1819. One bullet to Browne's brain ended the lengthy feud.

A politician at the time who was particularly dismayed at the duel's outcome was Rufus Pettibone. This Connecticut Yankee arrived in Missouri the year before the duel and had become a law partner of Rufus Easton. In a letter to Henry R. Schoolcraft, Pettibone described the pinpoint accuracy of Smith T's shot. Nevertheless, he added, "The public sentiment is strong against Smith, and is to be hoped he will be chased from this part of the world." The colonel, the letter went on to say, "has persecuted Browne's family for many years and the quarrel grew out of some old affairs between them." This section of the letter concluded with the following regret: "Every body here," Pettibone said, "regrets that Smith was not killed."[7]

Besides the successful duel with Browne, other less dramatic forces were shifting in Smith T's direction. By 1819–1820 the tide had turned somewhat in Missouri politics. The coming of statehood did not bring to fruition some of the dire consequences that men such as Smith T had feared. For one thing, the political landscape had become slightly more conservative. This allowed Spanish land claimants to hold out hope that their titles would eventually be validated. In addition, large landholders had feared that popular, democratic forces might be able to galvanize support for higher taxes on their lands and perhaps even to succeed in reducing the size of their holdings.[8] These fears, however, were allayed by the political makeup of the men who attended the Constitutional Convention and the document that they produced. Although John Smith T did not serve as a delegate to the convention, his political views, which would soon lead him into the Whig Party, were representative of the larger body.

7. Rufus Pettibone to Henry R. Schoolcraft, September 26, 1819, in "Missouriana," *MHR* 33, no. 3 (April 1939): 412.
8. March, *The History of Missouri,* 188–90.

Moreover, the Constitutional Convention had strongly supported the position that no restrictions concerning slavery should be part of the new constitution. In fact, the major reason for the more conservative composition of the delegates was their proslavery stance. Their concern over this issue seems, according to William Foley, to have preempted any attempts to make the subsequent election a referendum on broadening participation in the political process. Foley further suggests that territorial elites seized upon the antislavery fears and momentarily positioned themselves as the champions of the antirestrictionist majority.

Smith T, an ardent defender of slavery, undoubtedly agreed with this tactic. He also could take comfort in the fact that Missourians elected as their first governor Alexander McNair over William Clark. Though Clark generally supported the junto faction, McNair likewise supported the large Spanish land claimants. In addition to the new governor, Smith T was allied with Bernard Pratte, John Scott, and George C. C. Harbison. These men were all territorial leaders who had earlier petitioned Congress to remove Judge John B. C. Lucas from his post as land commissioner. Lucas had always been a thorn in the side of Smith T, and it was politically advantageous to have allies such as McNair and the others on his side. McNair may, in fact, have tacitly condoned the ill-fated Burr expedition in 1806. He had penned an essay to the editor of the *Pittsburgh Gazette* that year discounting rumors of a western insurrection by the former vice president. The insurrection and the resulting accusations of treason, he had written, were "unfounded."[9]

Another ally, if for no other reason than their mutual contempt for Lucas, was William Carr Lane. This enterprising individual was elected mayor of St. Louis in 1823 and served six consecutive one-year terms. Although at odds with Auguste Chouteau and many of the other old-line Creole families over municipal growth and urban development, Lane shared with the French and Smith T a thorough dislike of Lucas. Lane also supported the large land claimants and therefore was an indirect ally in their quest to protect their holdings.[10]

9. Kenneth W. Keller, "Alexander McNair and John B. C. Lucas: The Background of Early Missouri Politics," 243.

10. Ronald L. F. Davis, "Community and Conflict in Pioneer Saint Louis, Missouri," *Western Historical Quarterly* 10, no. 3 (July 1979): 347–50. English, *Pioneer Lawyer and Jurist,* 42.

As for Judge Lucas, his final demise did not occur until Missouri reached statehood. During this period, his bid for the U.S. Senate ended in failure. This defeat, coupled with the elections of Thomas Hart Benton and David Barton, signaled "the final repudiation" of the judge and his cohorts to uphold the small-land claimants against the influence of the large Spanish land grant claimants.[11] Admission to the Union, therefore, marked a temporary setback for the yeoman farmer. Benton would later emerge as a champion of small farmers, but in the early 1820s the conservative forces were securely in control. John Smith T, who had spent much of his career fighting squatters and small-land claimants, no doubt felt a degree of vindication with this turn of events.

If there was one group of individuals, however, who the newly crowned mineral king hated even more than squatters and small-claims jumpers, it was most certainly the abolitionists. During the tortuous period leading to Missouri's admission to the Union, no question seemed to unite the territory's denizens more than the attempt by antislavery forces in the North to place restrictions on Missouri's sovereignty.

In 1818 John Scott, Missouri's territorial delegate, had presented to Congress a petition for statehood. The following year an enabling bill cleared a committee in the House of Representatives and was presented to the full chamber for consideration. At that point in the early deliberations James Tallmadge, Jr., of New York proposed an amendment to the bill that would require the gradual elimination of slavery in the new state. After considerable debate and much to the consternation of southern sympathizers, Tallmadge's proposal passed the House.

Missourians were furious. No other territory had ever had restrictions placed upon its admission into the Union. The issue of sovereignty, combined with the considerable investment in the more than ten thousand slaves in the territory, produced an uproar. By 1820 the outlines of a compromise, sketched in part by Henry Clay and Senator Jesse B. Thomas of Illinois, were becoming clear. In June of that year a constitutional convention met in St. Louis. Of the forty-one delegates, not one was a restrictionist. Two months later the people went to the polls to select their leaders.

11. William F. Keller, *The Nation's Advocate: Henry Marie Brackenridge and Young America*, 244.

Thomas Hart Benton. During his thirty-year tenure in the U.S. Senate, Benton often represented Smith T in some of the colonel's most important legal cases. Courtesy of State Historical Society of Missouri, Columbia.

The twin issues of slavery and statehood, however, had not yet been resolved. Although the first Missouri Compromise allowed for no restrictions on slavery, questions arose over the rights of citizenship, especially for blacks, under Missouri's constitution. After considerable wrangling, Clay worked his political magic and a second compromise in 1821 erased all doubts as to Missouri's status within the Union.

It was within the context of this heated debate over slavery that Smith T committed what may have been his first act of cold-blooded murder. In the summer of 1821 rumor had it that abolitionists had visited the mining region with the intent of encouraging slaves to desert their masters. One abolitionist, Richard Rose, was identified as the individual whose objective it was to persuade Smith T's slaves at Shibboleth and the surrounding area to leave their owner. When Smith T got wind of the conspiracy, he decided to act. Upon learning that Rose might be at a stillhouse owned by Samuel Thompson, the colonel set out to find him. The stillhouse was approximately four miles northeast of Potosi, so the ride was not a long one. Smith T indeed did find Rose at Thompson's and promptly shot him dead.[12]

12. Statement of Account, Coroner to Washington County Court, February 12, 1822, Circuit Court of Ste. Genevieve, WPA Historical Survey, Folder 21589, Collection no. 3551, WHMC.

Another account of the killing was related by Harry Burke, as told to him by Emmy Goff. Goff said her father, William Goff, was employed by Smith T as a blacksmith. She said the colonel had come to see her father one evening and asked him to take a walk. William was at one of the stores at Shibboleth. Smith T told Goff that he had heard rumors that an abolitionist was tampering with his slaves and that he was at Fountain Farm, a plantation owned by the colonel. According to Burke, Emmy said her father and Smith T walked to Fountain Farm, and " 'There was the abolitionist sitting just inside the open barn door, playing cards with the niggers by torchlight.' " Goff later maintained that he did not actually see the killing and therefore could not testify against his employer. Nor could the slaves. Even though they may have witnessed the incident, under Missouri's slave codes they were not allowed to testify in court against a white man. According to Burke, Smith T lit out for Tennessee immediately after the murder to allow the situation to die down before he returned to Missouri.[13]

There appeared to be no other way to interpret this killing other than as a deliberate act of first-degree murder. In July 1821 the Washington Circuit Court handed down its first indictment for murder. The dubious honor went to Smith T. It has been suggested that the Rose encounter was indeed a gunfight, which would somewhat exonerate the colonel. This particular defense had a hollow ring to it. Nevertheless, owing to the political defendant, Smith T was never punished for his crime. It was a stern but sad lesson for would-be abolitionists in the mining region for years to come.[14]

The Rose murder aside, Smith T was indeed at the top of his game in the early 1820s. According to Henry Schoolcraft, an early-nineteenth-century mining expert, Smith T's mines produced approximately five hundred thousand pounds of lead in 1810. By the end of the decade and into the first years of Missouri statehood his diggings were producing nearly 2.7 million pounds per year. One must also remember that Schoolcraft was no friend of Smith T. He bitterly objected to many of the colonel's tactics and usually sided with Austin. In spite of this hostility, Schoolcraft ranked Mine Shibboleth first among seventeen mines in the region (Smith T likewise owned and operated some of the

---

13. Burke Papers, 17.
14. Roberts, *Roots of Roane County*, 20. *Goodspeed's History of Franklin, Jefferson, Washington, Crawford, and Gasconade Counties, Missouri*, 499.

other sixteen mines) in lead production and first in the number of men (240) working at one mine. The figures for the years may be inflated somewhat, but one must remember that some of the colonel's major competitors such as Moses Austin had left the field.

Austin's bankruptcy and premature death allowed Smith T to not only purchase many of Austin's mines but also to take advantage of the technological changes, especially in smelting and extracting, that Austin had pioneered. Prices also remained relatively steady. Lead during these years sold for roughly four dollars per one hundred pounds at the mines. Smith T, however, had no intention of letting go of the minerals at this juncture of the operation. Following the path pioneered by Austin, he built the Selma Road to link his mines to the Mississippi River.[15]

Smith T's land and mining empire was becoming ever more extensive. Even before he completely replaced Austin as Missouri's lead king in the early 1820s, his legal bills to only one lawyer in just one year equaled the average year's salary of a dozen men. From October 1816 to May 1817, for example, he paid legal fees to Edward Hempstead of $5,225. In addition, he employed the services of such other famous lawyers as John Scott, Rufus Easton, and Thomas H. Benton. Benton won a case for him against Nicholas Wilson, who had extracted lead from Mine Shibboleth. The figures in this case and some of the others in which the colonel was involved were staggering for those years. In a lower court Benton proved that the claim descended from a 1796 Spanish grant, and Smith T received $14,900 of a $15,000 suit. Ultimately, Benton had to argue the case on appeal before the Tennessee Supreme Court in July 1823 at Nashville. This too he won for his client.[16]

There was, however, a price to be paid for this mobilization of effort in the Show-Me State. For one thing, Smith T's considerable landholdings in Tennessee suffered from inattention. Numerous legal suits were filed against him in the Volunteer State for payment on

15. For further details see chap. 3. See also Litton, *History of Jefferson County*, 20, 147; Smith, Jr., "John Smith T," 10–11. Other evidence of his large and diversified holdings are documented in Higginbotham, *John Smith T*, 15–17. Many of these land records can be found in Washington County Land Records, Book A, and Washington County Deeds, Book B; Donald J. Abramoske, "The Federal Lead Leasing System in Missouri," 27.

16. Document, Edward Hempstead from John Smith T, May 1, 1817, Chouteau Moffitt Collection, MHS. William N. Chambers, "Young Man from Tennessee: First Years of Thomas H. Benton in Missouri," 207–8.

lands purchased but not properly recorded.[17] Back taxes, questionable deeds, and squatters' claims also required consideration. Although entrepreneurial "overstretch" had continually plagued Smith T, the 1820s were a particularly vexing time. One factor limiting such diversified and far-flung business enterprises was the growing complexity of laws and regulations relating to property rights. The violent and direct action methods that might have worked during pioneer days became more and more unsuited for developing societies. Another factor that may have been a drain on his financial resources pertained to the backlog of debts incurred during the filibustering campaigns, as well as his ongoing battles with enemies in the mining district.

Besides lead mining, Smith T's holdings provided employment in ironworks, lumber mills, timber cutting, crops and livestock, salt works, and shot towers. Each of the activities required great expertise and specialized management. Diversification, integration, and expansion all characterized what had to be one of the most extensive sets of business holdings in the state. His Missouri land grants during this time included deeds to salt springs up the Flat River, land in the St. Charles District, seventy arpents at the Lamine Creek on the Missouri River, and claims to a salt spring near the White River in Arkansas that was at that time part of Missouri's New Madrid District. Another mining operation that produced a very high grade of ore was called the Flat Mines. These diggings were situated on the Flat River, two and one-half miles from its junction with the Big River. In 1824, for example, these very profitable mines employed fifteen men. The mineral yielding to the smelter stood at 65 percent—a very high yield indeed.[18] Without excellent supervision, however, these vast business arrays could easily lead to overextension and possibly economic ruin.

Smith T was fortunate during this period to have competent men serving as his agents. In Missouri, Reuben, William Russell, and his sons-in-law served in this capacity, and in Tennessee he gave power of attorney to Major Thomas Brown of Kingston and to John Brown, Jr.,

17. W. I. White to T. A. Smith, July 25, 1821, Thomas A. Smith Papers, Folder 21. Also see *Smith v. Mounts*, May Term, 1827 in Louis Houck, ed., *Reports of Cases Argued and Determined in the Supreme Court of the State of Missouri: From 1821 to 1827*, vol. 1, 273, 363–64, 512.
18. Roberts, *Roots of Roane County*, 16. Higginbotham, *John Smith T*, 28. Book of Doom, 2.

to execute deeds. The Brown brothers were sons of a Revolutionary War soldier who settled in eastern Tennessee. Both men were respected members of their communities. Without their services, Smith T's holdings east of the Mississippi might very well have suffered a much more dramatic and ill-starred fate.[19]

During this period, Smith T decided to diversify his holdings even more. This decision was based largely upon the actions of his brother, General Thomas A. Smith. Thomas had purchased a seven-thousand-acre estate in what is now Saline County in central Missouri. He named his enterprise "Experiment." Although the brothers had often had their differences, the colonel decided to follow his younger brother west. John, like Thomas, had become intrigued with the flora and fauna of the Boonslick country as well as its potential for trade and commerce. Using his brother's farm as his first base of operations, Smith T began acquiring land. Later he used his own landholdings in Saline County to add another wrinkle to his economic repertoire.

Although Smith T had earlier sent Reuben on a disastrous trade mission to New Mexico, he continued to be fascinated with the possibilities of overland trade. His operation this time, however, was considerably more safe and simple. Thomas Smith produced a variety of agricultural products on his farm. The brothers arranged to have these farm goods sold in the mining region. The produce would be purchased by the men digging in Smith T's lead pits. Lead, lead products, and other items of trade not produced in the Boonslick could then be transported from the Potosi area on the return trip to central Missouri. Colonel John O'Fallon was quite impressed by these and other brisk and profitable business ventures between the brothers. The operation went so well for a time that Smith T decided to buy additional farms in Saline County. On one of his farms near the town of Marshall, Smith T manufactured salt. Some of the salt vats used by the colonel are still visible today. He purchased another farm in the Napton area, not far from the home of his brother.[20]

Local lore hinted that Smith T's major salt-making competitors in the Saline area were the sons of Daniel Boone. While tales of a clash

19. Higginbotham, *John Smith T,* 24.
20. Col. John O'Fallon to Thomas A. Smith, October 23, 1824, Thomas A. Smith Papers, Folder 24. Magre Slide Programs, 16.

between two of the most famous names in early Missouri gave a certain flare to central Missouri business history, it is highly unlikely that any rivalry existed. The Boones had sold their interest in the salt works prior to the War of 1812. Although salt making continued at the site until the 1830s, only the Boone name remained part of the overall operation.

Salt making, however, was not Smith T's only new enterprise during these years. Incredible as it may now seem, Smith T ventured out once more in the early 1820s. This time his economic target was southwest Missouri, where new deposits of lead had recently been discovered. Smith T claimed land close to the present-day town of Granby.[21] In this case, like so many others during this period, he took on more than he could handle. For one thing, the infrastructure of the region was not highly developed. Lead mining in eastern Missouri, especially with pick and shovel, had always been a labor-intensive operation. But the southwestern part of the state did not have that many men willing to dig. Roads in this region were also poorly developed. When confronted by a similar situation some fifteen years before, Smith T had built, largely from his own resources, the Selma Road. By this period, however, he was not convinced that the ore warranted such a large outlay of time, money, and effort. In addition, the region still contained some hostile Indians who were a source of anxiety, even to intrepid miners. For these reasons, the mining endeavor never materialized as planned. Somewhat later, however, Smith T's heirs would develop a thriving operation in these parts. By 1856 Ferdinand Kennett and Henry T. Blow were mining the claims. They believed that in the eventuality of a civil war, the lead they produced in the region could serve as a valuable reserve for southern forces.

Another factor contributing to Smith T's "overstretch," especially when it came to traveling back and forth to Tennessee, was the difficulty of travel and communication. Even though business activities had become far more complex, transportation technology had not. Although steamboats had ventured up the Missouri River as early as 1819, there was no systematic linkage of waterways until nearly 1830.[22] In the early

21. Judy Murphy, "Varmit's Salty Past, Geology Meet in Saline Springs," *Missouri Water Resources Research Center* (Columbia: n.d.). Located in Surname Vertical File, WHMC. E. R. Buckley and H. A. Buehler, *The Geology of the Granby Area*, 2.
22. The author is indebted to Dr. Lawrence Giffen for his assistance and input into early steamboat travel.

1820s it still required roughly a week to make the journey to Tennessee and another to make it back to Missouri. Such trips were dangerous, and especially difficult for a man now in his fifties. Finally, Smith T's diversified holdings required excellent overseers and managers as well as attention to detail and good record keeping. Although Smith T's agents served him well, none of them were in a position to coordinate and integrate all of these activities. As for the colonel, good bookkeeping and close supervision of every business enterprise was certainly not his forte. For these reasons, he began to cut back on his Tennessee holdings. "Innumerable references" relating to his land transactions in Roane, Knox, Bedford, and Marion Counties in Tennessee were made all the way up to and including the year of his death in 1836.[23]

The greatest of Smith T's land ventures, outside the area of filibustering, pertained to his incredible claims to the northern part of the state of Alabama. During the years from 1816 to 1826 he worked diligently to pull off the largest claims-jumping feat of his career. Some of the details are as follows. In 1795 the state legislature of Georgia, as it was prone to do in those days, fraudulently sold to Zachariah Cox, Matthias Mahea, and their associates (one of them being Smith T) nearly a million acres of land. Overall, the Georgians, in "a corruption without example in history," sold nearly fifty million acres for less than half a million dollars. Cox's particular group, calling itself the Tennessee Company, purchased its land for only sixty thousand dollars. The company then divided the purchase into 420 shares. Smith T bought some of these original shares.[24]

During the period from 1795 to 1803, Smith T continued to purchase shares in the Tennessee Company even though Cox and his associates conveyed its title to much of the land to the state of Tennessee and to the U.S. government. It was a high-stakes gamble, and the price paid for these shares of dubious validity is unknown. Nevertheless, his grants and deeds were duly recorded with the U.S. Department of State in pursuance of the act of Congress of 1803. His deeds had also been recorded three years earlier with the Tennessee Department of State.[25]

23. Higginbotham, *John Smith T,* 3.

24. Burke Papers, 4; "Col. John Smith T," Vertical File, MHS. U.S. Congress, *The Debates and Proceedings of the Congress of the United States,* 13th Cong., 2d sess., March 1814, 1839. U.S. Senate, *Report,* The Committee on Public Lands, 21st Cong., 1st sess., Document no. 129, April 22, 1830, 1–3.

25. U.S. Senate, *Report,* The Committee on Public Lands, 21st Cong., 1st sess., Document no. 129, April 22, 1830, 1–3. U.S. Senate, *Memorial of William Kelly, of*

After his move to the Missouri frontier, Smith T continued to sell provisional contracts on some of the land purchased under the Tennessee Company. He must have known that the federal government was also claiming and selling the same tracts of land. He probably anticipated that the government, in order to clear up the title to these lands and avoid further litigation, would offer him a handsome settlement. This possibility became somewhat dimmer in December 1816. On December 13 of that year, Congress passed a statute of limitations which decreed that any person not getting a clear title from the Board of Land Commissioners within three years would forfeit their claim. From 1816 to 1819 Smith T tried and failed to establish the validity of his claims. Subsequently, he challenged the constitutionality of the law, and the case worked its way through the courts. By the late 1820s the case reached the U.S. Supreme Court.[26] In 1836, the year of his death, the court decided against his claim.

The Tennessee Company litigation was the largest and most speculative legal gamble that Smith T undertook. But in many respects it was not the most critical, mainly because it stood such an unlikely chance of success. The St. Vrain grant of roughly ten thousand arpents was the claim that Smith T believed vindicated his life's work in Missouri. In 1811 he lost the original concession in a political decision of the Board of Land Commissioners, but he refused to recognize the decision.[27] In 1816 he forcibly refused to give up his land to Sheriff Daniel Dunklin. Throughout the entire period from 1816 to 1826 he continued the struggle to win back these properties.

Inattention to detail and the seemingly endless number of speculative activities no doubt also contributed to the rash of smaller lawsuits that occurred in the decade or so leading to the late 1820s. These legal disputes, sometimes over relatively small amounts of money, were often due to the fact that much of Smith T's mining operation was still being done by individual lead miners digging in small pits on his lands for a percentage of the profits. Since these miners also worked

---

Alabama in Relation to the Claim of the Said John Smith T for Land from the United States, 1st sess., Document no. 65, February 23, 1830, 1–4. Hereafter cited as U.S. Senate, *Memorial.*

26. U.S. Senate, *Memorial.*

27. U.S. House of Representatives, *Report,* The Committee on Public Lands, 29th Cong., 1st sess., Document no. 198, February 10, 1846, 1–2. Hereafter cited as U.S. House, *Report.* U.S. Senate, *Report,* The Committee on Public Lands, 29th Cong., 1st sess., Document no. 239, March 23, 1846, 1–3.

other jobs and lived on credit, it naturally followed that complications would occur over how much of the price, percentage, and amount of lead mined belonged to each partner in the claim. Confusion and poor records management rather than duplicity and outright fraud seem to best characterize Smith T's mining ventures.

Smith T's mining problems, however, paled in comparison with those of his arch rival, Moses Austin. Land values, which in the early territorial period had jumped 50 to 200 percent, had begun to stabilize. In addition, lead prices had not increased in value after the War of 1812 as many miners had trusted they would. Austin, who had overcapitalized during these years, deeded Mine à Breton in 1816 to his son, Stephen. Moses, for his part, went to Herculaneum, where he oversaw the shot tower operation. In the meantime, he began the search for a suitable buyer for both the mines and the shot towers. In a letter to James Bryan, an in-law, he wrote that "would to god my business was closed, I would leave this country in a week—." Austin also made some risky deals in New Madrid land certificates, and these too lost money. In addition, he and Stephen had purchased land in the Arkansas Territory but could not get it surveyed. This too forced him to begin disinvestment.[28]

Compounding Austin's economic woes was his decision to invest heavily in the Bank of St. Louis. After the 1819 recession the bank collapsed, and it took the fortunes of Moses Austin with it. Banks and public bonds were some of the few fields of investments open to pioneer entrepreneurs, and Austin had gambled heavily on their rise in value. Smith T may also have lost money in this banking venture, although exact details of his transactions have been more difficult to ascertain. In July 1825, however, Smith T did sue the president, director, and the entire St. Louis banking company. The case was to be heard in the St. Louis Circuit Court. Owing to the dire straits of the bank, the incomplete records seem to indicate that he received no compensation.[29]

28. Moses Austin to James Bryan, September 13, 1818, vol. 1, pt. 2, 1812–1820; Public Notice, February 26, 1819; Stephen Austin to William O'Hara, June 16, 1819; Journal Account of Moses Austin, February 25, 1819; all in Austin Papers.

29. Paxson, *History of the American Frontier,* 67. Summons, *John Smith T v. President, Director, and Bank of St. Louis,* July Term, 1825, St. Louis Circuit Court, MSA; *Missouri Republican,* September 19, 1825.

Austin was less fortunate than Smith T. By 1820 he was being hounded by his creditors for obligations long past due. A final blow came when his land and mines in Washington County were foreclosed. Austin had also gambled that he could persuade the state legislature to name Potosi as the new capital. In the years before the capital selection he had purchased on credit a great deal of land around the town. When Jefferson City was chosen instead, Austin was sorely pressed. " . . . I am ruined in this [country]" he wrote to a relative, James Austin. Smith T now took sweet revenge. The last curtain in the two-decade-old drama between the two lead magnates was finally drawn when he purchased Austin's properties at public auction.[30]

The early 1820s were not all filled with triumph. Rifts between Smith T and his brothers began to widen. He had yet to reconcile completely with Thomas, and Reuben also had begun to distance himself from his notorious brother. In 1822, Reuben, who had been the most loyal and ardent defender of Smith T's interests in Missouri, began to branch out more on his own. He, John Inglish, and James Stark were elected county judges in the first Cole County political contests.[31] Three years later Reuben finally married and began mining lead on his own lands, called Bellefontaine. These acts of independence no doubt are what prompted Smith T to revoke his brother's power of attorney to act for him. Although the brothers remained friends, their very close personal relationship had begun to wane.

The year 1822 also witnessed the death of Lucy Wilkinson Smith. She had been preceded in death eight years before by her husband and Smith T's father, Francis. From all indications Lucy was not proud of her eldest son, perhaps in part because of his ruthless and violent reputation and perhaps too because of the dire predicaments in which he had sometimes placed her other sons. It should not be all that surprising, therefore, that she left John totally out of her last will and testament. In fact, the will, dated March 4, 1822, mentioned each of her children by name except for John. She also gave each child except John an equal

30. Notice, Moses Austin to Citizens of the County of Jefferson, January 10, 1820, vol. 1, pt. 2, 1812–1820, Austin papers. Moses Austin to James Austin, April 8, 1821, vol. 1, pt. 3, 1821–1822, ibid. Lemont K. Richardson, "Private Land Claims in Missouri," 135–36; James A. Gardner, "The Business Career of Moses Austin in Missouri, 1798–1821," 241–46; Gardner, *Lead King,* 178.
31. J. E. Ford, *A History of Moniteau County, Missouri,* 3.

share of her slaves and "their future increase."[32] It was one insult for which Smith T could not obtain personal satisfaction.

The year following his mother's death, his only daughter, Ann, lost her first husband, Captain David S. Deadrick. No doubt Smith T was consoled by the fact that the marriage had produced two healthy grandchildren, John S. and Julia. Ann had most likely met the captain at Southwest Point, the U.S. military outpost across the river from Kingston, Tennessee. The couple had come to Washington County, Missouri, sometime before 1818 and had remained close to Smith T and his wife, Nancy. Smith T trusted Deadrick's business acumen and used his son-in-law to help him attend to his various and sundry activities. In the early 1820s he gave Deadrick power of attorney to act for him in land sales. Deadrick's unexpected death was no doubt a severe blow to the entire family.[33]

Smith T's only daughter did not remain a widow very long. With two young children, John and Julia, to attend to and a father with such a roving disposition, it was a virtual certainty that Ann would quickly look for another mate. She remained single only from September of 1823 until November 1824. In many ways she was an attractive catch since she stood to inherit the entire estate of her famous father. On the other hand, any son-in-law of the hot-tempered Smith T would have to tread cautiously. The suitor who quickly won her hand and heart was James M. White. In 1827 Smith T gave his new son-in-law power of attorney, and he too began to take an active role in the family businesses. On some occasions he may have questioned whether his courtship of Ann was a wise decision. Legend has it that when the colonel was "in his cups he would draw his pistol and make" White "who was a large, stout man, dance until exhausted."[34]

During these years of fame and fortune, Smith T gained an even greater reputation for bravery in a celebrated affair of honor with Sam Houston. Unlike the encounter with General Jackson, which is difficult to corroborate, Smith T's conflict with Houston has been well documented. The incident began when Houston, as a member of the House of Representatives from Tennessee, proposed to Congress that

32. Higginbotham, *John Smith T,* 2. Last Will and Testament of Lucy Wilkinson Smith, March 4, 1822, Tom B. Hall, III Collection.

33. Ibid., 33, 22–24.

34. *St. Louis Globe-Democrat,* September 25, 1887.

John P. Erwin, the son-in-law of Henry Clay, be removed from his position as postmaster of Nashville.[35] Although the ploy to remove Erwin failed, the postmaster sought personal satisfaction and secured the good offices of John Smith T. The latter would be the bearer of the challenge to Houston.

Due to his many business enterprises, it was not unusual that Smith T would be visiting Nashville at the time. But it was not clear why he chose to carry the challenge. As a man well into his fifties, his days of duels and youthful dangers should have been well in the past. In addition, gentlemen of disparate ages seldom journeyed to the field of honor, and Houston was more than twenty years Smith T's junior. The Houston people, as well as a biographer of Houston, believed the Erwin faction brought in the "professional duelist from Missouri" to goad him into a fight with him.[36] In any event, sometime in late August or early September 1826, Smith T went to the Nashville Inn, where Houston was staying. Contemporaries of Houston believed that if he rejected the challenge delivered by the colonel then he would be expected to fight the messenger. At this juncture Smith T confronted Colonel William McGregor, who refused to accept the challenge. Acting for Houston, McGregor told Smith T that the reasons for the declination included the fact that Smith T was not from Tennessee and that he had no reason to be involved in the quarrel in the first place. In addition, McGregor suggested that Houston did not feel compelled to accept any challenge delivered by one who was not a gentleman.[37]

Houston and McGregor realized that Smith T could be a volatile man. Consequently, they and between ten and fifteen friends had gathered at the inn when Smith T arrived with the challenge. Most expected, according to one Tennessee historian, "a fight" when the communication was delivered and rejected. Houston later recalled that he was prepared at that time to kill Smith T without any protocol if the situation became threatening. Nonetheless, even "a desperate man" such as Smith T, Houston later recalled, knew better than to

---

35. Sketches, Frank Laren Collection, Miscellaneous Files, Tennessee State Library and Archives, Nashville, 3–4.

36. Randolph B. Campbell, *Sam Houston and the American Southwest*, 14–15.

37. Seth L. Hardeman to Meredith M. Marmaduke, October 2, 1826, John Sappington Papers, MHS; Doctor L. Cooper to Abiel Leonard, October 1826, Abiel Leonard Papers, Folder 57, WHMC.

take on such a large group of well-armed men. When told that Houston would "receive no communication through your hands [Smith T] from Col. Erwin," Smith T returned to his quarters without a struggle.[38] He could, nevertheless, take some consultation in the fact that it took around a dozen armed men to deter him.

The entire matter was far from ended. General William White, "a brave and chivalric gentleman," had watched the proceedings and remarked to Houston that he did not "think the proper courtesy had been extended to Col. Smith." Houston then replied, "If you, sir, have any grievances, I will give you any satisfaction you may demand." White replied, "I have nothing to do with your difficulty, but I presume to know what is due from one gentleman to another."[39] Houston, obviously not wanting to push the point, allowed White's remark to stand and all the parties left the Nashville Inn with their dignity intact.

By the next day, however, rumors began to fly that Houston had "backed down" White. White could not countenance such an imputation and thus issued a challenge to Houston. To escape Tennessee law officials, the two antagonists, accompanied by their seconds and surgeons, traveled to Kentucky. Andrew Jackson, although not present on the grounds, tutored Houston in the fine art of dueling. The advice paid a handsome reward. In the duel, White was badly wounded but survived. Houston's friends believed that the affair of honor was the final stepping stone to the governorship for Houston.

Unwittingly, therefore, Smith T contributed in some small degree to Houston's political fortunes. As for himself, the affair was the capstone of a decade. During the period from 1816 to 1826 the myths and legends surrounding the infamous Missourian became even more widely circulated. True, his reputation as a gentleman had been called into question, but he had been vindicated by the sacrifices of a prominent Tennessee general. The notoriety of this Nashville incident was in retrospect about the last affair that would end with his character and reputation still intact. The last decade of his life would see a slow descent into loneliness, vexation, and disconsolation.

38. W. W. Clayton, *History of Davidson County, Tennessee,* 162–63. A. W. Terrell, "Recollections of General Sam Houston," 129. This episode will be interpreted in a later chapter.
39. Clayton, *History of Davidson County.*

9. The Twilight Years

The final decade of Smith T's life proved to be both personally and economically traumatic. Family losses, including the death of his wife and brother, exacted a heavy psychological toll. Compounding these personal setbacks were several economic reversals from which he never fully recovered. The decade was also unkind to him in the political arena. Efforts to rehabilitate his reputation and to win electoral approval proved to be equally unrewarding. Despite these hardships and failures, he persevered. While other men might have been content to enjoy a modicum of economic success and to spend their waning years enjoying the fruits of their acquisitions, Smith T never gave up dreaming of new adventures. Ever the venture capitalist, he remained until his final days as restless as in the days of his youth.

One factor urging him toward new economic challenges was directly related to the decline in lead prices, which began in the late 1820s and continued into the next decade. Lead had been the mainstay of his economic domain in Missouri, and its decline forced him to make some major changes in his business strategies. In addition, his Saline County farms, perhaps best known for their salt making, also declined in profitability. The salt was manufactured in five-hundred-gallon kettles. Smith T reportedly had more than fifty of these kettles in operation. At peak production, Salt Pond, in the western part of the county, produced nearly ten thousand barrels of salt at roughly 37 cents per barrel. Since Saline County was located very close to the prairies, it did not take long to deplete the forests in the surrounding area. Wood was essential to keep the fires burning under the kettles. As wood became increasingly difficult to procure, the salt-making operation declined in profitability.[1]

1. Smith, Jr., "John Smith T," 11–12.

In addition, other sources of salt had been discovered elsewhere, further contributing to the decline of the industry in the region.

In an apparent effort to obtain money to meet his ever-mounting expenses, Smith T applied for compensation from the U.S. government for military services rendered in 1814. His effort to secure the money was rejected by the Senate in 1827. While Thomas H. Benton promised to continue the fight, the Senate's rejection was final, and the colonel never received any compensation.[2] It appears that this and other financial setbacks did little to deter his varied and sundry plans. Rather than pulling back from such an overextended business empire, he actually diversified his activities even more. In the last days of his life, Smith T was in the process of expanding into new fields of endeavor in Tennessee. His ultimate price for this adventure, as will be discussed later, was to die virtually alone and forgotten.

Smith T was always a rather litigious soul, and the last decade of his life was no exception. In fact, he was engaged in an ever-increasing number of lawsuits. Foreclosures and sheriff land sales accompanied overextension, diversification, and an apparent lack of attention to detail. In March 1832, for example, Washington County officials sued him for back taxes. While the amount was only two hundred dollars, it indicated serious cash flow difficulties and an escalating degree of carelessness on his part. Many of the lawsuits filed by Smith T were against trespassers for damages. One such case was for ten thousand dollars, filed against Jacob Phillipson and Simon Black, most likely for digging lead without proper authorization. The same type of unrealistic suit was filed against a William Parkinson for one thousand dollars. This suit resulted in a restitution of a mere fourteen dollars. In the July term of 1835, he netted only $6.25 on damages of $1,837.14.[3]

Smith T was also having to contend with more and more slave desertions. A typical notice of one particular runaway slave appeared in the April 1, 1828, *Missouri Republican*. The notice described a slave, Nace, whose skin color was between "African and mulatto," who spoke

2. *Missouri Republican*, March 8, 1827, December 23, 1828; U.S. Senate, *Journal of the Senate of the United States of America*, 19th Cong., 2d sess., February 1827, 187.
3. Debt, Document no. 325, March Term, 1832, Document no. 315; Suit, *John Smith T v. Jacob Phillipson and Simon Black*, Document no. 219, June Term, 1828; Suit, *John Smith T v. William Parkinson*, Document no. 311, November Term, 1831; Suit, *John Smith T v.* [name illegible], Document no. 419, July Term, 1835; all in Washington County Circuit Court Records, 1822–1838, MSA.

a little French, and "plays tolerably well on the violin, fond of playing cards, and ardent spirits, and addicted to theft—a fit companion for his harborers." If found, the notice implored that he be returned to Smith T or to Captain James White at the Cliffs of Selma. Nace had been missing for nearly a year, and it was stated that he was most likely living at the residence of Jacob Woods of the Fever River Lead Mines in Illinois. Smith T offered a reward of $150 for his return. The notice went on to say, "every or any friend to justice, or to me will assist Mr. John Hensley, or any other person who may apprehend the said runaway, that has honesty enough to be trusted to bring him as above directed."[4]

Runaways, however, were the least of Smith T's sorrows, as death and tragedy paid their most memorable visits during the year 1828. The first loss was that of his brother Reuben. The second was the death of his wife, Nancy. During the mid-1820s Reuben had slowly begun to distance himself from his more infamous brother. He had purchased land in the central part of the state and had began to operate, independently of Smith T, the Bellefontaine Mine located in Township 40 of Washington County. In response to Reuben's growing autonomy, Smith T in May 1827 revoked the power of attorney he had given his brother earlier.[5]

In 1825 Reuben, already in midlife and in poor health, married a teenage girl, Susan Horine from Jefferson County. This union produced two sons. The couple named their first son Thomas McLanahan Smith, after Reuben's trading partner. The second son they named Francis Hidalgo. Some students of Smith T's life believe that Francis was named for Father Miguel Hidalgo, the father of the Mexican Revolution. They contend that the colonel, in an effort to free Reuben, McClanahan, and the other members of the disastrous 1810 trading mission to Santa Fe, aided the Hidalgo revolt in order to divert Spanish forces. This diversion then allowed Smith T to free the Americans and return safely to the United States. In appreciation of the priest's assistance, so goes the story, Reuben named his second son after the famous revolutionary.[6]

In any event, Reuben barely lived long enough to enjoy his sons. As his health took a last and fatal turn for the worse, Reuben in mid-1828

---

4. *Missouri Republican*, April 1, 1828.
5. Ibid., June 7, 1827.
6. Burke Papers, 14–16.

summoned his brothers, John and Thomas, to Bellefontaine to witness his last will and testament. He died shortly after their visit. Smith T was quite distraught over Reuben's death. Furthermore, he believed that foul play had entered into the death of his younger brother. He maintained that the slaves of Reuben's father-in-law practiced voodoo. The Horine Negroes, as he referred to them, while practicing black magic had poisoned Reuben and sent him to his doom.[7] However, no proof of these accusations surfaced, and it appears that Smith T took no revenge on the suspects. Reuben was buried near the mines but, like his more famous brother, his grave site remains a mystery.

Even more psychologically devastating than his brother's death was the demise of his wife. Nancy had always been the rock upon which Smith T anchored his turbulent life. Increasing the deep personal sorrow of Nancy's demise was the fact that her husband was, in all probability, on one of his many jaunts and not by her side when she died. The exact date of Nancy's death is unknown, but most likely it occurred sometime in late 1828. She was supposedly buried near Malta Bend, a small town approximately fifteen miles west of Marshall, Missouri.[8]

Smith T reacted to the dual losses of Reuben and Nancy with heavy drinking. Both alcohol and anguish increased Smith T's erratic behavior. On the one hand, the old pioneer became very protective of his only daughter, Ann. This overprotectiveness, according to some newspaper accounts, led to violent and retaliatory actions on her behalf. On the other hand, Smith T demonstrated a good deal of generosity, especially to causes that were close to Ann's heart.

During these years Smith T also experienced his last and most dangerous encounter with Henry Dodge, with whom he had nearly engaged in mortal combat in the Iowa Territory. This time the incident occurred in Ste. Genevieve. Dodge had not permanently left Missouri to carve out his new and illustrious political career in Wisconsin.[9] Although in earlier days Smith T and Dodge had been close allies, their relationship turned sharply for the worse when Dodge joined forces with the colonel's enemies to wrest control of his mining properties.

7. Goff, "Reuben Smith," 276–78; William Carr Lane to Thomas A. Smith, June 18, 1828, Thomas A. Smith Papers, Folder 32.
8. Higginbotham, *John Smith T,* 22.
9. Dumas Malone, ed., *Dictionary of American Biography,* vol. 9, 348–49.

Portrait of an older Smith T. This is the only known image of him in his later years. Courtesy of Union Pacific Corporation.

The only known portrait of Nancy Smith T. The death of his wife was a great loss to the colonel. Courtesy of Missouri Historical Society.

A fatal incident nearly occurred at the law office of John Scott. The attorney, with some very quick thinking, managed to separate the two heavily armed and hot-tempered men long enough to avoid a certain calamity. Scott later remarked that one spark might have set off a chain reaction that almost certainly would have led to the death of one or both of the antagonists.

The opposite side of Smith T's personality was evidenced by his generosity to causes most dear to Ann's heart. In 1830, he deeded Lot No. 7 of the Old Mines concession to Father Phillip Borgna, perhaps in recognition of his daughter's conversion to Catholicism. Local historians believed the gift of land was intended as a memorial to his deceased wife, Nancy. Twenty arpents were designated for building a church. Prior to the church's construction, mass was usually said in the homes of parishioners. The contribution no doubt helped to lessen some of the ill feelings of locals who believed that Smith T had bullied them over the years. Roughly six months after the land transfer, Bishop Joseph Rosati consecrated the Church of St. Joachim. Two priests on the consecration day preached the sermons, in English and French. One of the families that contributed considerable funds for the church's construction was the Etienne LaMarque family. They, like many other early settlers, purchased their land on Lot No. 7 from Smith T. Two years later the colonel donated another four hundred arpents in Lot No. 7 to Father Borgna. This land allowed the church to expand its activities. Over the years a parochial school, rectory, and convent were built on the donated land. Thus Smith T, despite his Presbyterian upbringing, made significant contributions to the religious and educational life of his predominantly Catholic community.[10]

Land and charitable donations, however, did not make up for his otherwise erratic behavior. Alcohol undoubtedly contributed to his penchant for violence. An Illinois acquaintance, John Gillespie, gave an interesting account of an 1834 meeting with him. Gillespie was headed north on the Mississippi River when Smith T and his slave Dave got aboard the same steamboat at Cairo, Illinois. Both slave and master, he later recalled, were "armed to the teeth." In addition, Smith T carried a gun made to resemble a large walking cane. When the passengers heard about their infamous and dangerous travel mate, there was "a hurried

10. Higginbotham, *John Smith T,* 17–19.

consultation," during which they "determined to make common cause should Smith have a difficulty with any one of them."

Smith T, sensing their apprehension, pushed his way through the onlookers. With "a scowl," recalled Gillespie, "they all fell back," and Smith T "took a seat on the guard at the rear of the wheel and looked out upon the scenery." Curiosity overcame fear, and Gillespie stepped forward and introduced himself. At first he was "coldly and superciliously received," but soon the dreaded gunman "became quite friendly, remarking upon the aversion" of the passengers toward him. Smith T admitted that he had killed many men but said "that circumstances had thrown him into the society of the most desperate and lawless men in the world." Nonetheless, he assured Gillespie he had never killed anyone without being able to swear before God that it was a "justified" act.

As the two men conversed on a variety of subjects, the colonel asked his young friend to take a drink with him. Gillespie, perhaps not realizing that declining could provoke a violent reaction, politely refused. "Young man," declared Smith T, "you are right; it is a very bad habit to fall into, and has been my besetting sin through life." Speaking of this adventure in later life, Gillespie said that when sober, Smith T was a perfect gentleman, but when under the influence of alcohol, he could become "as ferocious as a tiger." Luckily for Gillespie, Smith T on this particular trip did not get drunk.

That evening, as Gillespie slept in the berth above Smith T's, he watched his bunkmate disrobe. As he "divested himself of his armory," Gillespie wrote, pistols, knives, and a shooting-cane were all placed in a position where he could reach them instantly. Some of the fellow passengers warned the intrepid youth that he was risking his life sleeping in the bunk above his well-armed friend. Any sudden movement during the night, they cautioned, might provoke Smith T into a shooting frenzy. The evening passed without incident, and Gillespie lived to tell the tale of his encounter with one of the frontier's most remarkable men.[11]

Throughout his twilight years, Smith T continued to exhibit eccentricities that contributed to the stuff of legends. In addition to his buckskin wardrobe, which he wore long after it ceased to be in style, he also attempted to make a statement by his unique mode of travel.

11. *St. Louis Globe-Democrat,* September 25, 1887.

After acquiring his farms in Saline County, his favorite method of transportation across the state was by pirogue. Even after steamboats began traversing the state, he preferred his own boat, which was manned by slaves and well fortified with provisions, arms, and munitions. He traveled, reported the *Kansas City Journal,* "in all the splendor and ease of an Eastern monarch." John Darby, during his tenure as mayor of St. Louis, recalled how people on the city sidewalks would first stand in awe of the colonel and then scurry from his path. His river excursions exhibited the same type of panache. Smith T, especially in his later years, had a flare for the dramatic and desperately sought the people's attention if not their respect. It was on these trips up and down the Missouri River that he would stop and occasionally harass fellow travelers like James Rollins at riverside hotels.[12]

His illusions of grandeur were not confined to mere displays of bravado and ostentation. Throughout the waning years of his life, Smith T clung tenaciously and unrealistically to the hope that his land claims both in Missouri and in Alabama would eventually be settled in his favor. As for the latter petition, in 1830 he proposed through his attorney, William Kelly, a settlement on the shares he had purchased from Cox's Tennessee Company. He was prepared "to execute a deed of relinquishment to the United States, if the sum of $100,000 shall be paid in cash or land."[13] The national government, believing the land claims to be invalid, refused the proposal. Smith T's only chance of success now lay with the U.S. Supreme Court. This too eventually proved futile.

His Missouri land claims under the St. Vrain grant met with the same lack of success. After the failure of his petition before the Missouri courts, his lawyers in 1830 appealed to the Supreme Court. The case was taken under advisement and, ironically, was decided in the year of his death. Both the lower and upper courts agreed that his claim was invalid because the tract had been surveyed by a private rather than a public concern. The Supreme Court reasoned that "Spain never permitted individuals to locate their grants" in the manner of Smith T's survey. Furthermore, the Supreme Court held, according to historian Louis Pelzer, that "Congress did not contemplate the submission of claims" unless they "were in accordance with the laws and usages of

12. Ibid. For the story of Smith T and Major Rollins, see chap. 10.
13. U.S. Senate, *Memorial,* 4.

Spain." The decision, coming as it did in 1836, was left in the hands of Smith T's heirs to fight. By 1846 they had begun to hammer out "a compromise" that would ultimately give them a part of the original concession. These discussions, however, continued into the next decade and beyond.[14]

Smith T's hopes for profits from windfall land sales, however unfounded, were no doubt instigated in large part by a serious turn of economic misfortunes. The best illustration of these financial woes was a letter written in January 1829 to his brother Thomas, who at the time was in Washington, D.C. The letter has been very important to historians for a number of reasons. First, it was one of the very few pieces of known correspondence written by Smith T during the last half score of his life. Second, the letter was even more interesting since it was written to his brother—a gentleman whose relationship with Smith T was often as turbulent as the summer storms that swept across the Boonslick.[15]

Smith T wrote the letter on January 28 from his home at Mine Shibboleth. This in itself was noteworthy since it indicated that, notwithstanding all the legal and physical troubles he had sustained, he nevertheless had been able to hold onto the single most precious parcel of Missouri land in his vast array of holdings. The letter began by informing Thomas that he and his son-in-law, James, had just left Thomas's farm, Experiment. Always the hunter, Smith T remarked on the abundance of game near his brother's estate and how he hoped to purchase a farm close by it in the near future. Just exactly how he proposed to purchase new lands he did not explain. For in the next breath he lamented the decline in lead prices and how discouraged he had become. "Our lead has got down to three dollar and a half Pr. H. [per hundred pounds]." At this low price, he continued, "we cannot afford to make it."

The letter had already indicated that he had a serious cash flow problem. The next part of the same correspondence, however, was vintage

---

14. Pelzer, "The Spanish Land Grants," 34. U.S. House, *Report,* 2. Also see U.S. Senate, *Report,* The Committee on Public Lands, 29th Cong., 2d sess., Document no. 64, January 14, 1847, 1. Document, Surveyor General, October 22, 1847, Capitol Fire Documents, CFD, vol. 21, 505, MSA; Documents, General Land Office (St. Louis), February 23, 1850, Capitol Fire Documents, CFD, vol. 24, 89.

15. John Smith T to Thomas A. Smith, January 28, 1829, Thomas A. Smith Papers, Folder 33.

Smith T. "I must turn my attention," he exclaimed, "to something else." Always the schemer, he revealed the restless side of his nature and his absolute unwillingness, even in later life, to rein in his ambitions. The "something else" that he proposed was a very impractical scheme to make an "application to the Mexican Government for compensation for my services and money advanced in support of the patriots." This sentence more than any other in this remarkable letter has fascinated historians. It demonstrated that Smith T had in fact abetted the revolutionary cause, at least in his own mind, but to what extent or when is not fully disclosed. The belief, no matter how faint, that the Mexicans would even consider granting him compensation at this late date demonstrated either how desperate he was for money or how increasingly deluded he had become.

His lack of cash was also evident by the letter's next petition. Smith T proposed to leave for Mexico the following May and take with him around five thousand dollars in merchandise. Unwilling or unable to take the risk himself, he hoped that his brother would "think well of such an undertaking" and would procure the credit for the goods for a period of twelve months. These trade caravans could be highly profitable, but they were risky. Their importance to the commerce of the prairies was illustrated by the U.S. Army's instructions to Major Bennett Riley that he accompany the next caravan with two hundred troops.[16] Even with a military escort, this type of trip for a man nearing sixty years of age was hazardous enough. But owing to the unsettled state of U.S.–Mexican affairs, as well as the danger from both bandits and Indians, the trade stratagem smacked of vintage Smith T.

Land disputes had been part and parcel of the colonel's entire adult life, and they too appeared in this relatively short letter. "The appeal in my land case," he wrote, had been forwarded to one of his attorneys. More papers and documents, he added, had been sent to Senator Thomas H. Benton. Nevertheless, he beseeched his brother to take an active role in the case. "Do for me what you can," he implored. Coming from such a proud man, the request had a very humbling and anxious quality about it.

The last portion of the letter, and certainly the oddest, pertained to a remark concerning Smith T's antipathy toward Native Americans. It

16. Burke Papers, 14.

was his contention that the government should take more aggressive steps "with the hostile bands of Indians." Unfortunately for historians, he did not give specific impressions on what tribes or areas of the country seemed to be the most dangerous. The next-to-last sentence in the letter again showed that he had perhaps lost some of his common sense but none of his flare for the dramatic. "I have been manufacturing such arms," he wrote, "as will carry danger." Although he did not mention any particular weapon or design, he believed that his weaponry "would surprise a more enlightened enemy." The Indians of his displeasure obviously did not rank as "enlightened." Finally, in the same rambling sentence, he closed by saying that his "wish" was to be able to witness "their effect." The letter demonstrated that Smith T, always the adventurer, was willing, at least on paper, to face danger and to fight the last "good fight." It ended with a customary farewell and a reassurance that "nothing new" had transpired back home that could not be found in "the news papers." His closing was signed "Your brother Jn. Smith T."

It would be difficult to ascertain exactly when the letter arrived in Washington. Nor can historians know for sure how Thomas reacted to it, since no direct reply can be found among his papers. Perhaps Thomas realized that the best response was no response at all. He also must have been cognizant of the letter's style as well as its content. For in this two-paragraph letter occurred numerous mistakes of punctuation, capitalization, and spelling. Simply put, the correspondence appeared to be neither a carefully conceived plan nor the work of a man who attended a school as respected as William and Mary. Rather, it was more reminiscent of a troubled spirit unable to express clearly a variety of emotional vexations.

The economic frustrations of the late 1820s perhaps exacerbated Smith T's fiery temper. An object of his violent and erratic behavior was Samuel Ball. Little was known of Ball except that he had the misfortune of being in the wrong place at the wrong time. His 1830 rencounter with Smith T found the colonel drinking in a Ste. Genevieve tavern owned by William McArthur. According to most sources, Smith T had been drinking heavily. The exact nature of the dispute between the two men was never fully determined. Nor were there any eyewitnesses to what exactly transpired between them (although William McArthur was later paid one dollar for being a witness in the case). In any event,

Mrs. McArthur, who was in another room at the time of the killing, heard a single shot and rushed into the barroom to find Ball lying dead on the floor. According to the *Missouri Intelligencer,* he had been shot through the heart. Apparently the quarrel had escalated very quickly since she had no inkling of any impending difficulty. Rushing into the barroom, she demanded that Smith T turn over his weapons to her and stand trial for murder. Always the gentleman, Smith T supposedly replied, "Take them, my daughter." He then produced four weapons and handed them to her with a courteous bow. Thereupon, he surrendered to authorities. Unlike the outcome of his previous killings, this time he was arrested and placed in custody. Emily M. Perry, the wife of James, disgustedly wrote her husband about "another" killing by Smith T and said that he spent three to four days in jail before posting bail. She sadly believed he would be found not guilty. She further contended that a Dr. Robertson was present at the time of the killing, but "he will be put out of the way on the day of the trial."[17]

Within a few short weeks of the killing, as best as can be ascertained, the Ste. Genevieve Circuit Court acquitted Smith T of murder. An 1887 *Globe-Democrat* article suggested the real reason for the acquittal when it wrote, "No jury would have the temerity to convict him." Robertus Love, a newspaperman, concurred. "Jurors in those days," he wrote, "were careful, self-preservation being their first law." The *Kansas City Journal* agreed. Smith T's "reputation as a 'killer,'" it stated, led only to "a show of prosecution." No lawyer, the paper went on to report, could be found "with sufficient courage to encounter the opposition and enmity of so dangerous a character." The "killer" himself was more than adequately defended. John Scott, a former U.S. congressman from Missouri, as well as a prominent St. Louis attorney, Beverly Allen, served as his counsel.[18]

The Ball murder may have been an irrational and spontaneous act of violence, but it was by no means the only mysterious action taken by Smith T in the early 1830s. The most inexplicable act of his twilight

17. WPA Historical Survey, Ste. Genevieve Circuit Court, March 8, 1831, Collection no. 3551, Folder 19226, WHMC. Higginbotham, *John Smith T,* 51. *Missouri Intelligencer,* October 9, 1830. WPA Historical Survey, Ste. Genevieve Circuit Court, June 6, 1831, Collection no. 3551, Folder 21554. Emily M. Perry to James F. Perry, October 3, 1830, Eugene Barker Papers, Barker Library, University of Texas, Austin.

18. *St. Louis Globe-Democrat,* September 25, 1887. "Col. John Smith T," Vertical File, MHS. *Kansas City Journal,* August 7, 1896.

years was certainly his ill-fated decision in 1832 to run for governor of Missouri.[19] The *Missouri Intelligencer* thought so too. On June 16, 1832, about six weeks after his announcement, the newspaper stated that he and another long-shot candidate "cannot by any possibility be elected" to office. "It is therefore idle," the paper went on to add, "for these gentlemen longer to hold their names before the public." The editor of the *Intelligencer* believed that Smith T's candidacy might siphon off votes from a more viable political candidate, Dr. John Bull of Howard County. The paper was no friend of the Democrats. It accused Andrew Jackson of pushing "suffering and angry savages" into Missouri and perhaps instigating a future massacre. It also opposed many of Jackson's and Senator Benton's economic policies. The newspaper supported Henry Clay's American System and endorsed the Bank of the United States, internal improvements, and a protective tariff.[20] These were positions also held by Smith T. It was, therefore, the messenger rather than the message that concerned the *Intelligencer*.

The most that can be said for Smith T's bid for governor, as historian Perry McCandless suggested, was that it added "color" to the gubernatorial campaign.[21] Little can be ascertained, however, about what motivated him to take the political leap. Perhaps he was moved in part by his hatred for the front-runner for the office, Daniel Dunklin. It was Dunklin, one might recall, who some seventeen years earlier as Washington County sheriff had tried to remove Smith T from his residence at Shibboleth only to retreat in the face of armed resistance.

Dunklin, Smith T quite rightly believed, had been allied with the Henry Dodge faction that hoped to strip him of his considerable influence in the mining region. The colonel's political animus was not directed only toward county and state Democrats. His long-standing quarrels with such prominent political figures as Andrew Jackson and Sam Houston must also have played a role in his decision to seek the governorship. Philosophically, he could only have resented the social and political leveling that was sweeping the western states. While few leaders personified the ideals of self-reliance and individualism more

19. *Missouri Intelligencer*, May 5, 1832.
20. Ibid., June 16, 1832.
21. McCandless, *A History of Missouri*, 90.

than Smith T, he nevertheless believed that Democratic rhetoric was inimical to the entrepreneurial spirit. These differences likewise extended to Senator Thomas Hart Benton. Although the senator had represented Smith T in numerous court cases, he no doubt objected to Benton casting his lot with Andrew Jackson. Many of Missouri's wealthy merchants, mining operators, and large plantation owners along the Mississippi and Missouri River bottoms also believed that the Jacksonians' narrow construction of the U.S. Constitution jeopardized economic growth in the state.[22] His differences with Benton, though many, did not jeopardize their personal relationship.

The 1832 decision to seek the highest office in the state must also have been predicated upon Smith T's mistaken belief that his legendary career could be parlayed into political success. Perhaps, too, the declaration of candidacy was partly a search for public vindication for a lifetime of adventure and exploitation that encompassed more than its share of violence. His error was to confuse reputation with respect. Missouri in 1832 had barely shed its frontier skin. But it had matured to the point where his kind of swashbuckling held little political appeal. In the early 1830s Smith T had yet to become a caricature of those violent and reckless years of pioneer life. Nevertheless, Missouri was quickly making a transition from a rural, agrarian economy to a dynamic market economy. The colonel, who had always been in the vanguard of these capitalist changes, recognized the new commercial and financial forces. He did not, however, seem to realize that his style and persona were politically ill-suited to reflect and to direct these new economic changes.

His statement of political principles, however, was the clearest and most articulate piece of writing in the last decade or so of his life. In a circular dated July 13, 1832, Smith T insisted that no one should be elected to office "whom they [the people] do not know." The pamphlet, he hoped, would better acquaint the people with the aspiring politician. Without hesitation, Smith T endorsed the Bank of the United States. As for the constitutionality of that institution, he had no question. The bank, so stated the circular, "has been well tested" and would preserve the currency of the country. A sound financial system, he added, was a prerequisite for a healthy economy.

22. Meyer, *The Heritage of Missouri*, 178.

A second important position that he endorsed was a system of internal improvements. Although most Whigs believed that the government should support infrastructural development, Smith T used this issue to construct a political philosophy as well. "Man" he wrote, was not "stationary" and should ever be "on the advance towards moral perfection." The country likewise should "naturally improve" with the individual. Internal improvements, therefore, provided the perfect nexus between private initiative and public response. The product of this marriage was no less than "a more brotherly union; a confidence in each other; and a greater reliance upon our confederacy." The idea of binding the nation together through a network of internal improvements and creating a unified citizenry was perhaps a bit too utopian, but it represented a genuine belief in the efficacy of government to promote a more perfect union.

Smith T also endorsed a protective tariff to aid domestic manufacturers. Unlike the Democrats, who saw low tariffs as a means of enhancing agricultural exports, generating federal income, and helping consumers, National Republicans such as Smith T endorsed the principles of the American System. These principles became the foundation of the Whig Party. Smith T, however, failed to make a good case for the tariff. "We are a peculiar people," he wrote, "enjoying a portion of liberty unknown in any other country." Although the statement sounded appealing, it did not directly address the issue. His concluding remark on the tariff issue was equally off the point. "Our government," he exclaimed, "is a rebuke upon all the other governments in the world.— We will preserve it." Furthermore, he unequivocally supported Henry Clay for president. Unlike his Democratic opponents, he believed that the constitutionality of the above positions had been settled long before this particular election.

Whatever the merits of his positions, the citizens of Missouri soundly rejected his gubernatorial bid. In Washington County he received a paltry 120 votes. Throughout the rest of the state he garnered only another 194. The most ignominious rebuttal to his candidacy came in Saline County, where he received not a single vote.[23] By dismissing Smith T, the people of Missouri also rejected the type of swashbuckling bravado that characterized his life. In a sense the election debacle was

23. *Fayette Democrat-Leader,* April 20, 1974.

an important step in the transformation of the myths and legends surrounding his life. For one thing, it clearly signaled that his deeds had no political appeal. For another, the defeat suggested that it would be difficult to sustain intact the memories of frontier swashbuckling in the light of changing market forces and new economic and political elites.

If Smith T's detractors hoped that after the election debacle he would go quietly into the night, then they were sadly mistaken. It seems that he was not quite ready to give up the unofficial title as the most dangerous man in Missouri. The Ball killing, as well as the subsequent arrest and trial, seemed not to deter the irascible colonel. Four years after the Ste. Genevieve rencounter, Colonel James Kearny, writing from Jefferson Barracks near St. Louis, related another murder attributed to Smith T. Kearny was not a Smith T admirer. In correspondence to William Clark, who at that time was in Washington, D.C., Kearny wrote that Smith T "has killed another man—I believe it was in a drunken frolic and no one else present, so that he is at large, there not being testimony enough to commit him—."[24]

The details of the Kearny letter appeared to fit the description of the Ball killing some four years earlier. Yet it is doubtful, given the tone and immediacy of the letter, that he was referring to the earlier incident. Kearny may have been alluding to the Southern Hotel killing, but since it reportedly occurred in the hotel lobby, there would have been many witnesses. It would therefore appear that, notwithstanding a mistake in the date of the letter to Clark, Smith T chalked up another fatality in the fall of 1834.

Placed in this historical context, these violent incidents lent credence to the numerous accounts suggesting that Smith T's welcome in Missouri was wearing thin. It would also help to explain why he left Missouri in 1836 for his final trip to Tennessee. The debunkers of the Smith T myth have also suggested another reason. They contend that his sudden departure was due to the physical insult of Dr. John G. Bryan. The debunkers maintain that the Potosi physician and entrepreneur, frustrated by numerous legal delays over land disputes, slapped Smith T on the Ste. Genevieve Courthouse steps. Smith T lost face, according to this

24. Colonel James Kearny to William Clark, October 11, 1834, William Clark Papers, MHS.

rendition of the myth, when he did not promptly challenge Bryan to a duel.[25]

Bryan's admirers may have been the same group of debunkers who first perpetrated the stories of Smith T showing the white feather in the McConnell incident. They no doubt believed that their hero shared the same constellation of traits as the colonel. The doctor's business activities included mining, medicine, journalism, politics, farming, and industry. Like Smith T, he was ardently pro-slavery and an advocate of the *code duello*. Although he left no manuscript collection, public writings, or private papers, a series of secondhand typed notes from a variety of his admirers were presented to the Western Historical Manuscripts Collection in Columbia, Missouri. They were catalogued as the Bryan Obear Collection. Since the authenticity of these notes cannot be substantiated, historians have been left in a methodological quandary. Nevertheless, the various witnesses who stepped forth to challenge the stories of Smith T's bravery were the same ones who saw Bryan as the champion of frontier chivalry.[26]

Other than the Obear Collection, no other historical reference, except Hyde and Conard's *Encyclopedia of the History of St. Louis,* has been found to substantiate the claim that Smith T's flight from Missouri was due to his humiliation at the hands of Bryan. A far more plausible explanation for the trip that eventually cost him his life was the need to find a new and profitable source of income. He planned to develop a Tennessee cotton plantation on some forest land near the Mississippi River on Hale's Point. The Hale family had known the Smiths back in Virginia. This familial connection most certainly played a part in the Hales' decision to extend the invitation. As for Smith T, his idea of opening new cotton lands was a sound one, as Lauderdale County later became one of the leading cotton producing areas in the South.[27]

The move to Tennessee was logical in other ways as well. In the first place, Smith T's roots in Tennessee ran deep. A plantation near Hale's Point would be a homecoming of sorts and would allow him to live the life of a southern gentleman. Second, he may have felt somewhat

25. Note, George M. Wilson, n.d., Folder 7; Note, John B. Johnson, n.d., Folder 11; both in Bryan Obear Collection.
26. William Hyde and Howard L. Conard, eds., *Encyclopedia of the History of St. Louis,* vol. 1, 261–62.
27. Higginbotham, *John Smith T,* 54. Burke Papers, 18.

rejected after his drubbing in the 1832 gubernatorial election, and perhaps believed that a change of scenery would do him good. Third, Smith T's mining operations had relied upon a labor-intensive system of Negro servitude. But a number of factors militated against the continuation of this type of operation. Along with the decline in lead prices had also come more efficient methods of mining that made slave labor increasingly problematic. In addition, the mines lay precariously close to the Mississippi River and the free state of Illinois. The likelihood of more runaways became more than a distinct possibility. Although Missouri was still securely in the hands of the pro-slavery elites, the mining country was uncomfortably close to St. Louis and the incipient abolitionist movement.

Slaves, of course, could be used in Saline County in the salt-making business, but the ever-vanishing supply of wood made this aspect of the western operation more and more impractical. Smith T continued to make salt country purchases via his brother in the early 1830s, but the size and scale of these transactions began to diminish.[28] At the time of his death, Smith T's slaves in the west-central part of the state totaled about thirty-one. Since this area of Missouri was solidly pro-slavery, he was not concerned so much about abolitionists. Nevertheless, a Tennessee cotton plantation appeared to be a more productive way to use these human resources than did farming on the edge of the prairies. Thus he set out, with only his trusted slave, Dave, for Hale's Point.

The trip to Tennessee was not considered all that taxing, even for a man in his sixties. In addition, Smith T's good health was attested to by the fact that he had survived a cholera epidemic that swept the state in 1833, taking the lives of many notables, including Senator Alexander Buckner of Cape Girardeau. This time, however, luck deserted him. Contracting a fever, he died rather suddenly in the arms of Dave in 1836. His body was returned to Missouri and reportedly buried on the White Cliffs of Selma.

To many of Smith T's contemporaries, his demise on the banks of the Mississippi was hardly the stuff of legends. After all, frontier idols and icons were expected to meet a fate similar to that which befell folk heroes such as Mike Fink, who died by an assassin's bullet. Smith T's

28. John Smith T to Thomas Smith, c. October 2, 1831, Thomas A. Smith Papers, Folder 36.

passing simply did not measure up to the mythic standards later set by Jesse James and Wild Bill Hickock. Unlike those legendary figures, Smith T suffered no dramatic death that could transform him into a heroic victim. Even notorious villains such as Big and Little Harpe, as well as Samuel Mason, had died in a blaze of glory.

Unlike Daniel Boone, who had a myth-making biographer, Smith T's career had only fragmentary documentation. Nor, for that matter, did he succumb in a burst of self-sacrificing glory, like Custer, Bowie, or Crockett. His unremarkable passing was the last chapter in an unsuccessful bid for lasting fame and recognition. He had failed (unlike Benton, Dodge, and Dunklin) to achieve political recognition. His gubernatorial pursuits had ended in public rejection and, one might suggest, even outright derision. His lackluster death was the final and most lethal blow to the legends and lore of this remarkable character.

Few men, even in such a reckless era, possessed Smith T's passionate nature or matched his frenetic pace. It was the supreme irony that many a lesser man in this age of expansion did not escape violent and romanticized death. Fate, ever the manipulator, had conspired to rob Smith T of those last, fleeting moments of glory that could have amplified his fame and secured his name in the annals of history. Without the recognition a hero's death would have brought him, his life became as lost as his grave—both shrouded in mystery and submerged in a tangled web of blurred facts and forgotten lore. His final days and ordinary passing likewise handicapped those myth makers who would struggle valiantly but unsuccessfully to resurrect his image. In the end, only history could partially restore what myth, legend, and lore had failed to achieve.

10. *Smith T: The Myths, Legends, and Folklore*

S mith T's death did not begin or end the supplementation of frontier history with myth, legend, and lore. The manufacturing of tall tales had already begun before he died. The early writers who collectively shaped much of Smith T's persona, such as John Darby, Henry Brackenridge, and Firmin Rozier, generally embellished the heroic side of his nature. They did so because geography and history, or more precisely the lack of history, promoted exaggeration. In the first place, the vast stretches of unchartered lands lent themselves to the stretching of truth. A big country required big tales. In the second place, the relative newness of the white inhabitants afforded them little time to develop traditional heroes. Consequently, biographies and frontier narratives tended to mix the hyperbolic with the heroic. A third explanation for the stretching of truth pertained to its utility. Nowhere, claimed historians of the West, was the process of historical change greater than on the fringes of the frontier. This "heritage of change" challenged early writers to discover some cultural permanence in the westward experience. One function of historical myth-figures such as Smith T was their ability to inspire a sense of personal triumph and a sense of regional identity.[1] Lastly, myths, legends, and lore combined with biography to dramatize and to vindicate a one-dimensional, ethnocentric interpretation of civilization's mastery over frontier savagery. In this latter vein, stories surrounding Smith T functioned as a historical art form that often pitted progress against depravity.

1. Tristram P. Coffin and Henning Cohen, *The Parade of Heroes: Legendary Figures in American Lore*, xx–xxxiii.

194

For Smith T's nineteenth-century admirers, the purpose in writing history was not to objectively re-create past experiences, but rather to install in the historical account subjective values that could be derived from the heroic action. Sometimes the myth makers enlivened the Smith T narrative. At other times they distorted it. Either was permissible if it achieved the desired effect. Yet the juxtaposition of history and myth leads to an inevitable paradox. For while the historian studies the functionalization of myth, that is, how it has defined national or regional consciousness, he or she must search for not only meaning but also reality. The historian must give credence to the myth and the heroes thus created while proceeding with their demythification. In short, myths about people like Smith T are real if people, including historians, believe they are real. One purpose of history, therefore, is to scrutinize the purposes served by myths.

This chapter analyzes the deeds of John Smith T as related by the chroniclers of his life. It will explore the genesis of a frontier hero and will attempt to discover how and why the various tales and stories of his derring-do were exaggerated. It will also analyze the relationship of history with myth, legend, and folklore as they pertained to Smith T's life. The historian must also explore the structure of myth. The outline of this structure is found in the almost supernatural deeds of the hero. As in the case of Smith T, these deeds are often associated with a quest or extended journey such as the Texas rescue mission. Another vital structural element of myth is the culture of the people who construct it and the values they thus attach to the hero.

Myths are subjective, unconsciously accepted beliefs held by a society. They are generally conceptual and motivate society by their appeal to the theological, mythical, and/or metaphysical. From these myths, legends and lore are born. Legends deal with the human or superhuman residue of myth. Legends and lore verify myths just as heroes give life and form to myth. Legends suggest a nucleus of fact, albeit unsubstantiated, surrounding an individual or group that is written and passed down by tradition. Legends are popularly accepted as true. Folklore, on the other hand, might be more narrowly defined by its more limited audience and milieu. Generally, the people and environment are more rural and the stories are passed down more informally through oral traditions. Lore may take the form of tall tales, anecdotes, jokes, serio-comedy, or songs and ballads, to name a few possibilities. Much of the

Smith T lore, for example, emanated from the Tennessee hill people and then was accepted as true by friends and enemies in Missouri.

Myths, legends, and folklore are therefore not mutually exclusive. They all help to define a culture. All employ heroes and symbols to confirm the structural underpinnings of a society. Neither are they static. New myths and new legends are created as societal needs change. These modifications usually reflect the changing needs of the ruling classes. Folklore also adapts. It relies upon powerful images and visualizations that mesh with the socialization process. Folklore is a more democratic version of history and usually places the hero alongside the aspirations of the common people.[2]

In early Missouri, myths, legends, and lore played an important role in the socialization process. Social and cultural identification was closely linked to these western role models. In turn, the qualities of legendary figures such as Smith T operated in conjunction with a number of larger assumptions about frontier history. Some of the more prominent of these were the ideas of entrepreneurialism, egalitarianism, love of liberty, Christian compassion and charity, economic competition, self-reliance, rugged individualism, pragmatism, the resort to violence, survival of the fittest, and an American mission of a transcontinental empire. Cultural historians such as Richard Hofstadter and Henry Nash Smith interpreted these myths as a popularly accepted cluster of images that rationalized behavior and conditioned national character.[3]

Early Missourians such as Darby, Brackenridge, and Rozier employed the Smith T saga as a valuable tool in their search for a "usable past."[4] Smith T's life blended neatly into their renderings of memory and history. Missouri in the early nineteenth century was a microcosm of many a frontier community with an identity crisis. It was a land enriched

2. Richard Slotkin, *Regeneration through Violence: The Mythology of the American Frontier, 1600–1860*, 13–14; Donald Worster, "Beyond the Agrarian Myth," 7; Slotkin, *The Fatal Environment*, 19–22.

3. It should be noted that many anthropologists see myths and legends as stories that are regarded as true and folktales as fictional. Also, myths are interpreted as sacred while legends are seen as secular. Myths are classified as remote, very early, and otherworldly. Their principal characters are gods or animals. Legends, according to this interpretation, are historical and have humans in the major roles. Obviously, this work is dealing with myths, legends, and folktales in the American milieu of the past two centuries. Slotkin, *The Fatal Environment*, 16–20; Henry A. Murray, ed., *Myth and Mythmaking*, 117; Slotkin, *Regeneration*, 7.

4. Henry Steele Commager, "The Search for a Usable Past," 90–94.

with many heritages: Spanish, French, Indian, and English. Yet those who would stamp an identity on the land looked for some way to assert its distinctive western character, which had been forged from other regionally disparate elements. Schematically, the Smith T portrayals served this purpose. He had lived by and personified a western code of behavior and honor that bore witness to its own rewards. There was also, however, another facet of his personality that struck a responsive chord. The colonel was both a pragmatist (after all, he not only survived the wilderness ordeal but prospered in it) and a dreamer. His kinetic energy epitomized both sides of the American character.

To accomplish their task, the myth makers faced a formidable chore. Without exception they focused upon the narrative of the hero as the linchpin of the Missouri experience. But in so doing they confronted an intellectual quandary. The hero by definition must evoke the cultural norms of the group and yet stand apart. To solve their problem, popularizers of frontier culture generally constructed an environmental dialectic in which typical pioneers were pictured as a "generous and placable race" pitted against hostile forces that sought to destroy their way of life. These forces might be Indians, boatmen, outlaws, or squatters. Usually the pioneer family, "warm hearted, and hospitable," as was its nature, could not confront the adversaries of civilization without the hero's leadership. Then, the battle could be joined. The people, grateful for the hero's assistance, respond with affection. This was the portrait painted by Smith T eulogists. Wherever he journeyed, wrote biographer Vallé Higginbotham, friends named their sons after him. From Kingston, Tennessee, could be found the likes of John Smith T Brown, and in Washington County, Missouri, a Smith T Goff was named in the colonel's honor.[5]

The hero must embody the cause of good and defend it against the forces that would destroy it. To this extent he is the community's protagonist—the champion of its virtues. On the other hand—and this posed the dilemma—the hero must also be an individualist. He must possess a pragmatic and nonconforming personality and be able to triumph against enemies, both imagined and real, while at the same time

5. Hall, *Sketches*, vol. 2, 70. James Hall, *Legends of the West: Sketches Illustrative of the Habits, Occupations, Privations, Adventures and Sports of the Pioneers of the West*, 3. For an earlier work in the same literary vein, see Hall, *Letters from the West*.

distinguishing himself from the crowd by his disregard of conventions and precedents.[6] These culturally divergent qualities were reconciled in the John Smith T myth by the incorporation of his life into the great American success story. The frontier with all its savagery could only be tamed by men of similar ilk. Yet the archetypal hero such as Smith T must never succumb to his hostile environment. In the end he must confront the destructive, atavistic forces of the frontier while never descending to that same base level to defeat them. His triumph is the victory of civilization over barbarity. He becomes the exorcist of the wilderness.

Early popularizers of myth, legend, and lore usually portrayed their subject as a man of inordinate intelligence, possessing a formal education that distinguished him from the mass of ordinary folk whose forte was common sense and practicality. A biographer and champion of the Smith T legend pointed out that an inventory of the books in the colonel's home library revealed a man with "an educated and inquiring mind." Another local historian wrote of Smith T's "penchant for esoteric literary references" and his fondness for a fourth-century Gaelic poet, Ossian, and his poem "Fingal." Hyde and Conard in 1899 described Smith T as "mild of manner and courtly in address, a jurist, statesman and scholar, but a veritable demon when affronted."[7] The hero's cultural regression must, however, be short-lived. If he momentarily resorted to violence, it was an aberration soon corrected by his classical education and class indoctrination. This dual feature of Smith T's personality was best expressed by John Darby.

As he seized the economic possibilities afforded him and confronted adversity, Darby intimated, Smith T gained strength from his hardships rather than being overcome by them. He developed a kind of "courage, self reliance, and determination possessed by few men." Darby went on to say, "a man of more polished manners and more courteous demeanor I never met. He was a gentleman in every respect." To

6. Dale Van Every, *Forth to the Wilderness: The First American Frontier 1754–1774*, 100–101. For a sample of this style see John A. McClung, *Sketches of Western Adventure;* Hall, *Sketches;* Timothy Flint, "The Missouri Trapper," *Western Monthly Review* 1 (May 1827): 28.

7. *De Soto Press*, November 18, 1963. *Festus Courier Journal,* July 24, 1991. Frederic L. Billon, *Annals of St. Louis in Its Early Days under the French and Spanish Domination*, 109–19; Hyde and Conard, eds., *Encyclopedia of the History of St. Louis,* vol. 1, 261–62.

his eulogist, Smith T was not outside the law, fragile as it was, so much as he was above it. His extreme sense of individualism, at least according to myth, allowed him to establish his own jurisdictional parameters. Yet his fights were fair, "honorable, open, manly warfare." Darby believed he killed fifteen men, mostly in duels. Even though he frequently sought justice by his own hand, Smith T "always stood his trial" and was never convicted. His often-quoted remark summarized the contradictions in the life and legend of Smith T. He was, said Darby, "as polished and courteous a gentleman as ever lived in the State of Missouri" and as "mild a mannered man as ever put a bullet into the human body."[8]

Folktales of famous frontier figures not only alluded to their courteous natures but also portrayed another side of their characters. These western lions were depicted in a humorous or down-to-earth style, in balance against their ferocious natures. Henry Brackenridge amplified the point that the frontier had not degraded his hero. He told how Smith T had a falling out with old friend Samuel Perry over a mining dispute. One day, he overtook Perry as he was riding toward Ste. Genevieve. He told his friend that he regretted their differences but, referring to a brace of pistols he was carrying, suggested that the two settle the problem in a "rational manner" by dueling it out on the spot. When Perry sensibly declined, Smith T cordially accepted the verdict and continued to ride with Perry for some distance. They conversed on a variety of subjects, and the colonel did not broach the subject of a duel again.[9]

Another author who described Smith T's polite manners was Firmin Rozier. Smith T, he wrote, was "very hospitable at home, and charitable to the poor." His defenders cited numerous occasions when he donated land and timber to build churches, even for denominations other than his own. Others described his benevolence toward his slaves and how one slave in particular, Dave, always stood guard for his master and went so far as to care tenderly for him on his deathbed. Even in some of his fiercest fights, such as the one with a "ruffian" of "ferocious character and herculean frame" whom he stabbed with his knife, Smith T showed compassion. Although the ruffian was mortally wounded, the colonel,

8. Darby, *Personal Recollections,* 85, 97.
9. Brackenridge, *Recollections,* 217–21.

John Darby, eventual mayor
of St. Louis, was one of the
most important purveyors of
the Smith T legends. Courtesy
of State Historical Society of
Missouri, Columbia.

so goes the story, took the man home and tried unsuccessfully to nurse
him back to health.[10]

Heroes are also recognized as remarkably handsome, with finely
chiseled features and usually blond hair. Most of Smith T's contemporaries reaffirmed his physical attractiveness but did not at all agree
upon a physical description. Firmin Rozier, who during his youth may
have encountered the colonel, described him as "tall, slight of build,
wiry in person." Brackenridge, who stayed at Mine Shibboleth with
the Smith Ts, described him as a small man of "delicate frame" and
even somewhat "effeminate." He had mild blue eyes, fair hair, a fair
complexion, and a youthful appearance. According to Brackenridge,
Smith T was a mild and gentle person, and "kindness and benevolence
appeared to be the natural growth of his heart."[11] John F. Darby, also

10. Rozier, *Rozier's History*, 316. Deed Book B, 480, 484, 498, and Deed Book C,
58, Washington County Courthouse. *Missouri Republican*, April 1, 1828. Brackenridge,
Recollections, 221.
11. Rozier, *Rozier's History*, 312–13. Also see Rozier, "Address," November 13,
1879, MHS. Brackenridge, *Recollections*, 218.

a contemporary, agreed with Brackenridge. Smith T was a man small in stature yet with a "Daniel Boone aspect" about him. The earlier descriptions of Smith T's physique appeared to match reality better than the latter ones. The slightness of build also made many of his physical feats, especially hand-to-hand encounters with dirks, even more remarkable. Courage, therefore, and not physical size or strength, was the asset that ensured him fame.

Legendary heroes generally possess the undying love of a beautiful and faithful wife or lover, but their sense of adventure requires them to undertake long and perilous journeys fraught with many trials and tribulations. No single event in Smith T's life did more to enhance his status than the legends of his first Mexican adventure, particularly the attempt to rescue his brother Reuben. Rozier wrote that it was his "roving disposition" that led Smith T not only in the rescue effort but also "to aid to revolutionize Mexico, traversing a wild, vast country, surrounded by dangers."[12] Rozier had perhaps heard the story from John Darby, who a decade before had written that Smith T, "solitary and alone," rode to Chihuahua. Along the way he battled Spaniards and Indians: "Nothing would deter him from saving his brother." It was perhaps this tale of heroic quest that prompted Brackenridge to write of "a hundred instances" of his "desperate intrepidity."[13]

The myths and legends that surrounded the lives of western men such as John Smith T came alive at the ordinary level of existence when they were incorporated into folklore. Legends popularize myths and ingrain them into culture. As the tales are passed down from generation to generation, especially among the populace, folk heroes emerge. Folklore becomes the raw material for regional self-identification. Since many of the stories surrounding Smith T center around heroic struggle, the devolution is complete when the folk hero is thoroughly assimilated to his natural environment.

Brackenridge, more than any other author, popularized the yarns of Smith T. In the "Western States and Territories," he wrote, Smith T "stood unrivaled" in "the number and success of his personal encounters." "Nothing," he went on to say, "was wanting but a more extended sphere of action to have equaled or surpassed the fame of Marion or

12. Rozier, "Address."
13. Darby, *Personal Recollections*, 94–95. Brackenridge, *Recollections*, 221.

202 *Frontier Swashbuckler*

Putnam."[14] To the early chroniclers of Missouri, enlarging the legend was one means of giving the western lands this extended sphere of action. The Smith T drama fused southern characteristics with a frontier style to produce a distinctive regional folk legend. These stories developed during a time of intense nationalism and were expressed as part of the phenomenon called Young America. Missouri and her early heroes played a vital role in the expansionist movement, which enveloped nationalism and unity.

No far-fetched story quite captured the popular imagination, epitomized the symbiosis of myth and folklore, or fitted the hero within his environmental habitat like the tale of Smith T and the bear hunt. The story, no doubt apocryphal, gave rise to many a folk yarn. In Brackenridge's original account, Smith T tracked a bear to a cave and crawled into the cave to shoot it. The bear rushed out and ran directly over him before it died. "I asked," Brackenridge wrote, "whether he [the bear] had whispered in his ear as he passed." "Yes," said Smith T, "he told me whenever I wished to have a thing well done, I must do it myself."[15]

The story was quite in keeping with a number of western heroes who did battle with one of nature's most powerful adversaries. Hugh Glass, for instance, had fought and killed a bear. Although torn and shredded, he survived the ordeal only to be killed later by Indians. There was also the bear-fighting contest between mountain men Jim Bridger and Jim Baker. They too went into a cave to "skulp the varmints with their knives." It was a mighty battle and one in which they emerged battered but victorious. As Brackenridge's memories were transformed into our history, no story projected a folk aura as much as the bear hunt. Perhaps the author took his cue from another folk hero and famous bear hunter, Davy Crockett. Although bears were quite plentiful in the Missouri wilderness, wolves were by far a greater menace. As late as 1820, travelers to Jefferson City, the proposed capital site for the new state government, reported that more wolves populated the town than humans.[16] By crawling into a cave and in virtual hand-to-hand combat

14. Brackenridge, *Recollections*, 217.
15. Ibid., 219–20.
16. Coffin and Cohen, *The Parade of Heroes*, 252–53. Slotkin, *Environment*, 168. Alphonso Wetmore, *Gazetter of the State of Missouri*, 62; Dick Steward, "Selection of a State Capital: Vagaries and Vicissitudes," 144–45. For some hint as to why the

killing a bear, Smith T gave stature to the bear as a foe formidable enough to match his own courage. Even today, the bear graces the state seal as a projection of power, strength, and endurance. Finally, the bear's advice to Smith T as he crawled over him on his way out of the cave to die suggested a simpatico of man, beast, and wilderness. Not even a Marion or Putnam could top that!

In a day and age when not only courage but also shooting and hunting skills lent credence to one's right to enhanced status, Brackenridge staked out a mighty claim for Smith T. The author recalled Smith T's unerring aim and steadiness of hand as he shot hawks, deer, and other wildlife at incredible distances when the two men hunted together. As a sign of their lasting friendship, Smith T presented his host with two pistols and a rifle handcrafted at Shibboleth. He was, noted Brackenridge, "an unrivaled connoisseur" of guns. He was also "one of the most determined and intrepid men ever known in our frontier settlements."[17]

No one doubted that Smith T possessed composure in the midst of carnage. His violent demeanor had given local color to many western stories. As preceding chapters have suggested, much of this folk tradition was conceived during the early years of the mineral wars when he was pitted against Moses Austin. To many of the locals he became a folk hero as he battled Austin for control of the Ste. Genevieve mining area. Unwittingly, Austin added to the commissary of myth and folklore when he exaggerated his adversary's violent roots in Tennessee. Any "god of Darkness," as he described Smith T, who was capable of more mayhem than "forty men" could not be taken lightly. Austin also magnified his enemy's belligerence during the slander trial instigated by Smith T. The testimony revealed that on numerous occasions Austin had accused Smith T of fleeing "his country" to avoid prosecution for murder.[18] Other witnesses came forward in the civil suit instigated

---

Smith T legends did not survive see Timothy Flint, "Dueling," 453–61; Flint, "A Trait of Frontier Warfare," 139–41; Flint, "On the Formation of a National Character," 348. Also see two articles, authors unknown, "The Destiny of Women," *Western Monthly Review* 2 (January 1834): 137, and "Review of David Crockett, A Narrative of the Life of David Crockett, of the State of Tennessee," *Western Monthly Magazine* 2 (June 1834): 277.

17. Brackenridge, *Recollections,* 218, 222.

18. Rufus Easton to Moses Austin, July 29, 1805, Rufus Easton Papers; Thomas Oliver to William C. Carr, July 29, 1805, William C. Carr Papers; Timothy Phelps to

by Austin against his old foe. These trials collectively reinforced an impression, no doubt prevalent throughout the Missouri Territory, of Smith T's violent intrepidity.

Few if any of the colonel's contemporaries, however, spun a yarn containing as many facets of his character as did John Darby. In 1827, on perhaps one of the last formal meetings between the two men, Darby had traveled to Potosi and there, along with Senator Benton and Arthur L. Maginnis, dined at a hotel with Smith T. Even at this late date Darby was struck by Smith T's mild character. "A man of more polished manners and more courteous demeanor," he wrote, "I never met. He was a gentleman in every respect." Yet in virtually the same breath, the author vented his astonishment at how "every person seemed to have a dread and fear of him." Even in St. Louis, Smith T was the talk of the town. Stories of his desperate rencounters, Darby added, were "in the mouth of everybody." As he walked down the streets of the city, people would point at him "with dread and fear" and quickly "dodge into stores" to avoid his menacing presence. When the hotel guests at the St. Louis Planter's House discovered him in their midst one chilly autumn evening, "their dread of him was unbounded." Not surprisingly, he had the fireplace all to himself.[19]

Darby also recalled the story of how one old general, identified only by his last name of Street, exclaimed to his friends that he was not awed by the presence of so famous a gunfighter when he was told that the gentleman dining alone in a St. Louis hotel was none other than John Smith T. Street then bravely proceeded to strike up an uninvited conversation. To break the ice, the general related how he had known Smith T's brother, Thomas. It proved to be, however, a poor character reference. Smith T hastily pulled out one of his infamous pistols and exclaimed that brother Thomas "was born with a silver spoon in his mouth and did not have to work for his money like I did." The tone of voice left little doubt that General Street's stay at the table would either be brief or perilous. Choosing discretion over valor, Street gathered his

---

Moses Austin, August 6, 1807, vol. 1, pt. 1, 1765–1817, Moses Austin Papers; J. B. C. Lucas to William Crawford, November 9, 1828, in Lucas, *Letters,* 33. Moses Austin to Rufus Easton, August 14, 1805, Easton Papers. General Court Case Files, 1811 Term, Territory of Louisiana, 1804–1812, Record Group 1, Box 3, MSA.

19. Darby, *Personal Recollections,* 92, 97, 93. *St. Louis Globe-Democrat* (weekly), September 25, 1887.

wits and wisely excused himself from the table. No one else dared to invite himself to the colonel's table.[20]

Some of the Smith T tales, on the other hand, proved to be more humorous in vein. In this genre was James S. Rollins's story of his brush with death. Even in his later years, Rollins discovered, Smith T had not traded his weapons in for ploughshares. The two of them met one evening in a Jefferson City hotel. Smith T had just arrived at the City Hotel barroom from one of his legendary sojourns by barge to his plantation in Saline County. Rollins was preparing to deliver a speech at a local temperance rally that evening. Although only twenty-five years of age, Rollins had already made a successful tour of the state on behalf of the temperance cause. In the process he had attracted a considerable amount of attention as a gifted orator and future statesman. When Smith T discovered that he was in the presence of the man he described as "the silver tongue," the colonel, "considerably the worse for liquor," filled a tumbler with whiskey and offered it to Rollins. The young attorney respectfully declined the offer and told his uninvited guest that he had never taken a drink in his life. Pulling out his bowie knife, the colonel said: "No, sir, you never will unless you take this one right now."

At this point the various versions of the story differ. In one rendition, according to William F. Switzler, Smith T draws two pistols from his belt and exclaims: "Major James S. Rollins, the great Boone County temperance orator, take your choice. You have to drink or fight, by God, and that d—n quick." Switzler further maintained that what made the incident all the more unbelievable was the fact that the sheriff of Boone County had accompanied Rollins to the City Hotel, but he too was in no mood to challenge Smith T. William Napton, a historian of Saline County, recounted that he heard the story one day from Rollins when he was a member of the state senate. According to this account, Smith T was very polite at first but when Rollins continued to refuse his hospitality, the colonel angrily replied, "Sir! I allow no gentleman to decline to drink with me; you can either drink or fight." Rollins was not a man easily frightened, but when he discovered the identity of his would-be assailant, discretion became the better part of valor. After a few drinks, Rollins recalled, Smith T "became more amiable and agreeable." No one, certainly the least Rollins, could accurately recall

20. Darby, *Personal Recollections*, 93–94.

how many drinks Smith T poured for his reluctant guest that night. At long last the young "silver tongue" was allowed to excuse himself. Very intoxicated and very sick, he proceeded to the temperance meeting to deliver an oratory on the evils of drink. History does not reveal how well the speech was received.[21]

One nineteenth-century newspaper believed that "hundreds" of folktales concerning Smith T were told throughout Missouri. Many of the stories, it cautioned, were no doubt "apocryphal," but they added color to the myths and legends surrounding him. One tale, dismissed as "absurd," had to do with Smith T's mischievousness when drinking. Allegedly he would draw and fire his pistols at the feet of his son-in-law James M. White and make him dance until exhausted.[22]

Another tall tale recounted how a captain in the regular army passed through Saline County in 1835. The captain, according to lore, had become lost from his detachment and rode up to Smith T's house at sundown. He requested supper and lodging for the night and was generously received by Colonel "Jack." Seated by a large blazing fire, the two men made ready for a supper of hot, smoking corn-meal mush. After eating a large helping of the mush, the captain proclaimed himself satisfied. But this reply was not to Smith T's liking. He took down his dragoon pistols, cocked one, pointed it at his guest, and gave a command. At this juncture the story can best be told by an old Saline County history:

> "By G—; you shall eat, sir!" And thereupon the officer ate!
> He now thought he had fallen in with a maniac. As soon as operations had been resumed, Col. Smith became the pleasant, entertaining host of an hour before. Now, corn-meal mush is very "filling" sort of food. The captain had not long plied his spoon until he again announced himself satisfied. "Eat some more!" thundered Jack T. Remonstrances, and even entreaties were unavailing, and the captain ate "some more." In a few minutes, he again intimated his desire for a cessation of hostilities, as it were. The mush was very good, he said; it was indeed refreshing; there was nothing else he liked so well as mush, and this was decidedly the best he had ever eaten; but, if the colonel would pardon him, he had eaten

21. "Col. John Smith T.," Vertical File, MHS. William B. Napton, *Past and Present of Saline County, Missouri*, 355. *St. Louis Globe-Democrat*, September 25, 1887.
22. *St. Louis Globe-Democrat*, September 25, 1887.

quite a sufficiency, and begged to be allowed to retire. *"Eat some more!"* again demanded Old Jack, presenting a pistol.

The Captain ate "some more!"

O, how it would have delighted poor Oliver Twist to have been a guest of Jack Smith T!

But, at last, nature came to the assistance of the poor surfeited, if not "foundered," officer. And Col. Smith, perhaps touched by the spectacle, allowed him to retire.

The next morning the captain departed before breakfast. Not until he had mounted his horse and was out in the road, were his pistols and sword given him. As he rode away, his imagination, like his stomach, was distended, as he thought that it certainly did require all sorts of people to make the world, especially the Missouri part of the world.[23]

In addition to the mush story, the Saline County history recounted another far-fetched yarn of a time when "Jack T" met two horsemen as he made his way to Boonville. Smith T greeted the fellow travelers, but they did not return his greeting "very politely or ceremoniously." Drawing his rein, he ordered the men to halt and inquired where they were going and from whence they came. When informed that they were from Virginia and were headed west as "land-sharks," Smith T exclaimed: "By G—! That is just what I thought. Draw your pistols, gentlemen." The colonel then proceeded to fire, killing one of the men and badly wounding the other. Only later was it discovered that the men were not land sharks but "honest, reputable citizens" looking for suitable property to settle.[24]

The tall tales spun by the Saline County storytellers were reminiscent of the literary generation just prior to the Civil War. These writers were the first to transform the Smith T persona of duelist, entrepreneur, and adventurer into one of western desperado. One of the more notable of these new sensationalizers was Alfred Arrington, alias Charles Summerfield. This antebellum writer had no literary agenda except to parlay his considerable writing talent into financial gain. The back pages of his books contained a number of references advertising his own works as well as other works depicting western adventure. Collectively, these sensationalized monographs indicated that long before the popularization

23. *History of Saline County, Missouri*, 509.

24. Ibid., 507–8. The stories of the mush eating and the Boonville shooting were also told by Walter B. Stevens, *Centennial History of Missouri*, vol. 2, 543–44.

of cowboys and gunmen by post–Civil War writers, literary attempts had been made to familiarize eastern audiences with the exploits of trans-Mississippi men of action. During the late 1840s Arrington published three books, two by a publishing house in New York and one in Philadelphia, which transformed the Smith T legends and lore into an allegory of doom and fear. To many who read Arrington's works, this intrepid Missourian would become "the precursor of Bowie and the whole race of desperadoes of the Southwest."[25]

Arrington was one of the early eastern writers to make the distinction between southern theatrical dueling and those more deadly contests waged in the West. Thus he anticipated and contributed to the changing images of Smith T. According to Arrington, what made the duelist in the West unique was his only rule of honor, "to fight at all hazards, and against every disadvantage" and with "every implement of destruction" from bowie knife to cannon. Consequently, these duels, he noted, were "always fatal."[26]

To Arrington and other authors of his ilk, the word "desperado" had a different and far less pejorative connotation than it does today. In his 1847 book Arrington noted that the famous English historian Thomas Carlyle had been fascinated with the southwestern duelist. It was in this same work that he referred to Smith T as the most "notorious" of these men and one who "deserves to stand at the head of the whole class" of duelists. "What a hand," he wondered, "were Carlyle to paint the desperadoe of the backwoods! How would his congenial soul gloat over those daring deeds of semi-chivalry!" Arrington, like Darby and Brackenridge, described the dual nature of desperadoes such as Smith T. "His look is fierce," cautioned Arrington, "but not all ferocious; for in it there is a touch of deep tenderness, and a shoreless sea of wild-flowing, inexhaustible humor, and irrepressible, barbaric mirth!" Carlyle, he exclaimed, would have been proud.[27]

Smith T, one might recall, was identified as the dean of western duelists and desperadoes. As such, he certainly qualified as an Arrington knight errant of the western frontier. Every duelist, Arrington wrote,

---

25. *Nashville Tennessean*, March 20, 1983.

26. Alfred Arrington, *Duelists and Dueling in the Southwest: With Sketches of Southern Life*, 4–5; Alfred Arrington, *Illustrated Lives and Adventures of the Desperadoes of the New World*, 9.

27. Arrington, *Duelists*, 4, 54, 5.

A dueling pistol, representative of the weapons used in formal duels, including Smith T's duel with Lionel Browne. Courtesy of State Historical Society of Missouri, Columbia.

"considers himself solemnly conscience-bound, to protect, and if needs be avenge, the peaceable, the strange, the oppressed, and the feeble!" Smith T, he exclaimed, "killed eight men in a single combat, five of whom fell in a regular duel, and the remaining three in affrays, or sudden heats."[28] Dueling pistols, knives, dirks, and a rifle, "Hark from the Tombs," were all, for Arrington, pedagogical tools that conjured up images of a stern taskmaster, intent upon using force as a means of teaching miscreants the futility of challenging his authority.

As to Smith T's physical features, Arrington fell victim to his own literary imagination. This "Ajax" in both "size and in courage" wore long hair, "black as the feathers of a crow," which appeared "savagely grotesque to the whole man." His eyes "reminded one of the glittering orbs of a prairie rattle-snake," except, he cautioned, "when the tiger within him was let loose by rage." Then they flared "like two pits of burning brimstone." His cheekbones were those of "a wild Osage," and "the skin of his face was of a dead yellow, seamed and corrugated with innumerable wrinkles." "The whole man was savage," he exclaimed, but with a beautiful adoring wife and two daughters, both "paragons of virtue." The attachment of such women to such a violent man was, by the author's own admission, a "marvelous phenomenon, truly!" Arrington went on to add:

28. Ibid., 6–7. Alfred Arrington, *The Lives and Adventures of the Desperadoes of the South-West,* 54.

What! the man of blood so fierce and fearful to men, so coldly
cruel in thought and deed, whose home was like the den of a wild
beast, surrounded with the bones of the dead, and the very lintels
of his door stained with blood-spots . . . who was ugly as a satyr,
and his great hands hairy almost as the paws of a black bear, . . ."[29]

Although Arrington's depiction of Smith T expanded the boundaries
of historical imagination beyond credulity, he had at least done some
homework. He correctly identified, for example, Smith T's rifle. He
also correctly identified the colonel's favorite oath, "By Jesus Christ
and General Jackson."[30] In addition, he was undoubtedly familiar with
the Lionel Browne duel in which the former sheriff of Washington
County was, on first fire, hit squarely between his eyes and killed
instantly. According to Arrington, Smith T "usually took aim at the
head, and as he ever fired with the word, his victims almost always fell
dead without pulling a trigger." On one occasion, however, Smith T
cursed his trusted dueling pistol when he examined his victim and found
that his bullet had struck half an inch above the right eye. "It was," said
Smith T, "a d—d bad shot. I aimed at his right eye—." This story may
have been manufactured from the tall tales told by a friend of Sam
Houston, A. W. Terrell. "Smith," recalled Terrell, "was a dead-shot
who after killing his victim always walked up to him to see if he had
shot him in the eye."[31]

Arrington's polemics were for the most part aimed at a relatively large
and unsophisticated audience. One of the literary devices he used to
gain a certain rapport with his audience was to identify Smith T with the
causes and customs of the common man. "He was always very meanly
clad himself," Arrington wrote, "and though *rich,* hated the rich with
an intensity bordering on insanity." It was probably Arrington who
spawned the tale of Smith T's killing of "two costly robed gentlemen"
who ridiculed him. The old swashbuckler wheeled his horse around,
pointed two pistols at the dandies, and ordered them to halt. Then
he commenced to pronounce sentence. A man who insults him, he
exclaimed, must fight him. And a man who fights will also die. Believing
the men to be "d_ _ _ _d cowards," he offered to let them both draw

29. Ibid., 55.
30. Ibid.
31. Terrell, "Recollections of General Sam Houston," 129.

and fire first; this would ensure a "fair" fight. "But," he cautioned, "say your prayers first of all and don't forget to thank god for the honor of being shot by old Jack Smith T."

When they heard the name of this "redoubtable desperadoe," they "turned white as their own crimped and starched shirt bosoms." Immediately they begged for forgiveness. Their apologies might have saved them, except that Smith T knew their secret. They were land speculators, those "accursed land-robbers" who prowled the country seeking "to devour poor men's improvements." "I have sworn by Jesus Christ and General Jackson," he shouted, "to slay every d_ _ _ _d speculator that dares to set his foot in the State of Missouri!" With that declaration the two land sharks drew their pistols and fired. A split second later they lay dead on the road.[32] This tale was incorporated into a number of late-nineteenth-century county histories in Missouri and solidified Smith T's reputation as a psychotic, trigger-happy killer. It also predated the efforts of post–Civil War myth makers to depict latter-day villains such as Jesse James as anticapitalist heroes who felt honor-bound to defend the interests of the common folk. Arrington's tales predate the legends and lore of Jesse James by twenty years, but the transition from aristocratic dueling to plebeian gunfighting was well under way.

Arrington probably was also responsible for creating another fanciful episode that reportedly occurred at a St. Louis hotel. The *Globe-Democrat* years later identified the place as the Southern Hotel, where today the modern Busch Stadium stands.[33] According to Arrington, "a richly dressed youth" of about nineteen cast some "vulgar" glances at Smith T's lovely daughter. After escorting the young lady to her room, Smith T returned and demanded either an apology or a fight. The man chose the latter, gleefully exclaiming that he "had not shot any person now, for two weeks." Smith T graciously handed the man one of his prized pistols and headed outdoors for the duel. His adversary, however, did not wait. He cocked and fired the pistol at the back of Smith T's head. The bullet grazed his temple. "That was close cutting," observed the colonel. He then drew his bowie knife and plunged it "up to the hilt in the heart of his foe."[34]

32. Arrington, *The Lives and Adventures*, 55–56.
33. *St. Louis Globe-Democrat Magazine*, April 13, 1927.
34. Arrington, *The Lives and Adventures*, 56.

Arrington also recounted a tale combining the character traits of humor, courage, and coolness. But it was the role of the champion of the dispossessed that he found most admirable in his hero. This story was the "Joke of the Shot Tower." The setting for this yarn was likewise in St. Louis. It began when a wealthy general of that city, referred to only as General A, crossed paths with Smith T. The general, who moved in the highest social circles of the city, was, according to Arrington, "a speculator, and all-grasping stock-jobber" as well as "the arch-millionaire of all Missouri." This was enough, of course, to make him "unutterably odious to Jack Smith T." But the colonel refrained from killing him, because to do so would be "highly dangerous, not in the act but in the consequence," since the general had many powerful friends. Smith T brooded for some time until one day when the general "grossly insulted a poor mechanic." It was at this point that Smith T's feelings of fair play could be restrained no more, and he "instantly took up the mechanic's quarrel." A challenge to a duel was issued. Once again Arrington had projected the theme of knight-errantry into the corpus of myths, legends, and lore surrounding the desperado. Smith T proposed that both men go to the top of a St. Louis shot tower where their seconds would bind their right hands together. Then both principles would leap from the tower to a sure death. If General A. refused those terms, Smith T warned him that he would horse-whip him every time he ventured onto the streets of St. Louis. The prospects of either a jump or a whipping made the general turn "pale," and he fled the territory. Brackenridge, one might recall, had compared Smith T to Marion and Putnam, but Arrington did him one better. Napoleon or Caesar, he exclaimed, might be a better comparison. "I feel certain," he wrote, "that a braver hero never trod this world's stage since the beginning of time."[35]

Arrington likewise depicted the dual nature of Smith T's personality. By his own admission, Smith T was "as cruel as Nero and relentless, fierce as a fiend to his foes," yet this "lawless man," he implored, was not wholly evil. Otherwise he would not have been cherished by his wife, daughter, and friends. Even his slaves, Arrington noted, "were

35. Ibid., 56–58. For an anthropological-historical analysis of myth and its uses, see Marshall Sahlins, *Historical Metaphors and Mythical Realities,* chap. 5. Arrington, *The Lives and Adventures,* 58.

idolaters in the worship they yielded to his unalterable kindness." The author maintained that nothing could subsist but by virtue of the good that it contained. This applied even more to "the great desperate duelist of Missouri," who, "though sadly soiled and marred by sin," was still an image of the "All Divine." The love of his countrymen, Arrington maintained, was the reason no jury could be empaneled to find this "idol of the lower class" guilty of murder, no matter what evidence was presented against him.[36]

There was a goal other than commercialism served by accounts such as Arrington's. It was essentially the same purpose, albeit with an exaggerated style, of other literary figures in the period called Young America. It was a kind of rhetorical motif, wrote historian Elliott J. Gorn, "tailor-made for a young nation seeking a secure identity." "Bombastic" language aided in the creation of "unfamiliar social institutions," "salved painful economic changes," and "masked aggressive territorial expansion." It was "a circular pattern of reinforcement" in which past heroes begot future heroes and "great acts found heightened meaning in great words."[37] Smith T's prowess mirrored the budding strength of the nation, and his identification as a defender of the lower class lent credence to an expanding ideology of egalitarianism.

There were others besides writers who added to the myths, legends, and folklore of Smith T. These included Sam Houston, Andrew Jackson, and Jefferson Davis. Houston in 1859 told a friend, A. W. Terrell, of his near duel with the Missourian known as "Jack Smith T." Terrell recalled that Houston believed Smith T to be a professional duelist who had killed at least six men under the terms of the code. Houston, according to Terrell, always believed that his enemies had brought Smith T to Nashville in order to provoke a duel. "Smith," Houston went on to say, "was a heartless butcher." Unlike Arrington, Houston believed Smith T possessed no chivalry or bravery. In his duels, he told Terrell, "Smith wore a shirt of mail" to give him an extra advantage. Rather than dueling him, Houston intended, at the first act of provocation, to take a double-edged dagger and drive "the knife

36. Arrington, *The Lives and Adventures,* 58. Rozier, *Rozier's History,* 316; Arrington, *The Lives and Adventures,* 58.
37. Elliott J. Gorn, " 'Gouge and Bite, Pull Hair and Scratch': The Social Significance of Fighting in the Southern Backcountry," 29–30.

down the collar bone." If "insulted," Houston claimed, "I intended to slay him as I would a dog."[38]

Andrew Jackson was another name associated with Smith T's fighting abilities. Allegedly, some years after the Battle of New Orleans, the two quarreled over some land and hot springs that Smith T claimed in Arkansas. He applied for the grant to the General Land Office only to be informed that Jackson had encouraged the land officers to withdraw it from sale. Smith T believed that Jackson had betrayed his trust and, according to legend, issued a challenge. Jackson would have none of it. However, when the Missourian arrived in Nashville, tempers began to flare. According to Judge John Gillespie of Edwardsville, who heard the story from Smith T, Jackson mounted his horse and, with a number of armed allies referred to as "his myrmidons," set out to kill the colonel. Against such odds, Smith T beat a hasty retreat. Smith T, Gillespie recalled, "wanted a fair fight with Jackson," but when the general became excited "and this earth was a magazine of gun powder, he would hurl a firebrand into it and blow the world to atoms to obtain satisfaction."[39]

Jefferson Davis also contributed to Smith T's reputation. In a letter to General G. W. Jones on September 2, 1882, he discussed his early years as an army officer on the Iowa frontier and "a threat which was made that John Smith T was to come with a large part of riflemen to drive off my small party, so as to allow the mines [Dubuque] to be worked." An explanatory footnote on the same page referred to Smith T as an "old Indian Fighter" who "was a match for anyone in the act of defence and offence." To most individuals in government service, even the former president of the Confederacy, it might appear somewhat unusual that a private citizen and his army would challenge the authority of the U.S. Army, even on the Indian frontier. But not to Jefferson Davis. John Smith T, according to Davis, "was considered invincible by the people of the West, his name struck terror into the hearts of the men of that day." This "noted duellist," he reported, "had killed nine men outright." Davis recalled a case in point. One evening at an inn in Galena, "a brave and tried man" and his friends were

38. Terrell, "Recollections of General Sam Houston," 129; Campbell, *Sam Houston,* 14–15.
39. *St. Louis Globe-Democrat* (weekly), September 25, 1887.

conversing after supper about the infamous colonel. The venturous gentleman informed the group that he would like to see Smith T since "he could not be terrorized." At that juncture a "quiet little man arose and announced, 'I am Smith T., at your service.' The man went to the bannister and gave up his dinner, the instinctive terror made him sea-sick."[40]

The decades of the Civil War and Reconstruction witnessed the diminution of western frontier legends. It was not until the latter part of the nineteenth century that any serious revision of Smith T's life took place. One of the earliest post-Reconstruction revivifications of myth and lore was the previously mentioned *History of Saline County, Missouri,* published in 1881. The work established a new dimension in the caricaturing of Smith T. It began stretching the historical record by reporting on "three or four duels, in all of which he killed his man." The book inaccurately reported that Smith T fought at least one of these affairs of honor on Bloody Island. In an effort to make the subject larger than life and to inject some panache, the author wrote of Smith T's ability to instill fear. "His commands," it stressed, "were always obeyed, or there was a funeral if they were not."[41] This account also retold Arrington's tale of Smith T's killing of two travelers on a Boonville road. Only this time, the story changed. Rather than "land-sharks," the men turned out to be "honest, reputable citizens."

One of the most remarkable publishing feats, even more astonishing because it occurred without the aid of modern technology, was the publication of Goodspeed's county histories. During the late 1880s the company published scores of books that recorded local history, genealogy, folklore, and tradition. These handiworks, although hastily crafted, celebrated the victory of the American experience despite the ravages of the Civil War. In Missouri, as well as in Tennessee, the Goodspeed genre added to the lore of Smith T. In 1888, Goodspeed Publishing Company published two works, the *History of Southeast Missouri* and the *History of Franklin County,* which detailed Smith T's numerous adventures. While admitting that "he was generally feared on account of his success as a duelist," the accounts claimed that Smith T was reportedly "kind and good to the poor." Legendary

40. Varina Davis, *Jefferson Davis: A Memoir by His Wife,* vol. 1, 151.
41. *History of Saline County, Missouri,* 507–9.

heroes, a theme played very well by Goodspeed, may have a reckless, violent side, but they must also have ennobling traits as well. It was the same split personality presented earlier by John Darby. Another work similar to Goodspeed's histories was William Napton's history of Saline County. He too believed Smith T to have been the "most singular and remarkable man in some respects who ever lived" in the county.[42] Using Darby's figure of fifteen kills, Napton nevertheless presented one of the most balanced treatments the colonel's life had received for some time.

A turn-of-the-century figure who attempted to resurrect John Smith T's fame was Colonel William F. Switzler. This Boone County politician, newspaper editor, and Kentucky native had a talent for hyperbole and literary finesse matched by few writers of his day. Switzler began his account of Smith T by relating that his subject furnished, as could few men living or dead, "so abnormal a combination of characteristics." Smith T, a "bundle of contradictions" and "tangle of eccentricities," was to Switzler "an enigma difficult to solve." "Suave and courteous in manner, but terrible as a tiger when aroused by anger," Smith T "feared neither man nor evil." "Quick of ignition as tinder, and courageous and polite as a cavalier," the man was both "peaceable and warlike, mirthful and morose, of the most gentlemanly and decorous instincts, and at the same time ferocious as a catamount and pugnacious as a bulldog." Devoted and loyal to his friends, Smith T could be "unforgiving and merciless as a Comanche among the foothills of the Rockies" toward his enemies. Yet for Switzler and others of his social persuasion there was still an overriding sense of integrity that defined the essence of Missouri luminaries of the heroic age. According to Switzler: " . . . Smith was consistent with himself in this—he was the soul of honor. He was never corrupt enough to do a mean thing or desperado enough to plunge upon the thicksetting armament of a dishonorable action."[43]

Another turn-of-the-century author, Phil E. Chappel, likewise embellished the stories of John Smith T. Among the early settlers of Missouri who were "born and raised among scenes of bloodshed and crime," he wrote, no one created "so great a sense of fear" as

---

42. *Goodspeed's History of Southeast Missouri*, 313–14; *Goodspeed's History of Franklin County*, 499–500. Napton, *Past and Present*, 350.

43. "Col. John Smith T," newspaper article by William P. Switzler, Vertical File, MHS.

the colonel. Chappel, like most of his literary companions, marveled at Smith T's material possessions, his "fine plantation," "handsome home," and "princely style" of living. He was particularly impressed with Smith T's mode of river travel. In a boat manned by his own slaves, "he traveled in all the splendor and ease of an Eastern monarch." Yet it was "a life crimsoned with blood" that made the colonel "the most noted character, the most desperate, and in many respects the most remarkable, man known in the annals of the early history of Missouri." He killed, Chappel reported, "no less than fifteen men," most in duels "when his own life was in danger." Like his contemporaries, Chappel reveled in the tales of Smith T's challenges to Sam Houston and Andrew Jackson. With a straight face, Chappel added the following melodramatic epitaph for his swashbuckling hero. Smith T's presence, he wrote, "caused a cheek to blanche with fear," and his name "to the restless child, caused its little voice to be hushed into silence."[44]

Another far less complete description of John Smith T was printed in the *St. Louis Globe-Democrat* on September 27, 1887. This article downplayed Smith T's entrepreneurial side and stressed the violence. For the *Globe* article, there was no dichotomy. While admitting that a spirit of adventure and recklessness characterized territorial Missouri, the article left no doubt that the colonel's behavior went far beyond a reflection of the times. His victims, it reported, "would fill a whole volume." He had killed fourteen men "in duels and brawls," it further reported, and that constituted only a "portion of his bloody performances." The article (the author's name was omitted) perpetuated the violent image of Smith T more than any other of its kind during this period. The essay was also printed in a New York newspaper the same year. What little national recognition the by-gone colonel received, therefore, stereotyped him as the quintessential desperado of the early West.[45]

This dual theme of malevolence and magnanimity was again pursued by Howard L. Conard, editor of the 1901 multi-volume *Encyclopedia of the History of Missouri*. To Conard, Smith T was a small, calm, and courteous gentleman. He was "splendidly educated" and had "acquired some fame as a statesman and a jurist." He further noted that Smith T

44. *Kansas City Journal,* August 7, 1896.
45. *St. Louis Globe-Democrat* (weekly), September 25, 1887.

had a very quick temper and when angered could turn into "a dangerous man." Yet the following passage showed that Conard too believed the frontier had not corrupted Smith T beyond the point of social redemption:

> While he was quick to quarrel, he was just as quick to do a kindly act to those he quarreled with. . . . He was a scholar outclassing the majority with whom he had dealings, and was highly public-spirited, taking an active part in enterprises needed for the development of the country in which he was a pioneer.[46]

Conard's depiction contrasted sharply with the 1899 edition of the *Encyclopedia of the History of St. Louis,* which he coedited with William Hyde. In this work Smith T was portrayed as a coward who was run out of the state by another legendary figure, Dr. John E. Bryan. The two rather contrasting characterizations of Smith T written between 1899 and 1901 probably have less to do with a change of interpretation on the part of Conard and more to do with the fact that since many different authors contributed to these brief sketches there was no biographical consistency in the volumes.[47]

Post–Civil War historiographical trends, especially by the era of Populism and Progressivism, also worked against mythic and legendary figures such as John Smith T. The Populists no doubt harkened to the past in hopes of reviving agrarian democracy and the power of the individual yeoman farmer. Their predilections were of course decidedly anti-elitist. Although they did not reject the role of violence in American social history, they believed its cathartic effects could best be justified in the cause of economic justice. The monopolistic powers held by railroads, grain elevators, trusts, and banks in the 1880s and 1890s were all too reminiscent of the land grabbers, speculators, and big-time entrepreneurs of the antebellum periods. Socially, the Populists identified themselves with the virtues of the common man and not the

46. Howard L. Conard, ed., *Encyclopedia of the History of Missouri,* vol. 4, 9–10.

47. Hyde and Conard, eds., *Encyclopedia of the History of St. Louis,* vol. 1, 261–62; Note, George M. Wilson, n.d., Bryan O'Bear Collection, Folder 7, WHMC. Wilson also credited Bryan with seeing to it that Mason Brown, Mike Fink, Thomas Waller, Henry Renshaw, and Curt Forbis, all unsavory characters in early Missouri history, left the state. For the ritualization and transformation of myth see Slotkin, *Regeneration,* 12–14; Roberts, *Roots of Roane County,* 19–20.

self-styled gentleman. Their reading of history, therefore, did not lend itself to a kind viewing of the capitalist style of a John Smith T.

Progressive historiography was no less unforgiving to the John Smith T myth. Theodore Roosevelt, for example, sought to elevate western heroes. But he chose the medium of the cowboy/gunfighter and not the duelist. Another Progressive, Frederick Jackson Turner, took frontier historiography in a different direction. Whereas Roosevelt linked individualism and violence with the American character, Turner downplayed the role of violence and saw the frontier more as an environmental and collective force shaping history. Turner praised the yeoman farmer and his republican, egalitarian virtues. Although Roosevelt's popularization of the cowboy and Rough Rider greatly influenced mass culture, Turner's analysis of America's agrarian roots had a greater influence on the course of historical thought. For Missouri's Progressive historians it became intellectually difficult to reconcile the story of John Smith T with their rendering of history. The thrust of this new historiography led not to a healthy reevaluation of the Smith T myth but to his relegation as a mere footnote in history.[48]

As the twentieth century moved into its second decade, the exploits of John Smith T were increasingly downplayed by historians such as Walter B. Stevens and Robert S. Douglas. They believed that a certain amount of healthy debunking of popular myths was long overdue. Unfortunately, the contradictory elements of Smith T's character that had given marrow to his life were all but neglected.[49] Journalist Robertus Love in the late 1920s tried to keep the stories alive. He also had written some highly sensationalized tales of Jesse James. His intent was to popularize infamous characters and to remember some of their more daring exploits. In 1927, in a series on the Missouri frontier, Love perpetuated the one-dimensional violent aspect of the colonel's nature. One article recalled an incident at the St. Louis Southern Hotel in which Smith T took umbrage at a gentleman's perceived discourtesy toward his daughter Ann and promptly shot him dead. Love echoed the legendary tales of Smith T's killings, which he too estimated to be "at least fifteen." Most of Smith T's doomed targets, Love suggested,

48. Slotkin, *Gunfighter Nation: The Myth of the Frontier in Twentieth-Century America*, 22–39.

49. Stevens, *Missouri: The Center State*, vol. 2, 689–90; Stevens, *Centennial History*, vol. 2, 543–44. Douglass, *History of Southeast Missouri*, vol. 1, 60.

"were nicked in duels fought strictly under the code." He was "undoubtedly the fightingest Missourian that ever lived."[50]

By the 1930s the transformation of the Smith T myth was virtually complete. In a 1937 *Missouri Historical Review* article, Hattie Anderson placed him alongside "the reckless and unprincipled" adventurers of "depraved" character who frequented the frontier. Floyd C. Shoemaker, in his popular series entitled *This Week in Missouri History,* called Smith T a "savage fighter" who, it was claimed, had "killed fifteen men in fair fights or duels." Again in the 1940s, Shoemaker described the colonel as "a daring speculator," but left no doubt that he had little admiration for his entrepreneurial talents. In virtually the same line in which he lamented the host of criminals and swashbucklers who frequented the territory, he linked them to "the notorious John Smith T, speculator, duelist, and adventurer."[51]

The conflicting facets of his personality, i.e., the polished gentleman versus the intrepid duelist, as well as the ruthless entrepreneur versus the benevolent patriarch, had all but disappeared. There were, of course, other more subtle engines of cultural change at work. Legendary figures such as Smith T gave way to a more idealized version of western heroes. In this rendering of history, the frontier, due in part to the influence of the mass media, lost its place as a dynamic, ever-changing concept and became fixed in time and space as the West of Buffalo Bill and Wild Bill Hickock. The icon of mass culture became the cowboy/gunfighter. Industrial popular culture viewed the duelist as less romantic than the gunfighter and the entrepreneurial frontiersman as less glamorous than the cowboy.[52] Nor in Smith T's case was there a self-sacrificing death like Crockett's or Bowie's or political fame like Houston's or Jackson's with which to identify. Furthermore, Smith T did not have a notable biographer. John Filson, who popularized the life of Daniel Boone, turned his subject into a celebrity while he was a relatively young man. The Boone stories spawned a veritable cottage industry of myths and

50. *St. Louis Globe-Democrat Magazine,* April 3, 1927. These newspaper accounts were in the Miscellaneous File of the MHS. This particular account was in episode 17 of a series on the Missouri frontier.
51. Hattie M. Anderson, "Missouri, 1804–1828: Peopling a Frontier State," *MHR* 31, no. 2 (January 1937): 160. State Historical Society, *This Week in Missouri History,* April 30–May 6, 1933. Floyd C. Shoemaker, *Missouri and Missourians,* vol. 1, 139–43, 237, 260.
52. Slotkin, *Gunfighter,* 32.

tall tales that changed and grew as they spread across the country. Not so for Smith T. In most respects, his life has been frozen in time since the days of the Progressive historians. Modern scholarship has either reinforced the earlier caricatures with only a fleeting remark, or ignored altogether the career of this remarkable pioneer and his single duel.

Bibliography

Books

Abernethy, Thomas P. *The South in the New Nation 1789–1819.* Vol. 4. Baton Rouge: Louisiana State University Press, 1961.

Almaráz, Felix D., Jr. *Tragic Cavalier: Governor Manuel Salcedo of Texas, 1806–1813.* College Station: Texas A&M University Press, 1991.

Ammon, Harry. *James Monroe: The Quest for National Identity.* New York: McGraw-Hill Book Co., 1971.

Aron, Stephen. *How the West Was Lost: The Transformation of Kentucky from Daniel Boone to Henry Clay.* Baltimore: Johns Hopkins University Press, 1996.

Arrington, Alfred. *Duelists and Dueling in the Southwest: With Sketches of Southern Life.* New York: W. H. Graham, 1847.

———. *Illustrated Lives and Adventures of the Desperadoes of the New World.* Philadelphia: T. B. Peterson, 1849.

———. *The Lives and Adventures of the Desperadoes of the South-West.* New York: W. H. Graham, 1849.

Arthur, Stanley C. *The Story of the Battle of New Orleans.* New Orleans: Louisiana Historical Society, 1915.

Ashe, Thomas. *Travels in America Performed in 1806.* London: William Sawyer and Co., 1808.

Babcock, Rufus, ed. *Forty Years of Pioneer Life: Memoir of John Mason Peck.* Philadelphia: American Baptist Publication Society, 1864.

Baldwin, Leland D. *The Keelboat Age on Western Waters.* Pittsburgh: University of Pittsburgh Press, 1941.

Bannon, John F. *The Spanish Borderlands Frontier, 1513–1821.* New York: Holt, Rinehart, and Winston, 1970.

Barker, Eugene C., ed. *The Austin Papers.* Vols. 1, 2. Washington, D.C.: U.S. Government Printing Office, 1924.

Barry, Louise, ed. *The Beginning of the West: Annals of the Kansas Gateway to the American West.* Topeka: Kansas State Historical Society, 1972.

Bay, William V. N. *Reminiscences of the Bench and Bar of Missouri.* St. Louis: F. H. Thomas and Co., 1878.

Bean, Ellis P. *Memoir of Col. Ellis P. Bean: Written by Himself, about the Year 1816.* Austin: Reprinted Book Club of Texas, 1930.

Benton, Thomas Hart. *Auto-Biographical Sketch of Thomas H. Benton.* Columbia: State Historical Society, n.d.

———. *Thirty Years' View.* Vols. 1, 2. New York: D. Appleton and Co., 1854.

Billington, Ray Allen. *Westward Expansion: A History of the American Frontier.* 5th ed. New York: MacMillan Publishing Co., 1982.

Billon, Frederic L. *Annals of St. Louis in Its Early Days under the French and Spanish Domination.* St. Louis: Missouri Historical Co., 1886.

Botkin, B. A. *A Treasury of American Folklore.* New York: Crown Publishers, 1944.

Boyd, Julian, ed. *The Papers of Thomas Jefferson.* Vol. 9. Princeton: Princeton University Press, 1954.

Brackenridge, Henry M. *Journal of a Voyage up the River Missouri, 1811.* In Reuben Gold Thwaites, ed., *Early Western Travels 1748–1846,* vol. 6. Cleveland: Arthur H. Clark Co., 1905.

———. *Recollections of Persons and Places in the West.* 2d ed. Philadelphia: J. B. Lippincott and Co., 1868.

———. *Views of Louisiana; Together with a Voyage up the Mississippi River in 1811.* Pittsburgh: Cramer, Spear and Eichbaum, 1814.

Bradbury, John. *Travels, 1809.* In Reuben Gold Thwaites, ed., *Early Western Travels 1748–1846,* vol. 5. Cleveland: Arthur H. Clark Co., 1905.

Brooks, Charles B. *The Siege of New Orleans.* Seattle: University of Washington Press, 1961.

Brown, Richard Maxwell. "Historical Patterns of Violence in America." In Graham, Hugh Davis, and Ted Robert Gurr, eds., *The History of Violence in America: Historical and Comparative Perspectives— A Report Submitted to the National Commission on the Causes and Prevention of Violence.* New York: Frederick A. Praeger, 1969.

———. "Historiography of Violence in the American West." In Michael P. Malone, ed., *Historians and the American West*. Lincoln: University of Nebraska Press, 1987.

———. *No Duty to Retreat: Violence and Values in American History and Society*. New York: Oxford University Press, 1991.

———. *Strain of Violence: Historical Studies of American Violence and Vigilantism*. New York: Oxford University Press, 1975.

Brown, Samuel R. *The Western Gazetteer; or Emigrant's Dictionary*. Auburn, New York: H. S. Southwick, 1817.

Brown, Stuart G., ed. *The Autobiography of James Monroe*. Syracuse: Syracuse University Press, 1959.

Brown, Wilburt S. *The Amphibious Campaign for West Florida and Louisiana 1814–1815*. Birmingham: University of Alabama Press, 1969.

Bruce, Dickson D., Jr. *Violence and Culture in the Antebellum South*. Austin: University of Texas Press, 1979.

Bryan, William S., and Robert Rose. *A History of Pioneer Families of Missouri*. St. Louis: Bryan, Brand, and Co., 1876.

Buckingham, J. S. *The Eastern and Western States of America*. Vols. 1 and 3. Newgate St. London: Fisher, Son, and Co., 1842.

Buckley, E. R., and H. A. Buehler. *The Geology of the Granby Area*. Jefferson City, Mo.: Hugh Stephens Printing Co., 1905.

Burnett, Peter H. *Recollections and Opinions of an Old Pioneer*. New York: D. Appleton and Co., 1880.

Burr, Aaron. *The Private Journal of Aaron Burr*. Vol. 1. Rochester, N.Y.: Geneses Press, 1903.

Campbell, Randolph B. *Sam Houston and the American Southwest*. New York: HarperCollins College Publishers, 1993.

Campbell, Robert A. *Campbell's Gazetteer of Missouri*. St. Louis: R. A. Campbell, 1874.

Cash, W. J. *The Mind of the South*. New York: Alfred A. Knopf, 1941.

Cawelti, John. *The Six-Gun Mystique*. 2d ed. Bowling Green, Ohio: Bowling Green University Press, 1984.

Chambers, William N. *Old Bullion Benton*. Boston: Little, Brown, and Co., 1956.

Clark, John. *"Father Clark" or the Pioneer Preacher: Sketches and Incidents of Rev. John Clark*. New York: Sheldon, Lamport and Blakeman, 1855.

Clayton, W. W. *History of Davidson County, Tennessee.* Nashville: Charles Elder, repr. 1971.

Clokey, Richard M. *William A. Ashley: Enterprise and Politics in the Trans-Mississippi West.* Norman: University of Oklahoma Press, 1980.

Coffin, Tristram P., and Henning Cohen. *The Parade of Heroes: Legendary Figures in American Lore.* Garden City, N.Y.: Anchor Press/Doubleday, 1978.

Collins, A. Loyd, and Georgia I. Collins. *Hero Stories from Missouri History.* Kansas City: Burton Publishing Co., 1956.

Conard, Howard L., ed. *Encyclopedia of the History of Missouri.* Vols. 1, 4. New York: Southern History Co., 1901.

Courtwright, David T. *Violent Land: Single Men and Social Disorder from the Frontier to the Inner City.* Cambridge: Harvard University Press, 1996.

Cronon, William, et al., eds. *Under an Open Sky: Rethinking America's Western Past.* New York: W. W. Norton, 1992.

Cuming, Fortescue. *Sketches of a Tour of Western Country, 1808.* In Reuben Gold Thwaites, ed., *Early Western Travels 1748–1846,* vol. 4. Cleveland: Arthur H. Clark Co., 1905.

Cunliff, Marcus. *Soldiers and Civilians: The Martial Spirit in America, 1775–1865.* 2d ed. New York: Free Press, 1973.

Cunningham, Noble E., Jr. *In Pursuit of Reason: The Life of Thomas Jefferson.* New York: Ballantine Books, 1987.

Darby, John F. *Personal Recollections of Many Prominent People Whom I Have Known.* St. Louis: G. I. Jones and Co., 1880.

Dary, David. *Cowboy Culture: A Saga of Five Centuries.* Lawrence: University of Kansas Press, 1989.

Davis, David Brion. *Homicide in American Fiction, 1798–1860: A Study in Social Values.* Ithaca: Cornell University Press, 1957.

———. "Violence in American Literature." In Otto N. Larsen, ed., *Violence and the Mass Media.* New York: Harper and Row, 1968.

Davis, Varina. *Jefferson Davis: A Memoir by His Wife.* Vol. 1. Baltimore: Nautical and Aviation Publishing Co. of America, 1990.

Davis, Walter B., and Daniel S. Durrie. *An Illustrated History of Missouri.* St. Louis: A. J. Hill and Co., 1876.

De Grummond, Jane Lucas. *The Baratarians and the Battle of New Orleans.* Baton Rouge: Louisiana State University Press, 1961.

Denslow, Ray V. *Territorial Masonry.* Washington, D.C.: Masonic Service Association, 1925.

Deutsch, Sarah. "Landscape of Enclaves: Race Relations in the West, 1865–1900." In William Cronon et al., eds., *Under an Open Sky: Rethinking America's Western Past.* New York: W. W. Norton, 1992.

DeVoto, Bernard. *The Course of Empire.* Lincoln: University of Nebraska Press, 1952.

Dick, Everett. *The Dixie Frontier.* New York: Alfred A. Knopf, 1948.

———. *Vanguards of the Frontier: A Social History of the Northern Plains and Rocky Mountains from the Fur Traders to the Sod Buster.* Lincoln: University of Nebraska Press, 1941.

Dictionary of American History. Vol. 1, 2d ed. New York: Charles Scribner's Sons, 1940.

Douglas, W. B., ed. "Note." In Thomas James, *Three Years among the Indians and Mexicans.* St. Louis: Missouri Historical Society, 1916.

Douglass, Robert S. *History of Southeast Missouri.* Vols. 1, 2. New York: Lewis Publishing Co., 1912.

Ekberg, Carl J. *Colonial Ste. Genevieve.* Gerald, Mo.: Patrice Press, 1985.

Ekberg, Carl J., and William E. Foley. *An Account of Upper Louisiana by Nicolas de Finiels.* Columbia: University of Missouri Press, 1989.

English, William F. *The Pioneer Lawyer and Jurist in Missouri.* Columbia: University of Missouri, 1947.

Esselman, Kathryn C. "From Camelot to Monument Valley." In Jack Nachbar, ed., *Focus on the Western.* Englewood Cliffs, N.J.: Prentice-Hall, Inc., 1974.

Evans, Estwick. *A Pedestrious Tour, 1818.* In Reuben Gold Thwaites, ed., *Early Western Travels 1748–1846,* vol. 8. Cleveland: Arthur H. Clark Co., 1905.

Fagg, Thomas J. C. *Thomas Hart Benton: The Great Missourian and His Times Reviewed.* Columbia: State Historical Society, 1905.

Faragher, John Mack. *Daniel Boone: The Life and Legend of an American Pioneer.* New York: Henry Holt and Co., 1992.

Faulk, Odie B. *The Last Years of Spanish Texas 1778–1821.* London: Morton and Co., 1964.

Fisher, David H., and James C. Kelley. *Away I'm Bound Away: Virginia and the Westward Movement*. Richmond: Virginia Historical Society, 1993.

Flint, Timothy. *Recollections of the Last Ten Years*. Boston: Cummings, Hilliard and Co., 1826.

Foley, William E. *The Genesis of Missouri: From Wilderness Outpost to Statehood*. Columbia: University of Missouri Press, 1989.

————. *A History of Missouri, Vol. I: 1673 to 1820*. Columbia: University of Missouri Press, 1971.

Foley, William E., and C. David Rice. *The First Chouteaus: River Barons of Early St. Louis*. Urbana: University of Illinois Press, 1983.

Folsom, James K. *Timothy Flint*. New York: Twayne Publishers, Inc., 1965.

Foner, Philip S., ed. *Basic Writings of Thomas Jefferson*. Garden City, N.Y.: Halcyon House, 1944.

Ford, J. E. *A History of Moniteau County, Missouri*. California, Mo.: Marvin H. Crawford, 1936.

Franchere, Gabriel. *Narrative of a Voyage to the Northwest Coast of America, 1811–1814*. In Reuben Gold Thwaites, ed., *Early Western Travels 1748–1846*, vol. 6. Cleveland: Arthur H. Clark, Co., 1905.

Franklin, John Hope. *The Militant South, 1800–1861*. Cambridge: Harvard University Press, 1956.

Frantz, Joe. "The Frontier Tradition: An Invitation to Violence." In Hugh Davis Graham and Ted Robert Gurr, eds., *The History of Violence in America: Historical and Comparative Perspectives—A Report Submitted to the National Commission on the Causes and Prevention of Violence*. New York: Frederick A. Praeger, 1969.

Franzwa, Gregory M. *The Story of Old Ste. Genevieve*. St. Louis: Patrice Press, Inc., 1967.

Fulcher, Richard C. *1770–1790 Census of the Cumberland Settlements*. Baltimore: Genealogical Publishing Co., 1987.

Gard, Wayne. *Frontier Justice*. Norman: University of Oklahoma Press, 1949.

Gardner, James A. *Lead King: Moses Austin*. St. Louis: Sunrise Publishing Co., 1980.

Garrett, Julia K. *Green Flag over Texas: A Story of the Last Years of Spain in Texas*. New York: Cordova Press, Inc., 1939.

Gentry, North Todd. *The Bench and Bar of Boone County Missouri.* Columbia: E. W. Stephens Publishing Co., 1916.

Gerson, Walter M. "Violence as an American Value Theme." In Otto N. Larsen, ed., *Violence and the Mass Media.* New York: Harper and Row, 1968.

Gibson, Charles. *Spain in America.* New York: Harper and Row, 1966.

Gill, McCune, *St. Louis Duels.* St. Louis: n.p., n.d.

Goodspeed, Weston Arthur. *The Province and the States.* Vol. 4. Madison, Wisc.: Western Historical Association, 1904.

Goodspeed's History of Franklin, Jefferson, Washington, Crawford, and Gasconade Counties, Missouri. Chicago: Goodspeed Publishing Co., 1888.

Goodspeed's History of Southeast Missouri. Chicago: Goodspeed Publishing Co., 1888.

Gracy, David B., II. *Moses Austin: His Life.* San Antonio: Trinity University Press, 1987.

Graham, Hugh Davis, and Ted Robert Gurr, eds. *The History of Violence in America: Historical and Comparative Perspectives—A Report Submitted to the National Commission on the Causes and Prevention of Violence.* New York: Frederick A. Praeger, 1969.

Gregg, Josiah. *Commerce of the Prairies or the Journal of a Santa Fe Trader.* Vol. 1, 2d ed. New York: J. and H. G. Langley, 1845.

Griffin, Charles C. *The United States and the Disruption of the Spanish Empire 1810–1822.* New York: Columbia University Press, 1937.

Grossman, James R. "Introduction." In Grossman, ed., *The Frontier in American Culture: An Exhibition at the Newberry Library, August 26, 1994–January 7, 1995.* Berkeley: University of California Press, 1994.

Hall, James. *Legends of the West: Sketches Illustrative of the Habits, Occupations, Privations, Adventures and Sports of the Pioneers of the West.* Cincinnati: Robert Clarke, 1869.

———. *Letters from the West: Containing Sketches of Scenery, Manners, and Customs; and Anecdotes Connected with the First Settlements of the Western Sections of the United States.* London: Henry Colburn, 1828.

———. *Sketches of History, Life, and Manners, in the West.* Vol. 2. Philadelphia: Harrison Hall, 1835.

Hartz, Louis. "A Comparative Study of Fragment Cultures." In Hugh Davis Graham and Ted Robert Gurr, eds., *The History of Violence in America: Historical and Comparative Perspectives—A Report Submitted to the National Commission on the Causes and Prevention of Violence.* New York: Frederick A. Praeger, 1969.

————. *The Founding of New Societies.* New York: Harcourt, Brace and World, Inc., 1964.

Henry, John W. "Personal Recollections." In A. J. D. Stewart, ed., *The History of the Bench and Bar of Missouri.* St. Louis: Legal Publishing Co., 1898.

Higginbotham, Vallé. *John Smith T: Missouri Pioneer.* N.p., 1968.

History of Caldwell and Livingston Counties, Missouri. St. Louis: National History Co., 1886.

The History of Cass and Bates Counties. St. Joseph, Mo.: National Historical Co., 1883.

History of Howard and Chariton Counties, Missouri. St. Louis: National Publishing Co., 1883.

History of Saline County, Missouri. St. Louis: Missouri Historical Co., 1881.

Hollon, W. Eugene. *Frontier Violence: Another Look.* New York: Oxford University Press, 1974.

Homans, Peter. "Puritanism Revisited: An Analysis of the Contemporary Screen-Image Western." In Jack Nachbar, ed., *Focus on the Western.* Englewood Cliffs, N.J.: Prentice Hall, Inc., 1974.

Houck, Louis. *A History of Missouri.* Vols. 1–3. Chicago: R. R. Donnelley and Sons Co., 1908.

————. *The Spanish Regime in Missouri.* Vols. 1, 2. Chicago: R. R. Donnelley and Sons Co., 1909.

Houck, Louis, ed. *Reports of Cases Argued and Determined in the Supreme Court of the State of Missouri: From 1821 to 1827.* Vol. 1. St. Louis: Gilbert Book Co., 1890.

Hough, Emerson. *The Story of the Cowboy.* New York: D. Appleton and Co., 1930.

Hyde, Laurence M. *Historical Review of the Judicial System of Missouri.* Kansas City: Vernon Law Book Co., 1952.

Hyde, William, and Howard L. Conard, eds. *Encyclopedia of the History of St. Louis.* Vols. 1–3. New York: Southern History Co., 1899.

Ingraham, Joseph Holt. *The Southwest by a Yankee.* Vols. 1, 2. New York: Harper and Brothers, 1835.

Jackson, Donald, ed. *The Journal of Zebulon Montgomery Pike.* Vols. 1, 2. Norman: University of Oklahoma Press, 1966.

Johnson, Allen, ed. *Dictionary of American Biography.* Vol. 2. New York: Charles Scribner's Sons, 1929.

Jones, W. A. Burt. "Rice Jones: A Brief Memoir . . ." In Edward G. Mason, ed., *Early Chicago and Illinois.* Chicago: Fergus Printing Co., 1890.

Jordan, Philip. *Frontier Law and Order.* Lincoln: University of Nebraska Press, 1970.

Jordan, Terry G., and Matti Kaups. *The American Backwoods Frontier: An Ethnic and Ecological Interpretation.* Baltimore: Johns Hopkins Press, 1989.

Keller, William F. *The Nation's Advocate: Henry Marie Brackenridge and Young America.* Pittsburgh: University of Pittsburgh Press, 1965.

La Feber, Walter. "Foreign Policies of a New Nation: Franklin, Madison, and the 'Dream of a New Land to Fulfill with People in Self-Control,' 1750–1804." In William A. Williams, ed., *From Colony to Empire: Essays in the History of American Foreign Relations.* New York: John Wiley and Sons, Inc., 1972.

Larkin, Lewis. *Missouri Heritage.* Vol. 2. Point Lookout, Mo.: School of the Ozarks Press, 1971.

Lay, Bennett. *The Lives of Ellis P. Bean.* Austin: University of Texas Press, 1960.

Limerick, Patricia Nelson. "The Adventures of the Frontier in the Twentieth Century." In James R. Grossman, ed., *The Frontier in American Culture: An Exhibition at the Newberry Library, August 26, 1994–January 7, 1995.* Berkeley: University of California Press, 1994.

———. *The Legacy of Conquest: The Unbroken Past of the American West.* New York: W. W. Norton and Company, 1987.

———. "The Trails to Santa Fe: The Unleasing of the Western Public Intellectual." In Limerick et al., eds., *Trails toward a New Western History.* Lawrence: University Press of Kansas, 1991.

Limerick, Patricia Nelson, et al., eds. *Trails toward a New Western History.* Lawrence: University Press of Kansas, 1991.

Litton, Howard C. *History of Jefferson County, Missouri.* Festus, Mo.: n.p., 1982.

Lucas, John B. C. *Communications and Letters of J. B. C. Lucas and T. H. Benton.* Columbia: State Historical Society of Missouri, n.d.

Lucas, John B. C., ed. *Letters of Hon. J. B. C. Lucas from 1815 to 1836.* St. Louis: Lippincott and Co., 1905.

Malone, Dumas, ed. *Dictionary of American Biography.* Vol. 9. New York: Charles Scribner's Sons, 1936.

———. *Jefferson and His Time. Vol. 5: Jefferson the President: Second Term, 1805–1809.* Boston: Little, Brown and Co., 1974.

———. *Jefferson and His Time. Vol. 6: The Sage of Monticello.* Boston: Little, Brown and Co., 1981.

Manning, William R., ed. *Diplomatic Correspondence of the United States Concerning the Independence of the Latin-American Nations.* New York: Oxford University Press, 1925.

Marbois, Barbé. *The History of Louisiana.* Philadelphia: Corey and Lea, 1830.

March, David D. *The History of Missouri.* Vols. 1, 2. New York: Lewis Historical Publishing Co., 1967.

Marshall, Thomas M., ed. *The Life and Papers of Frederick Bates.* Vol. 1. St. Louis: Missouri Historical Society, 1926.

McCandless, Perry. *A History of Missouri, Vol. II, 1820 to 1860.* Columbia: University of Missouri Press, 1972.

McClung, John A. *Sketches of Western Adventure.* Louisville: Richard A. Collins, 1879.

McCurdy, Frances Lea. *Stump, Bar, and Pulpit: Speechmaking on the Missouri Frontier.* Columbia: University of Missouri Press, 1969.

McDermott, John F. "August Chouteau: First Citizen of Upper Louisiana." In McDermott, ed., *Frenchmen and French Ways in the Mississippi Valley.* Urbana: University of Illinois Press, 1969.

McDermott, John F., ed. *The Early Histories of St. Louis.* St. Louis Historical Documents Foundation, 1952.

———. *Frenchmen and French Ways in the Mississippi Valley.* Urbana: University of Illinois Press, 1969.

McGrath, Roger D. *Gunfighters, Highwaymen and Vigilantes: Violence on the Frontier.* Berkeley: University of California Press, 1984.

McWhiney, Grady. *Cracker Culture: Celtic Ways in the Old South.* Tuscaloosa: University of Alabama Press, 1988.

Meigs, William M. *The Life of Thomas Hart Benton.* Philadelphia: J. B. Lippincott Co., 1904.

Menchaca, Antonio. *Memoirs.* San Antonio: Yanaguana Society, 1837.

Merrick, George B. *Old Times on the Upper Mississippi: The Recollections of a Steamboat Pilot from 1854 to 1863.* St. Paul: Minnesota Historical Society Press, 1987.

Meyer, Duane. *The Heritage of Missouri: A History.* Rev. ed. St. Louis: State Publishing Co., 1973.

Moser, Harold D., et al., eds. *The Papers of Andrew Jackson.* Vol. 3 (1814–1815). Knoxville: University of Tennessee Press, 1991.

Murray, Ellen N. *The Code of Honor: Dueling in America.* Bryan, Texas: Newman Printing Co., 1984.

Murray, Henry A., ed. *Myth and Mythmaking.* New York: George Braziller, 1960.

Musick, John R. *Stories of Missouri.* New York: American Book Co., 1897.

Napton, William B. *Past and Present of Saline County, Missouri.* Indianapolis: B. F. Bowen and Company, 1910.

Nash, Gerald D. *Creating the West: Historical Interpretations 1890–1990.* Albuquerque: University of New Mexico Press, 1991.

The National Cyclopedia of American Biography. Vols. 1–20. New York: James T. White and Co., 1929.

Nobles, Gregory H. *American Frontiers: Cultural Encounters and Continental Conquest.* New York: Hill and Wang, 1997.

Ogden, George. *Letters from the West, 1821–1823.* In Reuben Gold Thwaites, ed., *Early Western Travels 1748–1846,* vol. 20. Cleveland: Arthur H. Clark Co., 1905.

Owsley, Frank L. *Plain Folk of the Old South.* Chicago: Quadrangle Books, 1965.

Parmet, Herbert S., and Marie B. Hecht. *Aaron Burr: Portrait of an Ambitious Man.* New York: MacMillan Co., 1967.

Parra Cala, Rosario, ed. *Documentos Relativos a la Independencia de Norteamérica* (1752–1822). Vol. 1, no. 2. Madrid: Ministerio de Asuntos Exteriores, 1977.

Parrish, William E., et al. *Missouri: The Heart of the Nation.* St. Louis: Forum Press, 1980.

Pascoe, Peggy. "Western Women at the Cultural Crossroads." In

Patricia Nelson Limerick et al., eds. *Trails toward a New Western History.* Lawrence: University Press of Kansas, 1991.

Paxson, Frederic L. *History of the American Frontier 1763–1893.* Boston: Houghton Mifflin Co., 1924.

Peck, John Mason. *Father Clark on the Pioneer Preacher.* New York: Sheldon, Lamport and Blakeman, 1855.

————. *Forty Years of Pioneer Life.* Philadelphia: American Baptist Publication Society, 1864.

————. *A Guide for Emigrants Containing Sketches of Illinois, Missouri, and the Adjacent Parts.* Boston: Lincoln and Edmands, 1931.

————. *A New Guide for Emigrants to the West.* Boston: Gould, Kendall and Lincoln, 1836.

Pelzer, Louis. *Henry Dodge.* Iowa City: State Historical Society of Iowa, 1911.

Peristiany, J. G. "Introduction." In Peristiany, ed., *Honour and Shame: The Values of Mediterranean Society.* Chicago: University of Chicago Press, 1966.

Perkins, James H. *Annals of the West: Embracing a Concise Account of Principal Events which Have Occurred in the Western States and Territories.* St. Louis: James R. Alback, 1850.

Pessen, Edward. *Jacksonian America: Society, Personality, and Politics.* Homewood, Ill.: Dorsey Press, 1969.

Peterson, Charles E. *Colonial St. Louis: Building a Creole Capital.* St. Louis: Missouri Historical Society, 1949.

Pitt-Rivers, Julian. "Honour and Social Status." In J. G. Peristiany, ed., *Honour and Shame: The Values of Mediterranean Society.* Chicago: University of Chicago Press, 1966.

Potterfield, Neil H. "Ste. Genevieve, Missouri." In John F. McDermott, ed., *Frenchmen and French Ways in the Mississippi Valley.* Urbana: University of Illinois Press, 1969.

Prassel, Frank R. *The Great American Outlaw: A Legacy of Fact and Fiction.* Norman: University of Oklahoma Press, 1972.

Primm, James Neal. *Lion of the Valley: St. Louis, Missouri.* Boulder: Pruett Publishing Co., 1981.

Prucha, Francis P. *The Sword of the Republic: The United States Army on the Frontier 1783–1846.* Lincoln: University of Nebraska Press, 1960.

Rehm, Eleanor Koch. *Jefferson County: Its Settlers, Origin and Development.* Herculaneum, Mo.: n.p., n.d.

Roberts, Snyder E. *Roots of Roane County, Tennessee 1792.* N.p., 1981.

Robertson, James A., ed. *Louisiana under the Rule of Spain, France, and the United States 1785–1807.* Vol. 1. Cleveland: Arthur A. Clark Co., 1911.

Robinson, William Davis. *Memoirs of the Mexican Revolution.* Philadelphia: Lydia R. Baily, Printer, 1820.

Rogers, Joseph M. *Thomas H. Benton.* Philadelphia: George W. Jacobs and Co., 1905.

Rosa, Joseph G. *The Gunfighter: Man or Myth?* Norman: University of Oklahoma Press, 1969.

Rothert, Otto A. *The Outlaws of Cave-In-Rock.* Cleveland: Arthur H. Clark Co., 1924.

Rozier, Firmin A. *Rozier's History of the Early Settlement of the Mississippi Valley.* St. Louis: G. A. Pierrot and Son, 1890.

Rutledge, Joe B. *Our Jefferson County Heritage.* Cape Girardeau, Mo.: Ramfre Press, 1970.

Rydjord, John. *Foreign Interest in the Independence of New Spain: An Introduction to the War for Independence.* Durham, N.C.: Duke University Press, 1935.

Sahlins, Marshall. *Historical Metaphors and Mythical Realities.* Ann Arbor: University of Michigan Press, 1981.

Sánchez-Fabrés Mirat, Elena, ed. *Situación Histórica de las Floridas (1783–1819).* Madrid: Ministerio de Asuntos Exteriores, 1977.

Scharf, J. Thomas. *History of Saint Louis City and County.* Vols. 1, 2. Philadelphia: Louis H. Everts and Co., 1883.

Schoolcraft, Henry R. *Journal of a Tour into the Interior of Missouri and Arkansaw, 1818–1819.* London: Sir Richard Phillips and Co., 1821.

———. *Scenes and Adventures in the Semi-Alpine Region of the Ozark Mountains of Missouri and Arkansas.* Philadelphia: Lippincott, Grambo and Co., 1853.

———. *A View of the Lead Mines of Missouri.* New York: Charles Wiley and Co., 1819.

Sesquicentennial Celebration Commission. *Battle of New Orleans.* Washington, D.C.: U.S. Government Printing Office, 1965.

Shackleford, Thomas. "Reminiscences of the Bench and Bar in Central Missouri." In A. J. D. Stewart, ed., *The History of the Bench and Bar of Missouri.* St. Louis: Legal Publishing Co., 1898.

Shoemaker, Floyd. *Missouri and Missourians: Land of Contrasts and*

People of Achievement. Vol. 1. Chicago: Lewis Publishing Co., 1943.

———. *Missouri—Day by Day.* Vols. 1, 2. Columbia: State Historical Society of Missouri, 1943.

———. *Missouri's Struggle for Statehood, 1804–1821.* Jefferson City, Mo.: Hugh Stephens Printing Co., 1916.

Slotkin, Richard. *The Fatal Environment: The Myth of the Frontier in the Age of Industrialization 1800–1890.* New York: Atheneum, 1985.

———. *Gunfighter Nation: The Myth of the Frontier in Twentieth-Century America.* New York: Atheneum, 1992.

———. *Regeneration through Violence: The Mythology of the American Frontier, 1600–1860.* Middletown, Conn.: Wesleyan University Press, 1973.

Smith, Elbert B. *Magnificent Missourian: The Life of Thomas Hart Benton.* Philadelphia: J. B. Lippincott Co., 1958.

Smith, Henry Nash. *Virgin Land: The American West as Symbol and Myth.* Cambridge: Harvard University Press, 1950.

Smith, Sam B., and Harriet C. Owsley, eds. *The Papers of Andrew Jackson, 1770–1803.* 3 vols. Knoxville: University of Tennessee Press, 1980.

Standard, Janet H. *Wilkes County Scrapbook.* Vol. A. Washington, Ga.: Wilkes Publishing Co., 1970.

Steckmesser, Kent L. *The Western Hero in History and Legend.* Norman: University of Oklahoma Press, 1965.

Steffen, Jerome O. *William Clark: Jeffersonian Man on the Frontier.* Norman: University of Oklahoma Press, 1977.

Stevens, Walter B. *Centennial History of Missouri (The Center State).* Vols. 1, 2. St. Louis: S. J. Clarke Publishing Co., 1921.

———. *Missouri: The Center State 1821–1915.* Vols. 1, 2. Chicago: S. J. Clarke Publishing Co., 1915.

———. *St. Louis: The Fourth City 1764–1909.* St. Louis–Chicago: S. J. Clarke Publishing Co., 1909.

Stevens, William O. *Pistols at Ten Paces: The Story of the Code of Honor in America.* Boston: Houghton Mifflin Co., 1940.

Stewart, A. J. D., ed. *The History of the Bench and Bar of Missouri.* St. Louis: Legal Publishing Co., 1898.

Stoddard, Amos. *Sketches, Historical and Descriptive, of Louisiana.* Philadelphia: Mathew Carey, 1812.

Switzler, William F. *Switzler's Illustrated History of Missouri from 1541 to 1877*. St. Louis: C. R. Barnes, 1879.

Taylor, William R. *Cavalier and Yankee: The Old South and American National Character*. New York: Oxford University Press, 1957.

Thompson, Henry C. *Our Lead Belt Heritage*. Flat River, Mo.: New-Sun Publisher, 1955.

Thornton, Mable H. *Pioneers of Roane County, Tennessee 1801–1830*. Rockwood, Tenn.: n.p., 1965.

Thwaites, Reuben Gold, ed. *Early Western Travels 1748–1846*. Vols. 1–22. Cleveland: Arthur H. Clark Co., 1905.

Townsend, John. *Narrative of 1834*. In Reuben Gold Thwaites, ed., *Early Western Travels 1748–1846*, vol. 21. Cleveland: Arthur H. Clark Co., 1905.

Trexler, Harrison A. *Slavery in Missouri: 1804–1865*. Baltimore: Johns Hopkins Press, 1914.

Truman, Ben Co. *The Field of Honor*. New York: Fords, Howard and Hulbert, 1884.

Turner, Frederick Jackson. "The Significance of the Frontier in American History." In Turner, ed., *The Frontier in American History*. New York: Henry Holt and Co., 1920.

Van Alstyne, Richard W. "The American Empire Makes Its Bow on the World Stage 1803–1845." In William A. Williams, ed., *From Colony to Empire: Essays in the History of American Foreign Relations*. New York: John Wiley and Sons, Inc., 1972.

Vandiver, Frank E. "The Southerner as Extremist." In Vandiver, ed., *The Idea of the South: Pursuit of a Central Theme*. Chicago: University of Chicago Press, 1964.

Vandiver, Frank E., ed. *The Idea of the South: Pursuit of a Central Theme*. Chicago: University of Chicago Press, 1964.

Van Every, Dale. *A Company of Heroes: The American Frontier 1775–1783*. New York: William Morrow and Co., 1962.

———. *The Final Challenge: The American Frontier 1804–1805*. New York: William Morrow and Co., 1964.

———. *Forth to the Wilderness: The First American Frontier 1754–1774*. New York: William Morrow and Co., 1961.

Violette, E. M. *A History of Missouri*. St. Louis: State Publishing Co., 1954.

Walker, Alexander. *Jackson and New Orleans.* New York: J. C. Derby, 1856.

Wandell, Samuel H., and Meade Minnigerode. *Aaron Burr: A Biography Written, in Large Part, from Original and Hitherto Unused Material.* Vols. 1, 2. New York: G. P. Putnam's Sons, 1927.

Warren, Harris G. *The Sword Was Their Passport: A History of American Filibustering in the Mexican Revolution.* Baton Rouge: Louisiana State University Press, 1942.

Webb, Walter Prescott, ed. *The Handbook of Texas.* Vol. 2. Austin: Texas State Historical Association, 1952.

Weinberg, Albert K. *Manifest Destiny: A Study of Nationalist Expansionism in American History.* Chicago: Quadrangle Books, 1963.

Wells, Carol, ed. *Davidson County, Tennessee County Court Minutes 1783–1792.* Bowie, Md.: Heritage Books, 1990.

Wells, Emma M. *The History of Roane County, Tennessee.* Chattanooga: Publishing Library, n.d.

Wetmore, Alphonso. *Gazetter of the State of Missouri.* St. Louis: C. Keemle, 1827.

Whitaker, Arthur P. *The United States and the Independence of Latin America, 1800–1830.* Baltimore: Johns Hopkins Press, 1941.

White, G. Edward. *The Eastern Establishment and the Western Experience: The West of Frederic Remington, Theodore Roosevelt, and Owen Wister.* New Haven: Yale University Press, 1968.

White, Richard. "Frederick Jackson Turner and Buffalo Bill." In James R. Grossman, ed., *The Frontier in American Culture: An Exhibition at the Newberry Library, August 26, 1994–January 7, 1995.* Berkeley: University of California Press, 1994.

Williams, Jack K. *Dueling in the Old South: Vignettes of Social History.* College Station: Texas A&M University Press, 1980.

———. *Vogues in Villainy.* Columbia: University of South Carolina Press, 1959.

Williams, William A., ed. *From Colony to Empire: Essays in the History of American Foreign Relations.* New York: John Wiley and Sons, Inc., 1972.

Wilson, Charles R., and William Ferris, eds. *Encyclopedia of Southern Culture.* Chapel Hill: University of North Carolina Press, 1989.

Wilson, John Lyde. *The Code of Honor or, Rules for the Government of Principals and Seconds in Duelling.* Charleston, S.C.: n.p., 1838.

Worster, Donald. "Beyond the Agrarian Myth." In Patricia Nelson Limerick et al., eds., *Trails toward a New Western History.* Lawrence: University Press of Kansas, 1991.

Wyatt-Brown, Bertram. *Honor and Violence in the Old South.* New York: Oxford University Press, 1986.

———. *Southern Honor: Ethics and Behavior in the Old South.* New York: Oxford University Press, 1982.

Wyatt-Brown, Bertram, ed. *The American People in the Antebellum South.* West Haven, Conn.: Pendulum Press, 1973.

Wyeth, John B. *Notes of 1832.* In Reuben Gold Thwaites, ed., *Early Western Travels 1748–1846,* vol. 21. Cleveland: Arthur H. Clark Co., 1905.

Yealy, Francis J. *Sainte Genevieve: The Story of Missouri's Oldest Settlement.* Ste. Genevieve, Mo.: Bicentennial Historical Committee, 1935.

Zinn, Howard. *The Southern Mystique.* New York: Alfred A. Knopf, 1964.

Articles, Essays

Ambramoske, Donald J. "The Federal Lead Leasing System in Missouri." *Missouri Historical Review* 64, no. 1 (October 1959).

Anderson, Hattie M. "The Evolution of a Frontier Society in Missouri, 1815–1828." *Missouri Historical Review* 32, no. 3, pt. 1 (April 1938).

———. "Missouri, 1804–1828: Peopling a Frontier State." *Missouri Historical Review* 31, no. 2 (January 1937).

Aron, Stephen. "Pioneers and Profiteers: Land Speculation and the Homestead Ethic in Frontier Kentucky." *Western Historical Quarterly* 23, no. 2 (May 1992).

Blunt, Roy. "The Smith-Tharp Incident and Dueling in Missouri." *Steelville* (Mo.) *Star,* September 27, 1989.

Bogue, Allan G. "The Significance of the History of the American West: Postscripts and Prospects" *Western Historical Quarterly* 24, no. 1 (February 1993).

Brooks, George R. "Duels in St. Louis" *St. Louis Globe-Democrat Sunday Magazine,* June 7, 1964.

Brooks, Philip C. "Spain's Farewell to Louisiana 1803–1821." *Missis-sippi Valley Historical Review* 17, no. 1 (June 1940).

Carter, Clarence E. "The Burr-Wilkinson Intrigue in St. Louis." *Bulletin of the Missouri Historical Society* 10, no. 4, pt. 1 (July 1954).

Chambers, William N. "Pistols and Politics: Incidents in the Career of Thomas H. Benton, 1861–1818." *Bulletin of the Missouri Historical Society* 5, no. 1 (October 1948).

———. "Young Man from Tennessee: First Years of Thomas H. Benton in Missouri." *Bulletin of the Missouri Historical Society* 4, no. 4 (July 1948).

Cleland, Hugh G. "John B. C. Lucas, Physiocrat on the Frontier." *Western Pennsylvania Historical Quarterly* 36, no. 1, pt. 1 (March 1953), and vol. 36, no. 2, pt. 2 (June 1953).

Coleman, C. W. "Genealogy of the Smith Family of Essex County, Virginia." *William and Mary Quarterly* 25, no. 3 (January 1917).

Coles, Harry L., Jr. "Applicability of the Public Land System to Louisiana." *Mississippi Valley Historical Review* 43, no. 1 (June 1956).

Commager, Henry Steele. "The Search for a Usable Past." *American Heritage Magazine* 16, no. 2 (February 1965).

Cronon, William. "Revisiting the Vanishing Frontier: The Legacy of Frederick Jackson Turner." *Western Historical Quarterly* 18, no. 2 (April 1987).

Davis, David Brion. "Ten-Gallon Hero." *American Quarterly* 6, no. 2 (summer 1954).

Davis, Ronald L. F. "Community and Conflict in Pioneer Saint Louis, Missouri." *Western Historical Quarterly* 10, no. 3 (July 1979).

De Arredondo, Joaquin. "Joaquin de Arredondo's Report of the Battle of the Medina, August 18, 1813." *Quarterly of the Texas State Historical Association* 11, no. 3 (January 1908).

Din, Gilbert C. "The Immigration Policy of Governor Esteban Miró in Spanish Louisiana." *Southwestern Historical Quarterly* 73, no. 3 (October 1969).

———. "Spain's Immigration Policy in Louisiana and the American Penetration, 1792–1803." *Southwestern Historical Quarterly* 76, no. 4 (January 1973).

Faragher, John Mack. "The Frontier Trail: Rethinking Turner and Reimaging the American West." *American Historical Review* 98, no. 1 (February 1993).

Flint, Timothy. "The Bar, the Pulpit, and the Press." *Western Monthly Review* 3 (June 1830).

———. "Duelling." *Western Monthly Review* 1 (April 1828).

———. "The Missouri Trapper." *Western Monthly Review* 1 (May 1827).

———. "National Character of the Western People." *Western Monthly Review* 1 (May 1827).

Foley, William E. "The American Territorial System: Missouri's Experience." *Missouri Historical Review* 65, no. 4 (July 1971).

———. "Antebellum Missouri in Historical Perspective." *Missouri Historical Review* 82, no. 2 (January 1988).

———. "On the Formation of a National Character." *Western Monthly Review* 1 (December 1833).

———. "A Trait of Frontier Warfare." *Western Monthly Review* 5 (March 1836).

"From the Director's Note Book." *Bulletin of the Missouri Historical Society* 5, no. 2 (January 1949).

Gardner, James A. "The Business Career of Moses Austin in Missouri, 1798–1821." *Missouri Historical Review* 50, no. 3 (April 1956).

Garrett, Julia K. "The First Newspaper of Texas: *Gaceta de Texas.*" *Southwestern Historical Quarterly* 40, no. 3 (January 1937).

Goff, W. A., "Reuben Smith." In Le Roy R. Hafen, ed., *The Mountain Men and the Fur Trade of the Far West,* vol. 7. Glendale, Calif.: Arthur H. Clark Co., 1969.

Gorn, Elliott J. " 'Gouge and Bite, Pull Hair and Scratch': The Social Significance of Fighting in the Southern Backcountry." *American Historical Review* 90, no. 1 (February 1985).

Greenberg, Kenneth S. "The Nose, the Lie, and the Duel in the Antebellum South." *American Historical Review* 95 (February 1990).

Hackney, Sheldon. "Southern Violence." *American Historical Review* 74, no. 3 (February 1969).

Harper, Herbert L. "The Ante-bellum Courthouses of Tennessee." *Tennessee Historical Quarterly* 30, no. 1 (spring 1971).

Harr, John L. "Law and Lawlessness in the Lower Mississippi Valley, 1815–1860." *Northwest Missouri State College Studies* 19, no. 1 (June 1, 1955).

"Historical Notes and Comments." *Missouri Historical Review* 31, no. 4 (July 1937).

Keller, Kenneth W. "Alexander McNair and John B. C. Lucas: The Background of Early Missouri Politics." *Bulletin of the Missouri Historical Society* 33, no. 2 (July 1977).

Kernan, Thomas J. "The Jurisprudence of Lawlessness." *American Bar Association Report* 29 (1906).

Malone, Michael P. "Beyond the Last Frontier: Toward a New Approach to Western American History." *Western Historical Quarterly* 20, no. 4 (November 1989).

Mangold, George B. "Social Reform in Missouri." *Missouri Historical Review* 15, no. 1 (October 1920).

March, David D. "The Admission of Missouri." *Missouri Historical Review* 65, no. 4 (July 1971).

McCandless, Perry. "The Political Philosophy and Political Personality of Thomas H. Benton." *Missouri Historical Review* 50, no. 1 (October 1955).

McClure, C. H. "A Century of Missouri Politics." *Missouri Historical Review* 15, no. 2 (January 1921).

———. "The Confines of a Wilderness." *Missouri Historical Review* 29, no. 1 (October 1934).

"Missouri History Not Found in Textbooks." *Missouri Historical Review* 19, no. 2 (January 1925).

"Missouri History Not Found in Textbooks." *Missouri Historical Review* 25, no. 2 (January 1931).

"Missouriana." *Missouri Historical Review* 26, no. 4 (July 1932).

"Missouriana." *Missouri Historical Review* 33, no. 3 (April 1939).

"Missouriana." *Missouri Historical Review* 35, no. 3 (April 1941).

Moore, Ike H. "The Earliest Printing and First Newspaper in Texas." *Southwestern Historical Quarterly* 39, no. 2 (October 1935).

Moss, James E. "Duelling in Missouri History: The Age of Dirk Drawing and Pistol Snapping." *Trail Guide* 11, no. 4 (December 1966).

Nobles, Gregory H. "Breaking into the Backcountry: New Approaches to the Early American Frontier." *William and Mary Quarterly,* 3d series, 46, no. 4 (October 1989).

Oliver, Lillian H. "Some Spanish Land Grants in the St. Charles

District." Miscellaneous File 1965, Collection No. 2904, Western Historical Manuscripts Collection.

Owen, Mary Alicia. "Social Customs and Usages in Missouri during the Last Century." *Missouri Historical Review* 15, no. 1 (October 1920).

Pelzer, Louis. "The Spanish Land Grants." *Iowa Journal of History and Politics* 11, no. 1 (January 1913).

Richardson, Lemont K. "Private Land Claims in Missouri." *Missouri Historical Review* 50, no. 1 (October 1955).

Robins, Ruby M., ed. "The Missouri Reader: Americans in the Valley." *Missouri Historical Review* 46, no. 3, pt. 3 (April 1952).

Sampson, Francis A. "Glimpses of Old Missouri by Explorers and Travelers." *Missouri Historical Review* 1, no. 4 (July 1907).

Shackleford, Thomas. "Early Recollections of Missouri." *Missouri Historical Society Collection* 2, no. 2 (April 1903).

Sibley, John. "Dr. John Sibley and the Louisiana-Texas Frontier, 1803–1814." *Southwestern Historical Quarterly* 49, no. 3 (January 1946).

Steffen, Jerome O. "William Clark: A New Perspective of Missouri Territorial Politics 1813–1820." *Missouri Historical Review* 67, no. 2 (January 1973).

Steward, Dick. "John Smith T and the Way West: Filibustering and Expansion on the Missouri Frontier." *Missouri Historical Review* 89, no. 1 (October 1994).

———. "Law, Politics, and Dueling in Early Missouri History." *Missouri Supreme Court Historical Journal* 6, no. 2 (March 1997).

———. "Selection of a State Capital: Vagaries and Vicissitudes." *Pioneer Times* 14, no. 4 (July 1990).

———. "Western Myth: History versus the Legends and Lore of John Smith T." *Missouri Folklore Society Journal* 15 (1993).

———. " 'With the Sceptor of a Tyrant' John Smith T and the Mineral Wars." *Gateway Heritage* 14, no. 2 (fall 1993).

Stowe, Steven M. "The Touchiness of the Gentleman Planter: The Sense of Esteem and Continuity in the Ante-Bellum South." *Psychohistory Review* 8 (winter 1979).

Strickland, Arvarh E. "Aspects of Slavery in Missouri, 1821." *Missouri Historical Review* 65, no. 4 (July 1971).

Sydnor, Charles S. "The Southerner and the Laws." *Journal of Southern History* 6, no. 1 (February 1940).

Terrell, A. W. "Recollections of General Sam Houston." *Southwestern Historical Quarterly* 16, no. 2 (October 1912).

Thomas, Kenneth H., Jr. "Georgia Family Lines." *Georgia Life* (winter 1979).

Trexler, Harrison A. "Slavery in Missouri Territory." *Missouri Historical Review* 3, no. 3 (April 1909).

Van Ravenswaay, Charles. "Bloody Island: Honor and Violence in Early Nineteenth-Century St. Louis." *Gateway Heritage* 10, no. 4 (spring 1990).

Viles, Jonas, "Missouri in 1820." *Missouri Historical Review* 15, no. 1 (October 1920).

Violette, E. M. "Early Settlements in Missouri." *Missouri Historical Review* 1, no. 1 (October 1906).

Warren, Harris G. "José Alvarez de Toledo's Initiation as a Filibuster, 1811–1813." *Hispanic American Historical Review* 20 (1940).

White, Lynn, Jr. "The Legacy of the Middle Ages in the American Wild West." *Speculum* 40 (April 1965).

Wilhelmy, Robert W. "Senator John Smith and the Aaron Burr Conspiracy." *Cincinnati Historical Society Bulletin* 28 (spring 1970).

Windell, Marie George. "The Background of Reform on the Missouri Frontier." *Missouri Historical Review* 39, no. 2 (January 1945).

Addresses, News Releases, Speeches, and Papers

Atwood, Cathy. "State Road Maps and the State Road System." Unpublished paper read at Lincoln University, Jefferson City, Mo., spring 1996.

Jefferson County Heritage Society. "Prologue, Tour of Selma Hall." Unpublished paper, October 24, 1984. Jefferson County Courthouse, Herculaneum, Missouri.

Johnson, Charles P. "Personal Recollections." Address to the State Historical Society and Press Association of Missouri, January 22, 1903. Missouri Historical Society Collection, vol. 11, no. 2, April 1903.

Magre, Frank. "Chronology in the Life of John Smith of Missouri." Unpublished document, c. 1975. Winston Smith T Collection, Opelika, Ala.

———. "John Smith T., Missouri Pioneer in the Lead Industry." Slide program, c. 1980. Frank Magre Collection.

———. "Notes on John Smith T." No. 23, unpublished document, c. 1965. Frank Magre Collection.

———. "Selma Hall, Symbol of Success." Slide program, c. 1980. Frank Magre Collection.

———. "Tracing the Old Selma Trail from Lead Mines to River Bank." Unpublished article, c. 1975. Frank Magre Collection.

McCandles, Gabe. "John Smith T: His Relationship to Smithland, Kentucky." Unpublished article, c. 1970. Thomas B. Hall, III Collection, Shawnee Mission, Kans.

Muenks, Janice. "Frontier Society and the Missouri Duel." Unpublished paper read at Lincoln University, Jefferson City, Mo., fall 1989.

Philips, John F. "Reminiscences of Some Deceased Lawyers of Central Missouri." Address to the Missouri State Bar Association, St. Louis, Missouri, September 24, 1914. State Historical Society of Missouri, Columbia.

Rozier, Firmin A. "Address of Firmin A. Rozier." Address to the Missouri Historical Society, November 13, 1879. Ste. Genevieve Papers, MHS, St. Louis, Missouri.

Richeson, Paul. "The Perrys of Potosi." Unpublished speech, June 18, 1977. State Historical Society of Missouri, Columbia.

Smith, George Penn, Jr. "John Smith T. Fact and Tradition." Unpublished article, c. 1980. Frank Magre Collection.

Smith, W. R. "History of Dueling in the State of Missouri." Paper read before the State Historical Society, December 9, 1904. State Historical Society of Missouri, Columbia.

Unpublished Theses and Dissertations

Forderhase, Rudolph E. "Jacksonianism in Missouri, from Predilection to Party 1820–1836." Ph.D. diss., University of Missouri–Columbia, 1968.

Westover, John G. "The Evolution of the Missouri Militia 1804–1919."
    Ph.D. diss., University of Missouri–Columbia, 1948.

Manuscripts, Diaries, Letters, Testimonies, Case Files

Arkansas History Commission, Little Rock
    Federal Writers Project, "Early Days in Arkansas"
    Subject File, Duels
    Research File
Barker Library, University of Texas, Austin
    Moses Austin Papers
    Eugene Barker Papers
    Colonial Archives of Texas
    La Real Audiencia de Mexico
    Military Muster Rolls
Cape Girardeau Circuit Court Records, Jackson, Mo.
Thomas B. Hall III Collection, Shawnee Mission, Kans.
Madison County Circuit Court Records, 1827–1855, Fredericktown,
    Mo.
Frank Magre Collection, Herculaneum, Mo.
Missouri Historical Society, St. Louis, Mo.
    Frederick Bates Papers
    Thomas Hart Benton Papers
    Harry R. Burke Papers
    William V. Byars Papers
    William C. Carr Papers
    William Clark Papers
    Alexander Craighead Papers
    Mary Louise Dalton Papers
    Duels Files
    Rufus Easton Papers
    James Fordyce Collection
    William Carr Lane Collection
    J. B. C. Lucas Collection
    David Murphy Papers
    Chouteau Moffitt Collection

Thomas Reynolds Papers
Ste. Genevieve Papers
Isaac H. Sturgeon Papers
Vertical File
Missouri State Archives, Jefferson City
Cape Girardeau Court of Quarter Sessions
General Court Case Files
Missouri Supreme Court Cases, Territorial Court Cases, 1804–1820
St. Louis Circuit Court Records
State Supreme Court Records
Washington County Court Records
Susan Richardson Collection, Copy, Book of Doom, Possession of
Andrea Biles, Millis, Mass.
Winston Smith T Collection, Opelika, Ala.
St. Louis Mercantile Bank and Library
John Mason Peck Collection
Ste. Genevieve County, Ste. Genevieve, Mo.
County and Circuit Court Records
Deeds Records
Tennessee State Library and Archives, Nashville
Deeds and Land Records
Frank Laren Collection
Legislative Material, Record Group 60
Miscellaneous File
Washington County, Potosi, Mo.
Circuit Court Records
County Court Papers
Probate and Deeds Records
Western Historical Manuscript Collection, State Historical Society of
Missouri, Columbia
Cape Girardeau County Court Records, 1800–1804
Daniel Dunklin Papers
Miscellaneous File
Missouri State Archives Collection
Bryan Obear Collection
Ste. Genevieve Archives and Court Records, 1756–1930
John Sappington Papers
Thomas A. Smith Papers

Robert M. Snyder, Jr., Papers
Roy D. Williams Papers
Sarah Lockwood Williams Scrapbook
Vertical File
WPA Historical Survey

Government Documents

Carter, Clarence E., ed. *The Territorial Papers of the United States.*
    Vols. 4–13. Washington, D.C.: U.S. Government Printing Office,
    1936–1948.
State of Missouri. *Acts of the Second General Assembly of the State of
    Missouri, 1822.* St. Charles: Nathaniel Paschall, 1823.
———. *Journal of the House of the General Assembly of the State of
    Missouri, 1824.* St. Louis: Duff Green, 1825.
———. *Journal of the Senate of the General Assembly of the State of
    Missouri, 1824.* St. Louis: Duff Green, 1825.
———. *Laws of the State of Missouri up to the Year 1824.* Jefferson City,
    Mo.: W. Lusk and Son, 1842.
———. *Treaty of Cession Laws of a Public and General Nature of the
    District of Louisiana, of the Territory of Louisiana, of Territory of
    Missouri and of the State of Missouri up to 1824.* Vol 1. Jefferson
    City, Mo.: Duff Green Publishing Co., 1842.
U.S. Congress. *American State Papers, Documents, Legislative and
    Executive, of the Congress of the United States in Relation to the
    Public Lands.* Vol. 2. Washington, D.C.: Duff Green, 1834.
———. *Biographical Directory of the United States Congress 1774–1989.*
    Bicentennial ed. Washington, D.C.: U.S. Government Printing
    Office, 1989.
———. *The Debates and Proceedings of the Congress of the United States.*
    13th Cong., 2d sess., March 1814. Washington, D.C.: Gales and
    Seaton, 1854.
U.S. Department of State. *Correspondence Relating to the Filibustering
    Expedition against the Spanish Government of Mexico, 1811–1816.*
    Record Group 59, National Archives, Washington, D.C.

————. *Correspondence from Special Agents, 1810–1815.* Record Group 59, National Archives, Washington, D.C.

U.S. House of Representatives. *Report.* The Committee on Public Lands, 29th Cong., 1st sess., Document no. 198, February 10, 1846. Washington, D.C.: Gales and Seaton, 1854.

U.S. Senate. *Journal of the United States of America.* 19th Cong., 2d sess., February 1827. Washington, D.C.: Gales and Seaton, 1826.

————. *Memorial of William Kelly, of Alabama in Relation to the Claim of the Said John Smith T for Land from the United States.* 1st sess., Document no. 65, February 23, 1830. Washington, D.C.: Gales and Seaton, 1854.

————. *Report.* The Committee on Public Lands, 21st Cong., 1st sess., Document no. 129, April 22, 1830. Washington, D.C.: Gales and Seaton, 1854.

————. *Report.* The Committee on Public Lands, 29th Cong., 1st sess., Document no. 239, March 23, 1846. Washington, D.C.: Gales and Seaton, 1854.

Index

Adair, Thomas, 136, 140
Alabama claims, 94, 168
Allen, Beverly, 186
Alvarez de Toledo, José: filibustering in Texas, 134–50 passim
American Revolutionary War, 8–9, 15, 81
Anderson, Hattie, 220
Andrews, John: opposes Smith T, 58; testifies, 69
Anti-junto: members 40, 158–59
Arkansas Territory, 157, 170, 214
Arnold, Benedict: connection with Burr and Wilkinson, 75
Arredondo, Jose: defeats filibusterers, 137–49
Arrington, Alfred: transformation of Smith T myth, 207–13, 215
Arroyo Hondo: and the neutral zone, 103, 132–35
Ashley, William H.: business activities, 31; partnership with Smith T, 49–51, 71; proposes road to Jackson, 59; resigns commission, 85
Austin, James, 171
Austin, Moses: builds road to shot towers, 52–60; criticizes James Maxwell, 44; declares bankruptcy, 170–71; expertise in mining, 27, 42–43; initial challenges by Smith T, 27, 29–33; integrates mining industry, 53–54; later conflicts with Smith T, 88–97, 123; miner hostility to, 42–43; mineral war

with Smith T, 42–49; Potosi politics, 171; power diminished, 50–51, 165; promotes Smith T legends, 68, 203–4; removed from office, 47–49; Spanish land grants, 29–30; supports Bates, 84–85; sued by Smith T, 69–72; supported by John Rice Jones, 48; mentioned, 65, 65, 118, 130, 155, 156, 163
Austin, Stephen A.: takes over Mine à Breton, 170; views on Texas, 143

Baker, Elisha, 49
Ball, Samuel: killed by Smith T, 185–87, 190
Bank of St. Louis, 170
Bank of the United States, 188
Barataria: pirates of, 142, 151
Barton, David, 40, 125, 161
Bates, Edward, 90
Bates, Frederick: challenged by Smith T, 84, 109, 119–23; opposes Smith T, 70–71; removes Smith T from office, 83–85; sides with Dodge and Austin, 83–85, 88–97; supports Iowa incursion, 113; takeover of Smith T mines, 115–19, 123–29; takeover of Reuben's mines, 117–18
Bay, W. V. N., 124
Bean, Ellis, 105, 141, 151
Bedford County, Tennessee, 168
Bedford County, Virginia, 8
Bellefontaine Mine, 30, 41, 171, 177

251